SEARCHING
FOR YOUR
ANCESTORS

GILBERT H. DOANE, F.A.S.G., & JAMES B. BELL, F.S.A.

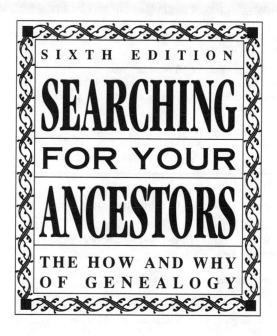

SIXTH EDITION

SEARCHING FOR YOUR ANCESTORS

THE HOW AND WHY OF GENEALOGY

UNIVERSITY OF MINNESOTA PRESS

MINNEAPOLIS

Copyright 1937 by Whittlesey House
Copyright 1948, 1960, 1974, 1980, 1992 by the University of Minnesota

Published by the University of Minnesota Press
2037 University Avenue Southeast, Minneapolis, MN 55414
Printed in the United States of America on acid-free paper.

First edition 1937
Second edition 1948
Third edition 1960
Fourth edition 1974
Fifth edition 1980
Sixth edition 1992

Library of Congress Cataloging-in-Publication Data

Doane, Gilbert Harry, 1897-1980
  Searching for your ancestors : the how and why of genealogy / Gilbert H. Doane and James B. Bell. — 6th ed.
      p.   cm.
  Includes bibliographical references and index.
  ISBN 0-8166-1990-5
  1. United States—Genealogy—Handbooks, manuals, etc.   2. United States—Genealogy—Bibliography. I. Bell, James B.   II. Title.
  CS16.D6   1992
  929′.1—dc20   91-32606
                                                                          CIP

The University of Minnesota is an
equal-opportunity educator and employer.

Think not that the nobilitie of your Ancestors doth free you to doe all that you list, contrarywise, it bindeth you more to followe vertue.

Pierre Erondell

CONTENTS

Preface

More than five decades ago, on the Great Plains of Nebraska, in Lincoln, Gilbert H. Doane took pen to paper and wrote the first edition of this book. At that time there seemed to him to be few people interested in the study of their family's past, and he wrote, he thought, for a rather small and special group of historians. But all of that has changed during the intervening fifty and more years, and the audience of a few has increased to a multitude: men and women, young and old, rich and poor, from every kind of national and ethnic background. The renewal of interest in genealogy was indeed stirring to his heart and imagination: he never dreamed there would be such broad interest in searching for ancestors.

You have much company in your search for your ancestors, since there has been an explosion of interest in family history during recent years. The bicentennial celebration throughout the country helped trigger a renewed interest in family history, as did the centenary jubilee in 1875 and 1876. Of course, Alex Haley's book *Roots* and the television series made from it popularized in a dramatic and powerful way one man's lonely and persistent pursuit of his family's history.

Interest in family history has sparked the introduction of courses on local history and families at colleges and universities, at high schools and grade schools, in centers for adult education from Maine to Hawaii. For students at every rung of education's ladder, the study of family history is really the study of the great themes and rhythms of history through a microscope. Every family stemming from nonnative roots has its immigrant ancestors: from England, or Ireland, or Germany, or Italy, or Poland, or Ghana, or China, or from some other country, to the United States. They may have arrived on one of the first ships in the early seventeenth century or on one of the flying ships of the twentieth century. It makes no matter: the important fact is to identify the members of your family who boldly moved from the Old World to the New. You will want to know as much about them as you are able to gather: their names, the dates of their arrival in the United States, and where they lived and worked.

Every family has encountered war—say, the Revolutionary War or Civil War, World Wars I or II, the Vietnam War, or the war in the Persian Gulf. Perhaps a father, husband, or brother, a cousin, loved one, or ancestor served in one or another of these wars. Some were wounded and crippled, and some died serving their country and lie buried in cemeteries near and distant.

Every family has experienced fear and loss during economic depressions and unemployment, not only in the 1930s but in earlier decades, and in the past fifty years, too.

When one visits a family doctor for an annual checkup, one is frequently asked about the medical histories and ailments of parents, grandparents, brothers, and sisters. A medical profile of a patient's ancestors' sicknesses is a vital reference tool for physicians in diagnosing and treating complaints.

It is fascinating to learn, too, the sort of work our forebears followed: Were they sailors or farmers, joiners or coopers, preachers or merchants? We want to know where our ancestors worked and lived. We want to identify the towns, villages, or farms in which they lived and determine whether or not their houses are still standing.

Someone asked me recently, "Why do you think there is such an explosive interest in family history today?" It is an interesting question, and I offer my observations for whatever they may be worth. First, as I noted earlier, I think the recent bicentennial ceremonies triggered a renewed interest in our country's history as well as that of local communities and of families. Second, Alex Haley's important book has stirred up a desire among people of every national and ethnic background to search for their ancestors. Third, we have lived through some difficult and turbulent times: the assassinations of prominent political leaders, a far-off and little-understood war, the damaging twin assaults of economic recessions and runaway inflation, and the hazardousness of nuclear and regional warfare. The uncertainties of the present day seem tempered and steadied by the study of the past, and family history can be a sort of anchor on the fast-moving, ever-changing time line of history. The images and events of the present day take on new hues, and are more comprehensible, with an appreciation of the past.

During the past ten years many important changes have taken place in the field of family history that assist us in undertaking and continuing our research on our families' stories. The most notable accomplishment during the last decade has been that at the Latter-day Saints Family History Library in Salt Lake City. The new facility, opened in 1985, was prepared to serve fifteen hundred readers a day. Today more than three thousand researchers stream through the doors every day to consult the books, films, indexes, and other materials in the library's collections. The facilities, which seemed more than adequate for readers' use in 1985, will be enlarged significantly in 1993, an expansion that will accommodate and serve the library's audience in the same high-minded, professional, and congenial manner as today.

Without a doubt the Family History Library is the best in the world in the field of genealogical research materials.

While regional libraries will assist you in the early phases of your research, you will want to travel to Salt Lake City again and again for a week or two to consult the family records that have been compiled there from nearly every country in the world. Visit the Family History Library before you fly to England, the Scandinavian countries, or some other distant country and city in search of your elusive ancestors on the pages of parish or civil registers. As we will note in greater detail in the pages ahead, the Family History Library not only has extraordinary collections to use but the professional staff have carefully integrated the use of high technology through the computer and the camera to gain control over tens of millions of pages of resource material. Their good efforts bring unlimited benefits to your persistent work in searching for your ancestors. I cannot speak too highly or supportively of the resources and staff of the Family History Library. Happily the resources of this library are in part available near your home through the church's more than fifteen hundred family history centers located throughout the United States and the world.

There are two other major national centers that have materials of assistance to family historians: the National Archives and the Library of Congress, both located in Washington, D.C. Each institution gathers and maintains different kinds of material, so you will want to consult the collections of both agencies. The National Archives maintains the federal government's records, such as census, land, and military records; ship passenger lists; and emigration and naturalization papers. Many of these records have been microfilmed and copies may be consulted at the National Archives or its regional archives (see Appendix C for locations) or at the Family History Library in Salt Lake City and its family history centers. Also, the National Archives offers an excellent loan program of the filmed materials, which you can request to use at your local public library.

The Library of Congress, located on Capitol Hill in Washington, D.C., maintains a rich collection of printed and copyrighted local histories and genealogies. The collection covers every state in the union and much material for other countries. The library's Local History and Genealogy Room, served by very able reference librarians, should be a scheduled visit for research when you are next in our nation's capital.

While the movement or migration of people has been a part of the American experience since the establishment of the first permanent immigrant settlements in the seventeenth century, it has accelerated in the years since the end of World War II. It is useful to draw on the research facilities of these three centers. There are also regional libraries that serve their geographical neighborhoods: libraries in Boston, New York, Atlanta, Cincinnati, Fort Wayne, Detroit, Dallas, Denver, Los Angeles, and Seattle are part of that list. The Allen County Public Library in Fort Wayne, Indiana, probably has the largest genealogical collection of any public library in the nation.

This book is intended to be an introduction to the methods of searching for elusive and forgotten ancestors. It has been prepared and written especially for the person who always thought that he or she would look up the family tree, but has never gotten around to it. The average person never does get around to it, mainly because he or she does not know how to start and feels a bit uneasy, perhaps, about asking a librarian for directions. This book is designed also for librarians in public libraries so that they may have something to put into the hands of patrons who have decided to look up their ancestors and come to librarians for advice.

A word of warning to prospective searchers for ancestors: do your own digging, at least at the beginning, or until you have found out enough about your family or have definite problems you want to solve. When you have done as much as you think you can or seem to have struck a ledge of rock in your digging, then consult with or take your problem to a genealogist of good repute. But beware of circular letters that come to you unsolicited, offering to supply a complete history of your family on receipt of your check. Do not waste your money on widely advertised genealogical services that appear to promise you your lineage back to the emigrant ancestor. If you fall for their subtle appeal to pride, you are likely to receive a pamphlet containing a few paragraphs on the origin of your surname, a few statements about the most prominent people of that name (which appeals, of course, to your vanity by implying that you are definitely connected with them), and a record, which may or may not be authentic, of the first few generations of the family in America. Proof of your own connection with the emigrants probably will not be given, and in the end you will in all likelihood find yourself with your same old problem and minus the money you have remitted.

There are reputable and reliable genealogists, many of them. As a rule they advertise very little and generally in genealogical magazines only, such as the *National Genealogical Society Quarterly*, the *New England Historical and Genealogical Register*, the *American Genealogist*, or the *Genealogical Helper*. But there are other ways and means of getting in touch with them. If the librarian of your public library or local historical society does not know any locally, the curators of the genealogical collections in the larger cities may have a list. Or write to the Board for the Certification of Genealogists, sponsored by the American Society of Genealogists, for an up-to-date list of certified genealogists, American lineage specialists, and genealogical record searchers. The address is P.O. Box 5816, Falmouth, VA 22403. The Family History Library in Salt Lake City maintains a roster of accredited genealogists, which may be obtained by sending a self-addressed and stamped envelope with your request describing your special geographical or topical interests. The address is 35 North

West Temple Street, Salt Lake City, UT 84150. The Association of Professional Genealogists publishes a directory of professional genealogists that may be purchased through the organization at P.O. Box 11601, Salt Lake City, UT 84147. You should remember that a capable genealogist, like any other competent professional man or woman, has spent a great deal of time and money acquiring competence to solve difficult problems. So do not be surprised if a genealogist's fee seems rather stiff. As a matter of fact, it is extremely difficult to fix an equitable charge for any professional service—try to figure out what your experience in your own line of work is really worth. When you pay a physician, a lawyer, an architect, you are paying for accumulated wisdom and expert knowledge. The same is true when you pay an experienced genealogist. Further, you must realize that no one can guarantee you a solution to your problem.

In the interest of accuracy, from the very start beware of using books that are made up of pedigrees and biographical sketches contributed by those who subscribe to the books—these are sometimes called "mug" books, as many reproduce photographs of the biographees. Some of these are good and some of them are bad, but all have to be checked against original records if possible. Until you have done this, you cannot be sure of their reliability. Some of the contributors to such volumes have undoubtedly been very careful in what they supplied, but others have pieced together their pedigrees from inauthentic sources or guessed at the connecting links. During the last hundred years a great many books of this kind have been published; they are to be found in every genealogical library. As you become familiar with the methods of genealogical research, you will learn to pick the flaws in them and to use them with discretion.

Since we last put to the printer's bench the fifth edition of *Searching for Your Ancestors,* my associate and colleague,

Gilbert H. Doane, has died. He was a learned and engaging
friend with handsome New England features and wide-rang-
ing interests; his gentle humor punctuated every meeting.
Born in Fairfield, Vermont, January 28, 1897, on land his
forebears had cleared from the wilderness in 1790, Dr. Doane
earned a bachelor of science degree from Colgate University
in Hamilton, New York, graduating in 1918. He later attended the Columbia University School of Library Services
and the New York State Library School.

During his lifetime Dr. Doane pursued several careers. He
was a distinguished bibliographer, serving as assistant librarian at the University of Arizona during 1921 and 1922; assistant librarian in charge of book classification at the University
of Michigan from 1922 to 1925; and director of libraries and
professor of bibliography at the University of Nebraska from
1925 to 1937. For twenty-five years he was associated with
the University of Wisconsin at Madison, where he held three
posts: director of university libraries and professor of bibliography, director of the library school, and university
archivist.

He was an active member and clergyman of the Episcopal
church, ordained as a deacon September 29, 1943, and as a
priest January 8, 1956. Dr. Doane served as honorary curate,
St. Andrew's Church, from 1943 to 1951, and as assistant at
Grace Church, Madison, Wisconsin from 1951 to 1967.

He served his country in the United States Navy during
World War I and in the United States Army in World War II.

Honored in every field of endeavor, he carried his achieve-
ments with lightness. Ever a gentleman, always gracious,
possessed of a keen sense of humor, he was good company.
I miss him but am grateful for his time with me, as he
touched my heart and mind.

For the fifth edition of *Searching for Your Ancestors*, I joined
with Dr. Doane, at his request, in preparing a new edition of
the book. For the sixth edition of the volume every line of the
earlier edition has been reviewed, revised when out of date,
and corrected when inaccurate. To reflect the extraordinary in-

terest in the search for ancestors today I have broadened the scope of the book a bit and added new material, in hopes of providing information and assistance to persons studying their family's genealogy in the United States and across the seas.

To those of you who read this book and are led into the pursuit of your ancestors, I owe you both congratulations and condolences: condolences because I know that you will never be able to rid yourselves of the desire to search one more family line, and congratulations because I know that you will have found an absorbing hobby that will enrich you in many ways.

I do want to express my special thanks to my friends Dr. James E. Mooney and Mr. Thomas Jay Kemp, who generously read this book in typescript and gave to me the full benefit of their editorial and bibliographical experience and knowledge. In Salt Lake City, Mr. and Mrs. Thomas E. Daniels graciously provided to my wife and me every courtesy of hospitality during our research visit to the Family History Library. Congenial and informative conversations on a wide range of topics contributed in a significant way to the strengthening of this book.

J.B.B.

PART I

How to Search for Your Ancestors

CHAPTER 1

Ancestors: Facts and Legends

Benjamin Franklin, in the introduction to his autobiography, observed, "I have ever had pleasure in obtaining any little anecdotes of my ancestors." When in England in the years before the Revolution, Franklin found time to check the parish registers and to visit the graves of his ancestors, just as has many a modern tourist.

"Who was your great-grandmother? What was her maiden name? Where did she live?"

If in the last census the enumerator had asked these questions of everyone and the results had been tabulated, the percentage of people who could give the answers would probably have been small indeed.

Yet an eighth of the blood flowing in your veins came from your great-grandmother, and possibly a much larger proportion of your individual traits: your sweet winning ways or your irascible disposition. Despite loose talk concerning the importance of heredity, we do take after people. A woman who lived in one of the New England states during the first half of the nineteenth century was noted for her temper and strength of will. By her first husband she had an only child, a son, who married and fathered a large family. Among his children two of the brothers fell into a dispute over some property and lived in the same small village for twenty years afterward without speaking to each other; two of the sisters got mad over something or other and refused to recognize each other again. When one of them died, thirty-five years later, the other deliberately mopped her own front porch while the deceased sister's funeral procession was passing! The same pertinacity cropped out in two of that same woman's grandchildren (brothers again) by her second husband.

Do you have a full quota of 1,024 great-great-great-great-great-great-great-grandparents in the tenth generation back, or are you, like most of us, a cousin of your own a few times? Are you one of those really rare individuals who can trace descent from every one of the fifty passengers on the *Mayflower* in 1620 from whom a blood descent has been proved, or merely one of the thousands living today who can trace a line back to one or two of that little band? Can you follow your ancestry to an old Cavalier family in Virginia, or are you stymied by one of your forefathers who dropped, apparently from heaven, into southern Ohio about 1820? Did this man quarrel with his older brother over the distribution of their father's estate, go west in a huff, change his patronymic, and never mention his rightful name again? Or possibly your ancestor arrived in one of America's port cities, Boston, New York, Philadelphia, or Baltimore, during the waves of immigration in the nineteenth and early twentieth centuries from Ireland, Italy, Germany, Poland, Russia, and other European nations.

Have you ever tried to verify the traditions that have been handed down from generation to generation in your family—say, that of the seven brothers who came from England in the *Lion's Whelp?* If your name happens to be Allen and your father told you that his father said that he was a descendant of the famous and impetuous Green Mountain Boy, Ethan Allen, have you ever attempted to confirm that statement from the records? Do you know that this particular Ethan Allen had but one living male descendant of the sur-

name Allen in 1900, and hence descent is possible in the female line only? Or did your father say that his father told him
that he thought the family was related to the Vermont hero?

The centennial celebrations in 1876 awakened an interest
in the part played in the American Revolution and the establishment of the United States by the grandparents and great-
grandparents of those whose awareness of history was
thereby stimulated. This, in turn, sparked the founding of
numerous patriotic and hereditary societies such as the Society of Mayflower Descendants, the Daughters of the American Revolution, and the Society of Colonial Wars. Their expanding membership created a continuing interest in family
history and tracing descents from more remote progenitors.
Hence the development of genealogy as a discipline in this
country. Since World War II, the establishment of the five-
day week, the expansion of Social Security and pension benefits, and enforced retirement soon after the presumed
"prime of life" have created a new leisure class. Many in that
category have turned to the study of family history as something more than a hobby; it becomes an engrossing occupation, a new vocation for an active and inquisitive mind.
There are some who, having acquired competence through
the years of pursuit when it was an avocation, have been
able to eke out inadequate annuities by capitalizing on the
expertise they have gained.

We Learn the Stories of Our Families

Digging for lost ancestors is far more than simply collecting
the names of your ascendants. It sometimes takes you into
strange places, and in the course of your excavations a considerable amount of history, geography, psychology, and
law very likely will be added to your store of knowledge. You
don't dig merely to accumulate a lot of dry bones, as it were;
or to change the metaphor, you simply cannot back-trail

your progenitors without becoming interested in the times in
which they lived and in the various phases of their lives and
activities. Suppose you are a midwesterner and are tracing
your line of ascent back to the emigrant. You find that your
grandfather came to Kansas or Nebraska as a homesteader. If
you are not apathetic to the past, you cannot help delving
into the history of the Homestead Act and learning its effect
on the migration to the Great Plains after the Civil War. You
go back further and find that your great-grandfather came to
Ohio from "York State" and you wonder how they traveled
in those days. You dig into the history of the great westward
movement that followed the War of 1812 and the building of
the Erie Canal, and perhaps you reread *Rome Haul* or *Drums
along the Mohawk* with excited interest because now you
know that that was the life your own people lived and knew,
or you see historical movies or documentaries with greater
interest, picturing your own ancestors in them. Then you go
back a generation or so further and learn that another ancestor took part in the capture of Ticonderoga in 1776 and was
one of the Green Mountain Boys. Suddenly all the glamour of
that exploit of Ethan Allen's assumes an intimate meaning
for you, for a man of your blood was with him and may even
have heard the actual words that he used as he demanded
the surrender of the fort from the British officer who was ner-
vously clutching his trousers in the dim, cold morning
light—a remark probably much more profane than the reputed "Open in the name of the Great Jehovah and the Continental Congress!" It isn't so difficult to visualize such
events when you know that your own people took part in
them. And incidentally you'll probably observe that in the
wake of every war in our history there has developed a rest-
lessness and dissatisfaction with life as it had been before the
war, and that a great movement of people has resulted in
each case.

Thus, step by step, generation by generation, you trace the blood back into the past, ultimately reaching the seaboard and the emigrant ancestor. You may be one of those fortunate enough to find records that take the line across the ocean to the "old country." Such a discovery, or the effort to make it, frequently results in a clearer understanding of the problems in the Europe of that time, or at least stimulates a desire to know more about it.

Work

In riding this hobby you can easily see what fascinating byways there are, lanes that look so inviting you cannot proceed without investigating them a bit. Consequently, you turn your hobby horse's head away from the main trail and explore a little, knowing that you can always come back again and continue along the main road. Let us suppose that one of your ancestors was a cloth manufacturer in central New York. Doesn't the history of that trade interest you, and aren't you keen to find out what economic conditions caused the family to give up and move westward? Or, again, maybe one of them was a potter and helped to make what is known as Bennington pottery. Now that funny-looking old brown china dog, which Grandmother insisted on lugging out to Iowa with her, comes to mean something, and perhaps you delve into John Spargo's book, *The Potters and Potteries of Bennington,* to learn about its manufacture.

Or what if you come upon the rather unsavory fact that your great-great-grandfather was killed by a revenue officer in a raid on the smugglers on Lake Champlain? Are you going to give up digging because you've struck such a rock? Or are you going to look into the history of smuggling in northern Vermont around 1800? If you decide to take up the spade again you will find that many of those people on the border—then truly frontier—had the courage to earn the best living they could and to sell their produce where it would bring them the best return. You'll find that they had many admirable qualities and were people to be proud of, in spite of their apparent lawlessness.

Migration Routes

All this and more will fascinate you. The Cumberland Gap will become more than a railway pass through the Allegheny range if your people came through it before the Baltimore and Ohio Railroad was built. The "State of Frankland" will be more than a mere phrase in a schoolbook if your people chanced to settle in Tennessee about 1780. "Natchez Trace" will cease to be a mysterious term when you follow your ancestors in their migration from the Carolinas to Louisiana and Texas. The settlement of the vast West will become fact rather than hearsay when you retrace the footsteps of your ancestors over the more than two thousand miles of the Oregon, or California, or Mormon trails in the 1840s and 1850s. Courageous men and women made their way from Independence, Missouri, to the mouth of the Columbia River in Oregon, or to Sutter's Fort in California, or from Council Bluffs, Iowa, to present-day Salt Lake City. History will become part of your blood.

Religion

Even religion may assume a new aspect, or your respect for it may be increased. Suppose you find that you are descended from Mary Dyer, the "Quaker Martyr," who was hanged in Boston, June 1, 1660. Wouldn't you want to know the reason for her fate? There is a saying among her descendants that they are all close-mouthed because she talked too much and got herself hanged. If you find that your family moved from Dartmouth, Massachusetts, to Nine Partners, Dutchess

County, New York, won't you want to know why there was a migration across Connecticut about 1735, and, moreover, why any town should have been called "Nine Partners"? You'll find that a large group of people who had become Quakers wanted to get away from the rather severe and unpleasant ostracism imposed by the predominate religious element in Massachusetts and have a place of their own, where they could worship as they pleased (and, perhaps, enforce their own ideas of religious belief). You'll learn the history of the grants in Dutchess County and perhaps find your family located in that curiously named area, the Oblong, no longer on the map. You may learn of the rise of the Hicksites, a group of Quakers who seceded from the main body of that faith and followed Elias Hicks, many of them moving westward into Kentucky and southern Ohio. You will run into a hundred and one other sects, each centered around some picturesque leader, such as the Shakers' Mother Ann.

Possibly your people became Mormons and followed Joseph Smith to Nauvoo, Illinois, and later accompanied Brigham Young across the plains to found Salt Lake City and the Mormon empire beyond the Rockies. After a visit to Salt Lake and to what is perhaps the most magnificent location for a city in the entire United States, admiration for the vision of the great Mormon leader grows apace.

Your interest in economic conditions in the past will develop amazingly as you explore. If you have a strain of Irish blood, you will find yourself investigating the great potato famine in Ireland in the 1840s, or going further back and delving into life in Ireland in the seventeenth century, for there was a migration from Ireland to America as early as that. You begin to understand the difference between Ulster and Ireland, the north and the south of the Emerald Isle, the Orangemen and the wearers of the green.

If your people are of Pennsylvania German ancestry, you may want to dig into the history of the Palatinate in the eighteenth century and find out why there was a great migration from Germany to Pennsylvania in the first half of that period. Then you will discover along what paths those people moved on, southward into Maryland and Virginia, and later westward over the mountains and through the Ohio Valley.

Perhaps you have a Huguenot line of descent. What was the history of that famous persecution? What were the conditions in France that caused a whole body of people to flee, first to England, and afterward to America? Where did they settle?

How long have there been Jews resident in America? Do you know about Judah Touro, that fine old patriarch whose remains lie in a wistaria-draped cemetery on Touro Street in Newport, Rhode Island? Does the name Abraham Redwood mean anything to you, and are you aware that the oldest library building in America, Redwood Library in Newport, was founded by him in 1752? This library, still a "subscription library," is located on Bellevue Avenue, one of the most noted streets in America, on which are to be found the summer villas of the Vanderbilts, Astors, and Whitneys. In front of it stands the first fern beech to be transplanted from Switzerland to America, a truly beautiful tree, well worth traveling to see in its lacy beauty on a bright summer day.

These are but a few of the fascinating byways of genealogy. Scoffers do not realize that digging for ancestors means far more than merely accumulating names. They think of it as "dry as dust" and even less interesting. They do not understand that it is a stimulating, living study, well worth pursuing, and that from it we may learn not only the histories of our own families but also a great deal about the history of our country, in which our own people have played a part, and also a great deal about ourselves.

Tools and Sources

Genealogical research doesn't call for a lot of expensive equipment—just a notebook, a few pencils, an inquisitive mind, and a willingness to ask questions and dig for facts.

Gather what you can from relatives; the older they are, the better. But all that comes to you from Great-Aunt Hettie, or garrulous Uncle Abijah, must not be accepted as the truth. The memories of some old folks are less reliable than those of others. Some like to make a good story out of a fact; some do not realize how much they have forgotten and how much they have added to the story in telling it. Your job is to note the details as best you can and check them later.

Once the memory of your older relatives is exhausted, you begin to dig in official records: vital records, probate records, church records, and the like. Each yields its quota of amusement as well as information, as does the following from the East Haddam, Connecticut, land records.

> John the sone of John Warner and of Mahittabel his wife was borne December ye: 18th: 1716
>
> Daniell ye sone of John Warnor and of Mahittabell his wife was borne May ye: 6th: 1717

To this the editor of the printed records has added the pertinent comment, "Quick work!"

Cemeteries, too, contain many things both puzzling and droll. Dr. Doane found a stone in a northern Vermont cemetery on which the inscription had been completely defaced. What is the story behind that vandalism? In the same cemetery he found the inscription:

> Sacred to the Memory of Inestimable Worth to Unrivaled Excellence and Virtue, Miss Cynthia Page, Whose Remains are Deposited here and Whose Ethereal Part Became a Seraph on the 4th of March 1824—Aged 20 Years.

Nearby lies:

Diah Sherwood, Died April 24, 1853, in his 90th Year.
A Soldier of the Revolution

and beside him:

Jayhannah, wife of Dyer Sherwood, Died May 22,
1833, in Her 67th Year

What a task Dr. Doane had identifying "Diah" or "Dyer"!
Alas for the New Englander's propensity for attaching *r* to
words ending in a vowel sound! After several years of
searching he finally discovered that "Dyer" (as his name was
spelled in most of the land records pertaining to him) was
identical with Jedediah Sherwood, who migrated from Connecticut to Vermont about 1790, later moved to Ohio, and finally returned to Vermont, where he died.

Wills, too, are more than records of bequests and dispos-
als. In a certain probate court there is a pre-Revolutionary
will in which the testator specified the actual rooms in his
house that each of his two daughters and his widow were to
have after his death. Each was to have right of way through
the central hallway and across the garden to the well. It is
easy to picture the family: a thrice-married man who at death
was survived by a daughter of each of his first two wives and
by his third wife. With each of the three women jealous of
the other two, the old man was wise enough to know that
there would be an unholy scramble, once he was gone, unless he made explicit terms in his bequest.

Sometimes the digger for ancestors is fortunate enough to
find a printed genealogy of the family into which he or she
has traced his line of ascent. These records must always be
checked for accuracy, and not followed blindly. Occasionally
humorous elements are found in them—another proof of our
contention that genealogy is not dry. In the Dewey geneal-

ogy one comes across this amazing collection of names in one family:

Armenius Philadelphus
Almira Melpomena
Pleiades Arastarcus
Victor Millenius
Octavia Ammonia

and last of all:

Encyclopedia Britannica

The last-named, the compiler states, was living unmarried at the age of 84. It is not surprising that she was a spinster. What man would want to marry an encyclopedia?

What a record is found on page 62 of *The Daniel Shed Genealogy!* There it is stated that Ebenezer Richardson, born in Billerica, Massachusetts, October 2, 1724, married first Elizabeth Shed, who bore him ten children and died about 1763. He married, second, in October 1764, Mary Crosby, who died before 1770, for in December of that year he married, third, Mrs. Lydia Danforth. She died, and he married, fourth, in December 1776, Mrs. Catherine Wyman. She succumbed, and he married, fifth, in May 1783, Elizabeth Bacon. She died, and he married, sixth, Mrs. Susanne Davis, who died. In October 1799, he married, seventh, Mrs. Keziah Wyman. As the compiler states, "after a long life, rich in marital experience, he succumbed in 1808 to the fell destroyer that had bereft him of so many wives."

The pension records of the survivors of the Revolutionary War not only yield a great store of genealogical data and military records, but present problems as well. In one such record there was found an affidavit stating that the soldier had married in Paris, Maine, and removed to "Thunderstood," Vermont. No atlas of Vermont ever noted such a place. It proved to be an old lady's mispronunciation and phonetic spelling of Hungerford, now Sheldon, Vermont.

Incidentally, the early census takers were marvels when it came to spelling, for in the first federal census, of 1790, we find the surname Reynolds spelled in thirty-four different ways, ranging from Ranals through Renholds, Reynull, and a few other spellings to Runnels and Rynolds. They managed to spell even Brown in seven ways: Bronn, Broons, Broun, Broune, Brown, Browne, and Brownes! Possibly some of this misspelling in the printed transcript is due to difficulty in reading the old handwriting, for it is hard to read, especially if the paper has become time-stained or the ink has been exposed to the light.

Surnames

Speaking of surnames, here is another absorbing byway of genealogical study: the history and development of names. When William the Conqueror established himself in England, surnames were almost unknown, even among noble, baronial families. They were not generally adopted until the thirteenth century or later. Most English surnames are derived from names of places or occupations, and a few from some peculiar trait or nickname. For example, the surname Atwood is derived from Atte Wood—that is, John Atte Wood, or John who lived at, or by, the wood, to distinguish him from John Atte Lea (now Atleigh, or more simply Lee), John who lived by the meadow. From these examples it is easy to see how the spelling has gradually simplified until the names have assumed the form with which we are familiar today. Sherman is an occupational name, meaning shear man, one who sheared cloth. Chandler derives from candlemaker; Thatcher from roof-thatcher. Names derived from places generally had the French preposition *de* inserted between the given name and the surname. For instance, the earliest occurrence of the name Hungerford applied to an individual is that of Everard de Hungerford, who lived at Hungerford in Berkshire in the twelfth century. By 1500 the *de* had been dropped and the Hungerford family was well established. Seymour is a phonetic spelling of Saint Maur, with a few elisions, thus de Saint Maur became Seymour in the course of a few generations. Powell is a corruption of Ap Howell, a Welsh name signifying son of Howell. Price was originally Ap Rhys, son of Rhys, a common Welsh given name. Thistlethwaite comes from two words: thistle and thwaite, the last an Anglo-Saxon word meaning a parcel of land (thistle patch, as we might say). Smith, the most common name, is occupational in origin—William the Smith, to distinguish him from William the Thatcher.

Thus it is easy to see that families of the same surname are not necessarily of the same common stock or origin. Smiths were common throughout England, hence the name had its origin in almost any hamlet in England. But occasionally a name is so unusual that you are justified in assuming that all people of that name living today are related in some degree. However, this is not invariably true, for such a name as Cobleigh when analyzed yields the two words *cob* and *leigh*, that is, a roundish lump and a meadow. Many a parish might have a field in which there is a rise of ground, and hence that name might originate in several different parts of England. (See chapter 15 for a further note on names.)

There may be some who still persist in wanting to know: "Now, why all this fuss about genealogy? Of what use is it?" One might as well ask: "Of what use postage stamps, Sandwich glass, Currier and Ives prints, baseball cards?" In the first place, it can be a hobby, an avocation. Psychologists tell us that it is good for people to have a hobby on which to spend spare time, something to study, something in the pursuit of which they can broaden their knowledge of the world and its ways. Genealogy is the study of family origins and the ways of individuals; individuals and families help to make history. The late Dr. LeRoy Crummer used to insist that "every man should study the past in order to understand the present and anticipate the future." The doctor applied that maxim to the study of medical history, but it is equally applicable to any other field. Also, individuals make up towns, towns make up counties and states, states make up nations, and nations make up the world and play their roles in its affairs. Thus, in the first or the last analysis, the individual counts.

All in all, you cannot escape the fact that your ascendants were human beings, not merely names that have survived in musty old records. They lived and breathed, had their joys and pleasures, their trials and tribulations, their work and play, however different these may have been from yours. Moreover, you will find that they, obscurely or prominently, took their part in the affairs of their times and contributed in some way to the development of civilization. By learning more about them and their times, you'll be the wiser in knowing "how we got this way."

CHAPTER 2

How to Search among the Relatives

If you really want to dig for your ancestors and have determined to learn something about your progenitors and ascendants, the material equipment is very slight. You needn't buy a lot of tools—spades, fishing tackle, clubs—or a horse. As we have said, all you'll need is a good notebook, preferably loose-leaf, of a size convenient to carry. Don't make the mistake of getting one that is too small, or one that holds only a few sheets of paper. We think you will find it best to have a page at least 5½ × 8½ inches (we like the size taking a standard sheet of typewriter paper, 8½ × 11). We recommend, also, one that opens like a book rather than one that opens at the end. If your notebook is hinged along the side, you can extend your pedigree charts across two pages, and thus be able to see a whole line of descent without turning a page. We prefer the larger size notebook, also, because we can put into it letters and other typewritten papers by simply punching the proper holes and inserting the sheets wherever we want them. A supplementary working notebook of pocket size is useful when you begin to take trips. Indeed, some genealogists always carry about with them such a notebook in which they keep notes of the details wanted on specific problems.

Using a Chart

Before beginning to question one's relatives, it is well to prepare an ancestral chart or skeleton outline of your ancestry.
Such a chart can be made easily with a pencil and ruler on a
sheet of your notebook paper—at least that is the way we
usually make them for working purposes; see Form 1. A similar one can be obtained from the National Genealogical Society, Glebe House, 4527 17th Street North, Arlington, VA
22207, or other firms dealing in genealogical supplies. You
can begin with your own name—if you propose to work out

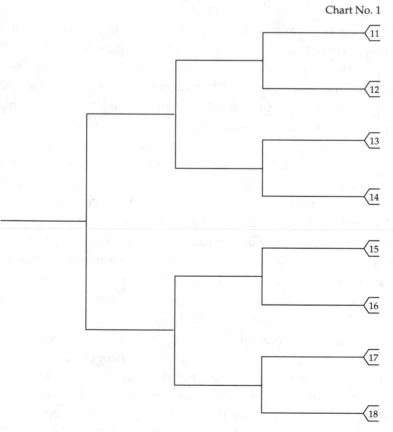

Chart No. 1

Form 1. Skeletal Ancestral Chart.

both paternal and maternal ancestry — on the single line of the left-hand side of this chart. On the upper of the next two horizontal lines, write your father's full name (start out right and never use an initial when you can get the full name), and immediately below it enter the place and date of his birth, the place and date of his marriage, and the place and date of his death (if he is not living). On the lower enter your mother's full maiden name. In the next column you will note that there are four horizontal lines, on and under which should be recorded the same data for your grandparents. Always record the wives under their maiden names, for in the next generation those become the names of the lines you are tracing. In the fourth column are spaces for your eight great-grandparents. Thus, on a single chart, when all the spaces are filled out, you will have the data on four generations, including yourself, if you have started with your own name.

You will notice the legend "Chart No. 1" in the upper right-hand corner of Form 1. If you look carefully, you will see that a two-digit number follows each of the eight great-grandparent spaces. This number refers to the chart on which that individual's line is carried along. To continue this line, let us say your paternal grandmother's paternal line, you start another chart, placing on the single line at the left-hand side the name of that great-grandfather; just as you have filled out Chart 1, you fill out his ancestry on this new chart, which gets its number, 13, from the number following his name on Chart 1. Thus this new chart becomes Chart 13. You may wonder why the numbers 2 to 10, inclusive, have been skipped. It is a little difficult to explain, but we'll try to make it clear.

If the charts are numbered consecutively, 1, 2, 3, and so on, it is necessary to figure out the whole number of charts that will be needed when a particular ancestry is complete. But because it is seldom possible to work out all the lines immediately, it is easier to use a system that allows you to insert new charts at any place at any time. So, after renumbering charts many times, we hit upon this system of numbering. Calling the first outline Chart 1, we then take that number and add it to the digit representing whichever great-grandparent is carried forward. Thus one's father's mother's father comes on the third line in the right-hand column, and his chart gets the number 1 plus the digit 3, or 13. If one carries out this great-grandfather's paternal line, that is, his great-grandfather's line, the next chart gets the number 131, that is, 13 plus 1, representing the first line at the right of that chart. If, at a later date, the mother's mother's line is worked out the new chart has the number 17 and is inserted in the loose-leaf notebook following Chart 13.

Another type of chart showing a skeleton of a complete ancestry, called the radial or semicircular chart, is illustrated in Form 2. It may be drawn in full circle, one-half for paternal and one-half for maternal ancestry. This type, too, can be either purchased or drawn by hand with compass and ruler. At the foot, or on the back, of each chart you should record the sources of your information for each generation, because if you or any of your descendants ever want to join a patriotic society, or any other organization in which one qualification for membership is based on heredity, you will need those references. As a matter of fact, since genealogy is a type of history, the history of an individual family, and since history should always be documented with references to sources, you should get into the habit of noting references so that you may easily recheck your data should the occasion demand it.

Another simple type of skeleton chart or record is the pedigree, shown in chapter 5 as Form 3, which gives only one line of descent. The angled rules show the "blood line" from the earliest known progenitor of the senior author of this book in his patrilineal line. This same type may be used to indicate the line of descent from any other ancestor, such as your mother's great-grandfather on her mother's side, who,

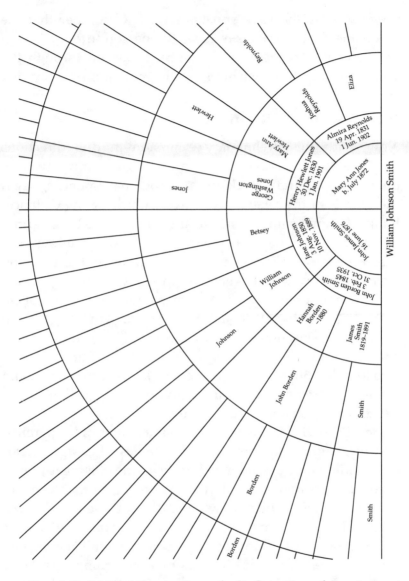

Form 2. Radial Chart Showing Spaces for Six Generations of Ancestors.

let us say, was one of the founders and first settlers of the town in which she was born and lived until she married your father, a descent in which she took considerable pride, so much so that she gave you his name. Remember that the blood line should always indicate the person through whom the descent is carried down; hence it may go through the wife instead of the husband in some generations.

Interviewing the Relatives

Now, with this preliminary excursion in dull directions ended, let us push on to our digging. With your trusty notebook in hand, and a pocketful of good sharp pencils, begin the rounds of the relatives who live within visiting distance. If any of your grandparents are alive, that is the best starting point for this journey of family relationships. Let us suppose that your father's father, your grandfather, is the first you visit. Most people of his generation enjoy telling a younger person about their own times, which almost invariably seem better to them than those in which we are living! So it ought to be easy to get him started on his reminiscences. The machinery of memory may creak a little at first, but as he gets into thinking about it, and you go back to see him again and again, he'll probably recall more and more of the details you need for your history of the family.

He will surely be able to give you the names of his parents, your great-grandparents—and the names of his grandparents, and he may even remember the name of a great-grandparent or two; and you will thus have five generations of ancestors. He may remember where most of these people lived or died. Don't let him off with providing simply given names or nicknames if he can possibly remember full names and proper names. If he says that his mother's name was Patty, try to find out whether it was actually Patty, or really Martha, Patience, or Patricia (Patty is used as a nickname, or diminutive, for all three). To illustrate this point: a friend had a difficult time determining the parentage of one of her great-grandmothers whose name was reported to her as Patty

Cobb. The name proved to be Martha Cobb in the birth record, although she had always been called Patty. Thus, for further search, in the event that your grandfather doesn't recall his grandmother's parentage, it is essential to know just what her full name was, as well as what she was familiarly called. Nicknames, or pet names, are sometimes given in parentheses or square brackets, so you can have the record of both.

Names, Places, and Dates

Try to get your grandfather to remember and tell you as many dates and names of places as he can. Although at first you may be interested in tracing your paternal line only, you will become interested, undoubtedly, in all lines sooner or later, so it is just as well to make note of everything Grandfather tells you. Thus, if he knows the names of his mother's parents, get them while you can. Dr. Doane recalled that when he was questioning his grandfather about his mother's people — for he started on that line rather than on any of his paternal lines, in response to a query from a genealogist who was compiling a history of that family — just out of politeness (or perhaps in response to some subconscious hunch), he asked him to tell him the names of the parents of his father, and what his grandmother's maiden name was. He told Dr. Doane that he thought she was born in Sherwood (she had died several years before he was born). It was a fortunate question, for after his death a year or two later, that slight clue was all Dr. Doane had as a starting point from which to work out that line, since he could not find in the official town records any mention of his great-great-grandfather's marriage.

Dr. Doane's experience in this matter indicates how important it is to get as much information as you can from old people while you are talking with them. They have a positive genius for dying just before you decide to go back to them for further information. Had he waited until he became interested in tracing his entire ancestry, the only source of information about a starting point on this particular line would have passed beyond his reach. "Gather ye rosebuds while ye may" is a good motto for an ancestor hunter. It is infinitely better to have too much information than not enough.

Do Take Notes

Always take notes as you talk with your relatives. Otherwise little details, which are frequently of importance to you in your pursuit of the elusive ancestor, may escape you, and you'll find yourself wishing that you had made more careful notes. If you are not sure of a point, ask about it again, or put a question mark after your note so that you may verify it more completely later. Let us suppose that Grandfather says that his father was born in Postville, Illinois, July 2, 1863, and tells you that his grandfather was fighting at the Battle of Gettysburg on that day and did not know his eldest son was born until several weeks later, because the letter giving the news did not reach him, owing to the movement of the troops. Moreover, since his grandfather was at war, his grandmother was living with her parents. This is all interesting and may furnish you with some facts that shed light on the history of the family. As he talks, he tells you that his grandparents had a pretty hard time financially after his grandfather returned from the war and that his father was four years old when the next child, his sister, was born in a covered wagon as they were crossing Iowa. Following up this lead, you question him further about the reason for the move and learn that his grandfather, as a soldier, located a homestead in Nebraska under the Homestead Act, which Congress passed in 1862.

As Grandfather has been talking you have filled in some of the spaces on your working chart, and the blank pages following it have been filling up with notes that you can later expand into a narrative account of the family. Now you might get him to tell you the names of his brothers and sisters and give you their birth dates or, at least, the order of their births and the names of the places where they were born. Perhaps he will remember the names of paternal or maternal uncles and aunts, and some details of their lives. These data aren't essential to you, but they help to complete the picture of the family (and may enable you later to help some cousin work out a line). If he says that his Uncle Harry disappeared and that the last the family heard of him he was with Custer in the Sioux Wars, record that fact, and later, if you wish, look up the history of Custer's campaign and the famous battle of Little Big Horn River. Perhaps Grandfather's father lost his life in the great blizzard of January 12, 1888, in Nebraska, and about 1893 his mother married again, say a widower on a neighboring farm. His stepfather's name and any details about possible half brothers and sisters will help to make the story more interesting and complete. As a matter of fact, while you are talking with older relatives, it is always wise to get the names of brothers and sisters (whole or half) as well as aunts and uncles, and names of their children. Sometimes recollections are handed down or remembered in one branch of the family that have been forgotten (if ever known) in another. One of our correspondents remembered that his grandfather had a brother. The official death record of the grandfather did not show the names of his parents and gave only New York as his place of birth; that of his great-uncle gave all their names and the town, which enabled him to trace his paternal ancestry back to the immigrant three centuries ago. The chances are that there are interesting anecdotes about the various migrations of the family, if they moved about at all. One of our friends told us that her grandfather was a baby when the family moved from western New York to Ohio and, as they were traveling to Buffalo to get the boat on which they were to go up Lake Erie to their new home, he, sleeping in the end of the bobsled in which they were traveling, rolled off and wasn't missed for a mile or so!

Possibly the story is entirely different and your grandfather was an adopted child and came from Michigan. In that case, urge him to recall as much as possible about himself: whether he came out of an orphanage or was given up by his mother because his father was killed in the World War I and she couldn't take care of him. Such a case presents a difficult problem but not necessarily an insoluble one. Local records of the community in which his foster parents lived may show something, if he remembers where they lived and who they were. Their blood descendants may recall details that he has forgotten. Orphanage records may show where he came from or who his parents were. Ask him to characterize his parents and tell you any traditions about his family. Although you yourself may not belong to any church or be of a religious turn of mind, don't forget that church records are a source of valuable information. He should also tell you to what church his family belonged; you can later try to find its records.

All such details should be noted down. But a word of caution about these questions: don't try to get too much information at any one time. Remember that old folks tire easily. Cultivate them and let them do most of the talking, and don't attempt to confine them to any one line of talk. One detail leads to another. As they turn over in their minds the incidents of their lives, more and more comes back to them. A forgotten detail is sometimes recalled the next day or later. An elderly man was repeatedly asked for information regarding his grandfather in the hope that a clue to his identity and occupation might be obtained. Finally, one day, a chance remark rang a bell and brought out the whole story with a wealth of detail.

Practice Diplomacy

Tact and diplomacy are very necessary in digging among the relatives. We know of one instance in which a problem is practically insoluble without the Bible records that are in the possession of a distant relative of the person interested. The latter has in some manner offended her relative cousin and now is at a standstill in her search, because the possessor of the records ignores her letters. Moreover, that relative is now suspicious of anyone else who tries to gain access to the Bible!

When personal relations are uncertain, it is not politic to demand access to a record; it is more diplomatic to play upon the owner's sympathy or to discover some roundabout method of obtaining the information. If you haven't ever gotten along with Cousin Emma, why not persuade George, her favorite, to copy those records or get the information you want? Don't risk a brusque refusal, and at the same time arouse her suspicion that everyone else who may approach her is working at your request. This art of getting along with irascible people is one of the things you can learn in genealogical work, if you haven't acquired it already.

Another thing that must be handled with tact is the matter of private scandal. You should know all family scandal—not as dirt for dirt's sake, but rather because it is often necessary to the proper carrying on of the investigation. While Dr. Doane was gathering material for a genealogy of his mother's maternal family, he went to a much older cousin for data about her aunts and uncles. She was very reluctant to talk about them, didn't even remember their names! He was surprised, for he had never before detected in her a failing memory. Later, he asked his mother why she wouldn't talk and was told that one of the aunts had been divorced and later sent to a state mental hospital. So the genealogy was published without a complete record of that branch of the family. When this cousin read it and saw that Dr. Doane did not mention the cause of the divorce, she recalled—when it was too late to use them—all the details for which he had asked the year before. If he had known this "scandal" before going to her, he probably would have been able to indicate more clearly the reason for his inquisitiveness and assure her of his discretion in using what she told him. There is no need of raking up too much past scandal, but one should know enough of it to be able to handle such situations tactfully. More- over, what seemed scandalous fifty years ago is now accepted without an eyelash being batted, at least in many circles.

Exchanging Letters

If there are any other relatives alive, get their addresses and begin a correspondence with them. Check the details re- ceived from one against those from another. Note the dis- crepancies, as well as the coincidences, and try to sift the facts as you go along. It is sometimes very difficult to recon- cile statements made by different members of the family, but generally there is an element of truth somewhere. What an old person recalls about one member of the family may prop- erly apply to someone else, only the names have been mixed.

Sometimes old friends of the family, living in the commu- nity from which they came, can supply the missing data. One very interesting case has come to our attention. A friend was trying to prove his wife's descent from a passenger on the *Mayflower* to secure for her membership in the Society of Mayflower Descendants. Although she knew her grand- mother's parentage, they could not find a single record to prove it. They knew that this woman's father had lived in a certain town in Connecticut, but that she had actually been born in Vermont or New Hampshire and raised by her moth- er's relatives, since her mother died soon after her birth. The records of Canterbury, Connecticut, indicate that her father

died unmarried. That was a hard hurdle to take. But, by going back to Connecticut and talking with the old men in that
town, they found one who had been the lifelong chum of
this great-grandfather—a very old man fortunately possess-
ing a clear mind and memory. He said that he was about the
only person who knew that Septus Ensworth had gone away
as a young man, that he had met a girl and married her, and
that she had died at the birth of their child a year later. Bro-
kenhearted, he left his baby daughter with his wife's family
in Vermont and returned to his native town in Connecticut,
where he died at an advanced age without ever seeing his
daughter again. He never remarried, and, in order not to be
reminded of his sorrow, hadn't talked about his early marriage except to this one very close friend. The old man,
whom our friends had found, made an affidavit about these
details before a notary public. With this as documentation,
the line of descent was accepted and our friend's wife was
admitted to the society. Two years later they went back again
to see the old man, but he had died very suddenly just a
month after they had met him. This incident again shows
that you must dig while the weather is good or the circumstances permit, and leave no stone unturned.

Whenever possible, it is best to talk with old people in person. People find it difficult to write letters, especially if there
are many details. In talking person to person, one question
leads to another, or a chance remark leads to further queries
and brings out information that they wouldn't think of writing down. Alert for facts, you can seize upon slight clues and
get them to elaborate in conversation, but this is difficult to
do in correspondence. Sometimes, however, geographical
distance prevents a personal interview. In this case, make
your questions as specific and clear as possible when you are
writing. It is helpful to write out questions on a separate
sheet of paper, leaving spaces for the answers, so they can be
filled in on the same sheet, which is to be returned to you

and inserted in your notebook. It is always a mark of courtesy, if nothing more, to enclose with your sheet of questions a self-addressed and stamped envelope: this makes it simpler for your correspondent to answer and helps to ensure a reply. Old people sometimes find it a task to write letters, and so they have a tendency to put off doing it—sometimes until it is too late—so it is best to do all that you can to lighten the task.

Dr. Doane recalled that, in the early days of his genealogical experience, he wrote to a great-aunt and asked her to give him the names of the descendants of her grandfather and tell him all she knew about them. Although she was a good correspondent and loved to write letters, she was a little slow in answering this one. Finally, however, Dr. Doane received a reply. She began to enumerate the grandfather's children and tell about their marriages. After she had listed about four of them (he had twelve, this hardy old pioneer!), she wrote: "Oh, this is too much to write, I'll tell you about them sometime." It was too much, for when Dr. Doane finally completed the records of all these descendants, there were about three hundred of them! Later, when he was able to visit her, she told him much that she did not have the patience to write.

Visiting Cemeteries

If you can persuade your grandfather, or another older relative, to go to the cemetery with you and explain the relationship that existed between those buried in the family lot or near it, you will often save much time and trouble. Sometimes different generations of the family are buried in different cemeteries. For example, Dr. Doane's grandparents, great-grandparents, and great-great-grandparents are buried in different cemeteries in the same town. If he hadn't had his great-aunt go the round of those cemeteries with him, and point out the graves of these ancestors, he would have had a great deal of trouble finding them and securing the data from their gravestones, for there are ten graveyards in that town and over three thousand stones in those yards. He has since copied the inscriptions.

CHAPTER 3

What about Those Family Traditions?

As we have suggested, don't accept as gospel truth all that your Great-Aunt Hettie, or Uncle Abijah, tells you about the history of the family. People do not always realize that they have confused two different episodes and telescoped them into one, and sometimes they do not discriminate between fact and fiction. Some are natural-born storytellers and quite unconsciously embroider the facts a little here and there to make the tale more dramatic, all the while really believing that they are relating the details as they heard them from their grandfather. Others, who give every evidence of a remarkably retentive memory, tell a clear and straightforward account of the family as they received it from an older generation without realizing that the tradition may have been distorted before they heard it.

You Are a Detective

So listen carefully and attentively to what your elderly relatives pass on to you. Remember, many people talk more or less at random, skipping back and forth as the wheels of memory begin to turn more easily, or they remember more clearly some detail and go back, without warning, to correct it or add to it. Sometimes they will tell the same story twice, having recollected something they have left out. It is often really quite difficult to follow the thread of the story, so you may have to ask for the connection with what you have already heard.

Make an effort to remember the details as faithfully as you can, especially if you have to trust to your own memory rather than take notes. Your pencil and pad may disconcert a speaker as you try to write down details or even key points in the story. Moreover, unless you have had stenographic training, or have learned speedwriting, it is virtually impossible to write fast enough to get down on paper the full story while it is being told. If you own a tape recorder, take it along with you. Later, the sooner the better, while it is still fresh in your mind, write down what you have heard, or transcribe your notes or your tapes, so you can sort out the details and will not have to depend on your own memory to put in the connecting links.

When you have got all that Aunt Hettie told you arranged in some sort of order, you may want to go back and ask her to tell you more about one point or another. This has a double advantage: your own recollection may be clarified, or she may, by that time, remember names and facts that she left out in her earlier account of it. Names and even dates do sometimes "come to you" hours later—we have discovered, with our own advancing years, that this happens quite frequently! Moreover, with the family saga somewhat organized in your own mind, you may well try to get another version of it from Uncle 'Bijah, or at least give him an opportunity to verify it. It is always an advantage if you can get two independent accounts and check to see if they tally. One cousin, aunt, or uncle may remember what another doesn't recall. The mind of one may retain details that didn't interest the other and were not remembered. By comparing and piecing together two or three independent recollections of the details, you may be able to put together a better history.

Even if accounts do not differ significantly, you must check the details as best you can against such sources as you can find, preferring public records, such as those discussed in later chapters, or any written or printed evidence you may find. This is especially important before you accept as true what your narrators have told you about an episode that happened before their own time. What a person does not know from his or her own participation in, or recollection of, a given event is hearsay, not bona fide evidence. Hearsay may be distorted or inaccurate. A mother may tell her daughter the date on which she married that daughter's father, the names of her parents and her husband's parents, as well as the date the daughter was born. Presumably such information is true, but you should make an effort to verify it if possible. When the mother tells her daughter what her father told her about his grandparents or great-grandparents, she is passing on tradition, which may be true, or distorted, or erroneous.

Speaking of differences in memory, Dr. Doane's father, sixty years ago when he was first quizzed about his mother's family, could tell his son very little about that side of the house. At first, he couldn't recall even the maiden name of his grandmother, his mother's mother, who, to be sure, died when he was a boy; later, having learned her name from his sister, his father remembered some details about his cousins. Fortunately, Dr. Doane's father's only sister, fifteen months younger than he, remembered much more about her mother's people (her mother lived with this sister during the last twenty years of her life, so the sister had much more opportunity to hear those relatives mentioned). From her Dr. Doane got the names of her grandparents, a great-grandfather, several cousins, aunts, and uncles, and a couple of great-aunts and great-uncles, so he could construct quite a pedigree of that family, which he verified from gravestones and public records. From one of the second cousins, a remove or two from him, whom he discovered almost by

chance, he gleaned even more about their common progenitors. The cousin was quite a bit older than his aunt so he remembered some people whom his aunt never mentioned.
From his recollections, Dr. Doane learned two interesting
and significant details: one, that the great-grandfather of his
grandmother, having come from Canada into northern Vermont, spoke French Canadian patois, the language of his
childhood, fluently, but quite broken English; and, second,
that there was Indian ancestry in the family. When Dr.
Doane expressed interest in the latter, his cousin became
confidential, apparently having decided to trust him, and
told him quite a gruesome story about a great-great uncle
which was really something! When he got the progenitor's
pension record from the National Archives—he served in the
Revolutionary War—and noted that his birthplace was given
as Saint Ours in Lower Canada (now Quebec), the French-
speaking tradition seemed verified, at least circumstantially.
It wasn't until he found his will in a Vermont probate office
that he learned his father's name. Going to Saint Ours, he
found no record, civil or ecclesiastical, of either him or his father. He was unable to verify, after half a century of searching, the Indian ancestor, although certain facts seemed to
suggest it. The gruesome story is confirmed by an account of
religious fanaticism and cruelty found in Crocker's *History of
the Baptists in Vermont*, which lends credence to the family
tradition of Indian ancestry—at least, he was willing to accept the tradition in the hope that he may find more convinc-
ing evidence.

This leads us to summarize the experience of a friend who
successfully tracked down a similar tradition in his family.
He grew up believing the tradition that was current in his father's family. When he wanted to know the facts, his father
told him that his grandmother, Rachel Rice, later Perin, was
of partly Indian descent. Whenever he had leisure, he studied the family history and began to compile and verify the

facts. He tried to study the appearance of as many of Rachel's descendants as he could, noting the hair and features of uncles, aunts, and cousins of one degree or another. According to Mendel's law, a percentage of them should have had black hair and Indian features, if the tradition was true. When he found that none of his relatives looked the least bit Indian, he concluded that there was no truth in the tradition, but he still wanted to know how it came about that his father and grandfather believed that there was an Indian ancestor. So he continued his search for the progenitors of Rachel Rice, his great-grandmother. One of his cousins gave him his first clue, which she found in a history of Tompkins County, New York. This mentioned the migration of his great-grandparents, John and Rachel Perin, from western Massachusetts to that county. In reading over the chapter, he found that a family with which he had a possible connection was said to have come from Charlemont, Berkshire County, Massachusetts, so he centered his search there. He soon discovered that Captain Moses Rice was living there when he was killed by the Indians, and his grandson Asa was carried away captive. Asa lived with his captors for about six or seven years before he was redeemed at the age of fifteen; therefore, it seemed quite unlikely that he had taken an Indian girl as a wife. Continuing his search, our friend learned that Asa married, not once but twice, white women, and fathered quite a family, among them Rachel, whom he named as Rachel Perin in his will. Thus the tradition of Indian ancestry was disproved, and in its place our friend found that he had a great-great-grandfather who, in his youth, was a captive among the Indians for several years. If you are sufficiently interested in how our friend followed step by step the clues that he picked up along the trail into the past, you will find the full story and the surprising happenstance by which the final, conclusive evidence was found in the *New England Historical and Genealogical Register* (vol. 121, January 1967,

pp. 29-36). The author is Stanley E. Perin; the title, "A Tradition in Search of Its Origin." It is not only an exciting story;
it is also an excellent example of first-class genealogical
research.

Beware of Fantasy

So much for one type of tradition. Now we want to discuss
the fanciful type. If the basic fact in the tradition in Mr.
Perin's family became distorted in three generations, consider the following letter, which another friend of Dr. Doane's
asked him to read about fifty years ago. He had written to
one of his distant cousins asking her to talk with her aged
grandmother about the history of the family and where they
had lived before moving to the West. (Dr. Doane copied the
original letter verbatim, changing only the names, as his
friend requested.)

> Here is all Grandma can think of about the fore fathers.
> Lord John Whiting, Great Grandfather, was born in
> 1735, near London. He came to America on the May
> Flower in 1776 soon after the Revolutionary War,
> bringing his two daughters, Lady Jane and Mabel
> (Not sure of the name). She, Mabel, went back to
> England with her father.
> Lord Whiting bought some land in Connecticut and
> gave it to Lady Jane for a wedding present when she
> married grandfather James Dupey (he was a French
> nobleman) in 1796 or 1798. James Dupey was Captain
> of the May Flower. Ten sons were born to them.

We cite this fantastic account simply to point out some of
the incongruities which, we trust, will strike you immediately. In fact, you might stop at this point and test your skill
in spotting the anachronisms before you read on. Surely
most of the school histories of our country still contain an account of the historic voyage of the *Mayflower*, overloaded

with 102 passengers and all the alleged heirlooms, the date of its arrival, and the horrors of that first winter, 1620-21. Most high-school students know that the Revolutionary War was not over until the surrender of Cornwallis at Yorktown in 1781, and that the independence of the United States was not formally recognized until the signing of the Treaty of Paris in 1783. These facts are sufficient to give warning that this story must have been told by an elderly person whose memory was no longer accurate. Consequently, it is of almost no value to one searching for ancestors and trying to discover something about the history of his or her family. The only clue of immediate value lies in the mention of Connecticut as the place of settlement, and there research should be centered once the trail has been followed back to New England. You may be interested to know that Dr. Doane's friend found that this was true. Following up some of the distaff families he discovered a line of descent from one of the passengers on the historic *Mayflower*, although the name was not that mentioned by Grandma, and another from a Huguenot who fled from France after the revocation of the Edict of Nantes in 1685 and settled in Connecticut.

In these two examples of family traditions, the one had on the face of it the semblance of truth, but, after careful examination, followed by tracing the pedigree of the great-grandmother involved, proved to be a distortion of fact; the other, which seemed to be a figment of the imagination, or at most the tale of one whose mind, perhaps weakened by illness and age, wandered from one vague recollection to another in strange fancy, did have, deeply buried in its fantasy, some basic facts.

Oral History

There was, however, in the history of our progenitors, a time when oral tradition was remarkably clear and accurate. Pedigrees were memorized and handed on from generation to generation, with appropriate additions in each. There were uncounted examples of such oral pedigrees among the ancient Scandinavians, the Irish, the Welsh, the Scots, the Icelanders, the Maoris in New Zealand, and the tribes of Africa. In Ireland, for example, for many centuries, the *filid*, or the hereditary historians, of the clan, or *sept*, were trained to memorize and recite, without error or omission, the descent from the founder or progenitor, not only of the main stem of the family, but also its agnate branches. In Iceland, there were handed down from generation to generation lines of descent from the first settlers who came across the sea from Scandinavia in the ninth century to colonize that uninhabited island. These pedigrees were not written down until the twelfth century, when Ari Thorgilsson compiled the *Landnamabok* in which they were entered. In New Zealand it took a Maori chieftain three days to recite, before a government land commission, the descent of his people for thirty-four generations in order to justify their claim to certain territory. From generation to generation he gave the names, not only in the direct male line, but in the agnate branches stemming from each generation. Many Welsh pedigrees, traced back to the early kings of both North and South Wales, were handed on by trained bards for many generations before they were finally written down. Historical scholarship has found the documentary proof that substantiates the authenticity and accuracy of many of those ancient pedigrees, so their reliability should not be denied.

There is at least one famous black family in the United States whose history has been faithfully and accurately memorized and handed on from generation to generation, beginning with the progenitor who was brought from Africa on a slave ship in the eighteenth century. Probably there are many others. The story of this one family has been so poignantly told by one of the descendants, Alex Haley, in his book *Roots* that we cannot refrain from abridging and para-phrasing it as an example of what may be done to verify a family tradition such as his. As a boy in western Tennessee, he squatted beside his grandmother's chair and listened while she and her visiting sisters and cousins talked about their forefathers and their traditional lineage; those conver-sations made a deep impression on him.

In maturity, Mr. Haley remembered that his grandmother always referred to her progenitor as "the African" who came to "Naplis"; she sometimes called him Kintay, and she said that he was cutting down a tree to make a drum when he was captured. Also, she used words that were strange to the boy, often enough to impress them upon his memory, words like *ko* for a banjo and Kamby Bolongo, which referred to a certain large river, and others, some of which she repeated to herself while working about the house. She talked also about the successive generations from the African, telling the names of each individual, what he or she did, and where he or she lived. Then, one day in 1965, when he was walking by the National Archives in Washington, he suddenly remem-bered his grandmother's account of the family history. On impulse, he went in and asked if there were census records of Alamance County, North Carolina, where her people had lived about 1860-70. In these records he found the first con-firmation of the accuracy of his grandmother's recollections: her grandfather and his family were listed! Another step was to identify the language or dialect to which those strange words that she used belonged. At the University of Wiscon-sin he found Dr. Vansina, an African professor of linguistics, who, listening intently to Mr. Haley's repetition of them, told him that the dialect was known as Mandinka, in which the word for river was *bolong*, which, combined with *Kamby*, undoubtedly referred to the Gambia River in West Africa.

With this knowledge, Mr. Haley went to Bathurst, at the mouth of the Gambia, where he learned the location of the tribe that spoke that dialect; but he had to return to America before he could organize a trip to the spot. Finally, months later, the officials in Bathurst wrote him that they had learned that a *griot* (an oral historian) who could recite the history of the Kinte tribe was living at Juffure, miles away up the river in the interior, and invited him to return to Africa, which he did. From the *griot*, then a very old man, he heard the history of the Kinte tribe and was told that a young man of the village, named Kinte, went into the forest one day to cut a tree and make a drum—the very tradition Mr. Haley had heard his grandmother repeat. Kinte was captured and was never seen again. The *griot* also told him about the tribe from the time it left Old Mali and migrated to Mauretania, whence, later, Kairaba Junta Kinte, a Muslim *marabout* (a holy man), came into Gambia and settled in Juffure. This man was the grandfather of Kinte, "the African" who came to 'Naplis (Annapolis, Maryland) in 1767.

CHAPTER 4

Out of the Family Papers

While you are talking with Grandfather and the other older relatives, try to find out if they have any written records of the family. Sometimes, as we have said, this requires tact, for the owners may be perversely inclined to think that you want to run off with some document; at other times, you can ask outright to see the family Bible and other papers and easily obtain permission to make a copy of the records they contain, so you have to play it by ear. If Grandfather happens to be in the right mood, he may even give you the Bible, but beware lest by accepting it you are going to offend Aunt Mamie. A timely refusal may win her eternal goodwill and perhaps, later, even the Bible itself.

If you are at a distance from these older relatives and have to seek by correspondence any records they may have, be sure to tell them that you are compiling a history of the family (promise them a copy, if need be), for sometimes they may suspect, however far it may be from the truth, that you are getting ready to claim some mythical estate. It is truly amazing how many people have a notion that their family is entitled to some great estate overseas. They have heard of the "Drake estate," or the "Buchanan estate," or the "Edwards estate"; or they have read in the newspapers about the litigation over the Wendell estate and seen printed lists of the great number of claimants. Colonel Green, the famous

Hetty's son, hadn't been dead a month when three women came into the genealogical library in Newport, Rhode Island, to attempt to find records proving that they were among the rightful heirs to the Green and Howland millions. The old estates, so frequently dangled before the eyes of the susceptible, have long since been settled; those recently in the courts are of such a nature that very explicit proof must be established by any claimant. So be careful to avoid suspicion that you are going to steal evidence that will enable you to claim property.

Bible Records

Sometimes old letters, diaries, and other family papers exist. One or two old letters, in faded handwriting, badly worn along the creases, may contain clues to places of residence or details of family history that would otherwise be completely lost in the obscurity of the past. Sometimes a dull old diary will contain, interspersed among accounts of the weather, notes of baptisms, weddings, and funerals. Old family account books are another source of information, perhaps meager, but sometimes very illuminating. Even the framed sampler, worked by Great-Great-Aunt Hannah at the age of eleven, may prove to be of value. Don't overlook such items, for everything is grist to the genealogist's mill.

Let us take a look first at the family Bible. If other evidence is lacking, Bible records can be most useful. But the genealogist should use them with care. Occasionally someone has tampered with a Bible record, attempted to change a date or erase an entry altogether, although generally any alteration that has been made can be easily detected. An instance of such tampering comes to mind. Dr. Doane was gathering data for a history of the family and wanted the record of the immediate family of a double cousin of his, a woman of his grandfather's age (the grandfather was then in his eighties).

She was inclined to be a bit vain and couldn't "remember" her own age! So he finally persuaded her to let him see her husband's family Bible (it was his second or third visit). When he came to the entry of her birth (her husband's father had meticulously entered the birth dates of the husbands and wives of his several children), he found that the year had been scratched out, although the month and day were there. He always carried a magnifying glass in his pocket for use in deciphering old handwriting and faded records. So, with a pretense of being unable to read some of the writing, which really was faded, he looked at the date she thought she had eradicated and, catching a faint residue of the ink, was able to make out "1831." Later, he verified this through his grandfather (she was his first cousin), who remembered that she was just about two years younger than he was. Really, there is little that can be done to a written record that cannot be detected upon careful examination.

The genealogist may puzzle for hours and perhaps worry for months over certain problems connected with the use of Bible records. Some such records are remarkably full; others, unusually scant and inadequate. In one old Bible with which we are familiar (the volume was printed in 1609), the records begin about 1650 and give the name, the exact hour and minute of birth, and the sign of the zodiac under which each child was born (in those days astrology and the casting of horoscopes were taken seriously, so it was considered important to know these details). We have seen some eighteenth- and early nineteenth-century Bibles containing this same sort of meticulous record. Other Bibles have such exasperatingly meager data as "My wife was delivered of a son at six o'clock P.M. November the 12th, 1785"—with no name given. Often one comes across a Bible with a record beginning like this:

Grandfather David Richardson, born 1700, died
August 1770

Remember Richardson, born 1703, died August 1760

followed by a list of their children, with dates of birth and death given. Such a record is obviously not a contemporary record, and was made many, many years after "Grandfather" was born, for David Richardson would never have called himself "grandfather." On the face of it, it looks as though David Richardson had married Remember Richardson (indeed, the present owner of this very Bible had interpreted the record in that way); but one should be suspicious of such a record, for, although occasionally cousins of the same surname did marry, it was not a very common practice. Further search in this particular case disclosed the fact that David Richardson's wife was Remember Ward. The granddaughter who made this record knew her only as Remember Richardson and, therefore, entered that name in the Bible.

Very few Bibles contain records dated before the eighteenth century, and most of the many we have examined commence with records dated in the 1780s and 1790s. Most of the older Bibles have disappeared, although once in a while they do turn up in unexpected places. For example, the Greene family Bible, containing records dating from early in the seventeenth century, turned up in the possession of a descendant of an entirely different surname out in Nebraska, sixteen hundred miles away from Rhode Island, where the first record was entered in it. So, however remote the possibility, don't entirely give up hope of finding one you are looking for. It may turn up in the possession of a third or fourth cousin, or even in a bookshop.

One of the first things to do when examining a Bible is to determine when the book was printed. If the title page has the date 1817 on it, or the preface or translator's note is signed 1817, you know at once that any records dated before that year were entered from memory (or, perhaps, copied from some older Bible). In this event, these records should

be carefully verified, if possible, from other sources—
gravestones, town or church records. Records of births, marriages, and deaths occurring after that date were probably
entered soon after they occurred. If, on the other hand, the
Bible was published in 1609, and that printed date is found
on its title page or on the half titles that mark the beginnings
of the Old and New Testaments, and if the *handwriting in
which the records were written* is of several different periods,
then you may be reasonably certain that you have a genuine
old record, containing, perhaps, several generations of the
family births, marriages, and deaths.

Occasionally a son was sufficiently interested in his family, when he was married and was about to start his own
family life, to copy from the original Bible, kept by his father,
the data it contained. But this rarely happened, for, we re-
gret to say, our ancestors were not always of a genealogical
turn of mind, and generally did not think of doing such a
thing. Young people are always more interested in the future, as they should be, than in the past, however much they
can learn from it.

Generally speaking, late in the eighteenth century and
early in the nineteenth, a young couple, newly married and
just starting out in life, either received a brand-new Bible as a
gift from parents or well-wishers, or bought one with their
first spare cash. It was a period during which "respectable
people" still belonged to a church and read the Bible regularly. Sometimes such a couple would enter their family
names, but more frequently they were content to enter only
the dates of their own births, that of their marriage, and
then, from time to time as the children came along, the
records of their progeny. Fortunately, in many nineteenth-
century Bibles parents entered the name of the place as well
as the date of birth. This was a century of great movement,
as families by the thousands were migrating westward, stay-

ing but a few years in one place and then moving on as they heard of richer lands.

Not infrequently there is a question about the authenticity of the dates of the records in the family Bible. If the handwriting in which the records are made gives evidence of contemporary entry, there can be little question, however. You all know that your handwriting has varied from year to year as you have grown older. Just compare your diary of ten years ago with that written last month, if you want an example. So, if the handwriting of these old records varies from entry to entry, if the ink seems to be of a different quality in each of them, you may be certain that the data were entered as each child came along. But if there is a "copperplate" evenness about the handwriting, then, if the records do not tally with others you have found, you will have to prove the correctness of one record or the other. For instance, there may be a difference between the record of your grandmother's birth as it is given in the Bible and that which you have found in the official records of the town in which she was born. Perhaps the baptismal record on the church books may settle the question, if it is the matter of the correct year, and sometimes the gravestone will determine it, although gravestone inscriptions are quite likely to have been made from Bible records. Sometimes it is impossible to settle the question. In that event you should carefully give both of the dates you have found, one in parentheses following the other, indicating, of course, which is which, thus:

Sarah Richardson, born in Newton, Massachusetts,
April 14, 1774 (Newton records; her Bible record gives
the date 1773); died January 23, 1848, "aged 74"
(according to an obituary notice).

Generally, in the case of such a discrepancy, the town records should be accepted as more reliable. In this particular case, Sarah (Richardson) Clough wrote up her Bible record when she was well along in years and may have made an error of a year in her age (although people are generally given credit for knowing their own ages). If she was born in 1773, as her Bible states, she would not have been seventy-five until three months after her death, and therefore the newspaper obituary was correct in stating that she was "aged 74" at the time of her death. But sometimes, when the birthday is approaching, the age on that birthday is given in such a notice, and even on the gravestone. Generally, we have noted that, in such a case, the person concerned was within a few weeks of the birthday—not as many as three months. The genealogist, however, to protect himself or herself against the accusation of inaccuracy, should always note such a discrepancy, give both of the dates found, and perhaps also explain the reason for accepting either one or the other. Sometimes a Bible record was begun by a young married couple in this way:

Luther Whitney, born February 23, 1781
Hannah Whitney, born December 27, 1777

This type of record, unlike the one of identical surnames in the Richardson family Bible quoted above, offers no hint that Whitney may not have been the maiden name of the wife. Ostensibly Luther Whitney married Hannah Whitney (the date and place of the marriage were not entered in the Bible), but we are always skeptical when we come across such a Bible record, especially when no other record verifies the wife's name. We feel reasonably certain, in this case, that Hannah's maiden name was not Whitney because it has been impossible to establish her in any of the Whitney families in or around Adams, Massachusetts, where their first two children were born. It is, of course, possible that she was a cousin, or belonging to some other Whitney family; the name is not uncommon.

If you cannot get possession of the Bible record that is important to you, get either a certified copy, sworn to before a notary public, or a photocopy or photostat of the record for your notebook. Moreover, if you cannot have the Bible to keep, it is always wise to make a careful note of the full name and address of the person who owns the Bible and the date on which you made the copy. Then, if you ever need to use that record for legal purposes or as a basis for membership in one of the hereditary or patriotic societies, you have certified evidence of this link in your ancestry, for you can submit your copy of this record to the society, with the name and address of its owner, and their genealogist can probably gain access to it for verification if desired.

Diaries

Another sort of family record unfortunately much less common in occurrence than a Bible, but very valuable when it is found, is an old diary. Some diaries are exceedingly interesting, not only because they contain a wealth of genealogical details but also because they were written by keen observers and display considerable evidence of the writer's personality. Unfortunately, sometimes the keeper of the diary was more interested in the affairs that were going on about him or her than in the details for which the genealogist is looking. In that case, however interesting it may be, the diary is a disappointment; it should be carefully read, nevertheless, for there may be some important clues buried in it.

One mid-nineteenth-century diary, which we happen to know, is almost purely a business record. The author was a miller in a small town, so he recorded each day just how many bushels of corn, wheat, and oats he ground in his mill, and how many feet of lumber were sawed. But he generally noted also the name of the individual for whom he ground or sawed. This has made the diary valuable to us in helping others trace their ancestry, and has enabled us to determine when some of the houses in the town were built. But this diarist also recorded which members of his family went to church each Sunday, so, in the absence of other records, we have been able to determine just when his sons and daughters moved away from home. When he mentioned a funeral, he was exasperatingly brief and made such statements as "Went to Florence's funeral." No clue to Florence's identity. One entry puzzled us a long time: "Went to Aunt Debbie's funeral." We knew of no Aunt Debbie or Deborah in the family. She proved to be a local character of such kindliness that she was "aunt" to everyone who knew her. Another exasperating entry was "Thomas started back West." Finally we learned that this Thomas was his cousin, the only son of his only uncle, who had moved west to Illinois. That is the last record we have been able to find about Thomas, for this branch of the family appears never to have heard of him again.

Often fruitlessly tantalizing as such diaries are, they must be carefully studied, for the alert mind will find much of use in them. It is a good plan to make careful notes of any names mentioned in them, for sometimes such names may prove to be of importance to you. In this same diary we noted that the diarist went to "Thomas Morse's funeral" on a given date. This entry, although it was of no immediate use to us, later enabled us to help a correspondent who was searching for the date of her great-grandfather's death. The town records did not contain the required information, and it was not until some time later that we found his gravestone in a forgotten cemetery.

While we are on the subject of diaries, let us note that there are many invaluable colonial diaries that have been found and printed. These very old diaries frequently enable a genealogist to prove a line of descent, and sometimes they make very good reading, furnishing a picture of the times in which their authors lived. Samuel Sewall's *Diary* (we have used the 1973 edition) is one of the most important documents that we have, for he loved functions and attended every christening, wedding, and burial that came to his notice. He tells also just what dowry he had to give each of his several wives. It is amusing to note that they came cheaper as he and the prospective spouse got older. The judge—for he was a judge, and even sat on the famous witchcraft trials—lived in Boston, so his diary was concerned with that vicinity. He kept a diary during the latter half of his life, which covered the period from 1674 to 1729. An even older diary, the years including 1653 to 1684, is that of Thomas Minor, born in England, who became one of the first settlers of Stonington, Connecticut. It is replete with information regarding those who lived there during the pioneer days of the settlement and was published in 1899 by one of his descendants. Joshua Hempstead's diary, covering thirty-seven years between 1711 and 1748, does much the same thing for New London, Connecticut. John Winthrop's journal, which has never been published in its entirety, is another invaluable source for Massachusetts and Connecticut families. He was a physician of a sort and made detailed records of many of his cases.

Family Letters

Family letters are likewise worth reading. Not unlike diaries, they frequently present a wealth of detail, although surnames are seldom mentioned in them, and they may shed considerable light on the character and personality of the writer. The one surviving letter written by Dr. Doane's great-great-grandmother gives a vivid picture of her personality and amplifies and confirms the family tradition concerning her characteristics in pecuniary matters. This particular letter was written to her son in Michigan about a month after her mother's death in 1839. She baldly states the fact that "Mother has been dead nearly a month and I haven't gotten my share of her things yet!" Even without the tradition that she quarreled with her husband because he loaned some of her money without her consent, and that she refused to speak to him again until it was repaid (about seven years later), we get from this single sentence in her letter an unforgettable picture of the redoubtable lady and her determination that no one should do her out of what was rightfully hers.

Another old letter among the family papers set Dr. Doane on the right road to determining the descendants of a different branch of the family. This was written in a fine schoolgirlish hand on dainty paper such as, about a hundred and fifty years ago, could be found only in cities. In it were mentioned all such parties and visits as a young girl loves, and a number of names of cousins of whose existence he had been unaware. Another such letter, written in the 1840s and full of news about widely scattered relatives, enabled its finder to trace her family back several generations because it gave her the necessary clues to the places in which they had lived.

Other Family Record Sources

Family account books also help considerably. Once, while attending a country auction in a Vermont hamlet, Dr. Doane pulled out of a basket of trash that was set aside to be burned (not even put up for auction) a long, narrow daybook. The entries dated from about 1803 to 1825 and contained many names of individuals and places. Through it he was able to establish the locality from which a migration was made. Aside from such details, of importance in a family history, this old account book sheds light on the prices of labor and materials at that time, especially in a rural community.

An account book, or ledger, in the possession of a gentleman in New York, proves to be practically a census of a small community in Dutchess County, for it was kept by a storekeeper. It contains evidence of the approximate dates of marriages, deaths, and removals, as the accounts are opened and closed or as the names of the customers are changed. From it he was able to prove almost to a month the date of the migration of his own family from that Dutchess County village to northern Vermont, for he noted the date on which the account was closed and marked "Paid in full." By comparing that date with those of some deeds in Vermont, he could set the date of migration. R. E. Dale, of Lincoln, Nebraska, edited this old account book of Dunkin's Store, Dover Furnace (Pawling Precinct), New York, and published it in the genealogical department of the *Boston Evening Transcript*, June 28, July 10, and July 18, 1935, as note 2751.

Although you may never have examined very closely the sampler hanging in its frame on the wall, it may contain data for your history. Sometimes a young seamstress, doing her cross-stitching, worked into the sampler a list of her brothers and sisters and their ages. If she dated the sampler (many samplers are dated), you know approximately when each of the relatives was born. Sometime, if you are interested, get Edith Standwood Bolton's *American Samplers* from the library and examine it. Not only a fascinating account, it is a genealogical source book as well, for Mrs. Bolton has illustrated a number of samplers and given the family data from many more. Other excellent volumes for such information are Glee F. Krueger's *New England Samplers to 1840* (1978) and Betty Ring's, *Needlework: An Historical Survey* (2d edition, revised, 1990).

Another type of needlework of value to the ancestor hunter is the so-called friendship quilt and its variations. About a hundred and seventy years ago it was the vogue to work quilts made up of pieces on which were embroidered or signed in indelible ink the names of the maker's close friends and relatives. Sometimes the girls who inscribed their names even embroidered the pieces themselves and presented them to the maker, who put them together. One quilt of this kind, in the possession of a descendant of the Standish family, contains the names and dates of all the female members of the family, including aunts and cousins.

Another coverlet enabled one ancestor hunter to trace her family back across half a dozen states to the locality from which her ancestors came. It was embroidered by a great-grandmother for her hope chest. Taking a justifiable pride in her skill, she worked into one panel of the spread her maiden name, the date, and the name of the town in Maine in which she was then living. Even old family silver may prove useful to the genealogist. Although very old silver is uncommon, an occasional piece has survived and been preserved as an heirloom. An old spoon engraved thus:

A B

C

has its clue, for initials placed in this manner on really old silver generally mean that the piece belonged to a husband and wife jointly; in this case, let us say to Abijah and Betsy Cole. It may have been a wedding gift. Old tankards and silver mugs are frequently engraved in the same manner. Sometimes it is difficult to identify such initials, but they do serve as a clue that may put you on the right track. Recently, reading the will of Captain Lawrence Clarke, of Newport and Middletown, Rhode Island, instead of depending upon the published abstract of it, we noted that he bequeathed to his son Lawrence the silver cup marked L T which belonged, he had written, "to my grandfather." Captain Clarke's mother's maiden name had not been known hitherto; his own given name is not found in any of the earlier generations of his father's family. There was a Lawrence Turner living in Newport in the seventeenth century, but, as far as the town records show, no other man with the initials L T. Was Margaret, the second wife of the Reverend Joseph Clarke, the daughter of Lawrence Turner? We think so. One other slight bit of circumstantial evidence seems to confirm this assumption: Lawrence Turner was called a "brick maker" in one document; Lawrence Clarke, when he was not much over sixteen, was granted permission by the town council to dig clay for bricks. This indicates that he may have been apprenticed to his grandfather, whose silver cup he later possessed.

Thus you see an important adjunct to the family memories is any record that may exist in the family archives. You should always try to locate such records and with their aid get the older relatives to explain as much about the family as possible. Sometimes the sight of an old letter or a bit of silver recalls to an aging mind the story back of it or relationships that have been forgotten and might not otherwise come to mind. In digging for ancestors, no stone is too small or too insignificant to be left unturned.

CHAPTER 5

Digging in Books and Libraries

By the time you have talked to or had correspondence with the older relatives and perhaps the older friends of the family, and have dug what you can out of the old family papers and records, you will probably have gathered sufficient data in your notebook and on your chart to begin searching in printed material. Perhaps you are lucky enough to live near a library containing a genealogical collection, say in Boston, New York, Philadelphia, Washington, Fort Wayne, Chicago, Seattle, San Francisco, or Los Angeles, to mention only a few of the larger cities in which there are well-known genealogical collections. This material may be found in public libraries or other libraries, such as the outstanding collection of the Family History Library in Salt Lake City, Utah (see chapter 9 for a discussion of its resources), the Library of Congress in Washington, D.C., the New England Historic Genealogical Society Library in Boston, or the Newberry Library in Chicago. Even though your public library may not contain a special collection of genealogical material, ask the librarian where such collections can be found and consult P. William Filby's *Directory of American Libraries with Genealogy and Local History Collections* (1988). If you do not live near a genealogical library, large or small, perhaps you can plan your vacation to include a visit to a city in which there is a good collection. One of our friends, whose family likes an annual trip to some city, always manages to go to a place such as Chicago, San Francisco, or New York for his vacation. While his family enjoys the shops and city sights during the day, he, with his notebook and the problems on which he is working, spends the time in the library, digging for his ancestors. Each year he comes back with a problem or two solved and a sheaf of notes that will keep him busy through many of the long winter evenings.

If you have never used a genealogical collection before, the first thing to do is to have a good talk with the curator or assistant in charge, who, from long experience in serving genealogists, knows how to help a beginner get started. He or she knows the collection and can efficiently direct your use of it. The curator will explain its arrangement to you and show you any special indexes that have been made for it.

Printed Genealogies

Once you have explained your problem to the curator, he or she will get out for you any printed genealogies of the family or families in which you are interested that are available in this collection. You may be fortunate enough to have such a genealogy put into your hands immediately and to find in it your line of descent—once you have become familiar with the system on which it is arranged. (A certain amount of study is required in order to pick up any genealogy and use it intelligently, for the system of arrangement varies a great deal from one volume to another.) In the event that you have such good fortune, you can either copy the complete line of your descent from the book before you or plan to buy a copy of it from one of the booksellers who handle genealogical books, such as Goodspeed's Book Shop in Boston, the Genealogical Publishing Co. in Baltimore, Maryland, or Tuttle Antiquarian Books in Rutland, Vermont. Sometimes the volume is rare, for genealogies are almost always printed in small editions; hence a copy may be very difficult to find and very expensive when found. But even if you are fortunate enough to be able to afford to buy a copy, you will want to make a working pedigree from the copy in the library as a basis for running back the female lines. No one printed volume will be likely to contain all your ancestry; otherwise you would know about it and probably not be reading this book.

Such a working pedigree will look something like Form 3, shown here. You will note that we have given, at the top of the column at the left-hand side of the page, the exact title of the volume used, and in that column, opposite each generation, the references to the pages on which the data for each generation were found. It is essential that you take such references as you go along. Otherwise you will have to check back through the volume to get them later. Many a genealogist who started out without these references has cursed himself or herself for the oversight when they were needed later, especially if the book was in a distant library.

This pedigree is based on what Dr. Doane happened to find in first consulting the book entitled *The Doane Family*, by Alfred Adler Doane (1902), in the New York State Library in Albany many years ago. Harry Harvey Doane, listed on page 298 of this book, was Dr. Doane's father, so here he found his complete Doane line back to the immigrant John Doane (or Done, as the name was then spelled), who appeared in Plymouth, Massachusetts, about 1630. As you will note on this working pedigree, when Dr. Doane found this line he discovered his descent from the Bangs, Hamblen, Bearse, Higgins, Howe, and Randall families as well, and so he began to dig for the ancestors in those lines and work those pedigrees back to the immigrants, and, in one or two cases, across the Atlantic into England, and for two or three generations there. He found printed genealogies for the Hamblen (that is, Hamlin) and Higgins families but he had to do a lot

The Doane Family by A. A. Doane

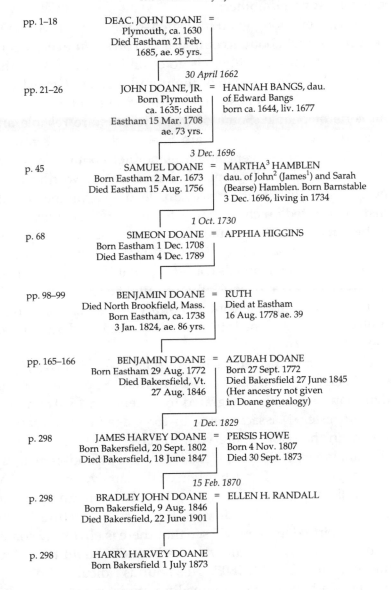

pp. 1–18   DEAC. JOHN DOANE =
              Plymouth, ca. 1630
              Died Eastham 21 Feb.
              1685, ae. 95 yrs.

              30 April 1662
pp. 21–26   JOHN DOANE, JR.   = HANNAH BANGS, dau.
              Born Plymouth   of Edward Bangs
              ca. 1635; died   born ca. 1644, liv. 1677
              Eastham 15 Mar. 1708
              ae. 73 yrs.

              3 Dec. 1696
p. 45   SAMUEL DOANE = MARTHA³ HAMBLEN
              Born Eastham 2 Mar. 1673   dau. of John² (James¹) and Sarah
              Died Eastham 15 Aug. 1756   (Bearse) Hamblen. Born Barnstable
                                          3 Dec. 1696, living in 1734

              1 Oct. 1730
p. 68   SIMEON DOANE = APPHIA HIGGINS
              Born Eastham 1 Dec. 1708
              Died Eastham 4 Dec. 1789

pp. 98–99   BENJAMIN DOANE = RUTH
              Died North Brookfield, Mass.   Died at Eastham
              Born Eastham, ca. 1738   16 Aug. 1778 ae. 39
              3 Jan. 1824, ae. 86 yrs.

pp. 165–166   BENJAMIN DOANE = AZUBAH DOANE
              Born Eastham 29 Aug. 1772   Born 27 Sept. 1772
              Died Bakersfield, Vt.   Died Bakersfield 27 June 1845
              27 Aug. 1846   (Her ancestry not given
                                           in Doane genealogy)

              1 Dec. 1829
p. 298   JAMES HARVEY DOANE = PERSIS HOWE
              Born Bakersfield, 20 Sept. 1802   Born 4 Nov. 1807
              Died Bakersfield, 18 June 1847   Died 30 Sept. 1873

              15 Feb. 1870
p. 298   BRADLEY JOHN DOANE = ELLEN H. RANDALL
              Born Bakersfield, 9 Aug. 1846
              Died Bakersfield, 22 June 1901

p. 298   HARRY HARVEY DOANE
              Born Bakersfield 1 July 1873

Form 3. The Doane Pedigree.

of digging for the rest. He never found Azubah Doane, his great-great-grandmother!

Now, even though you find such a line in print, you must be very careful about accepting it as correct in every detail. Not everything that glitters is gold, and not everything that is printed is true, in spite of the popular belief. Genealogies are compiled and published, sometimes at great expense, by all sorts of people. Some of these records are reliable and trustworthy; some of them are filled with glaring errors. A beautifully printed genealogy, elaborately bound in tooled leather, may be full of mistakes and almost worthless, or even worse than that, grossly misleading. Another family history, printed on cheap paper from worn type, may prove to be notable for its accuracy. You cannot tell from the outward appearance and the physical makeup, although as a general rule a book breeds confidence if it is carefully printed on good paper and substantially and tastefully bound in cloth. By studying the contents of a volume you can form a pretty good idea of the intelligence, acumen, and accuracy of the author or compiler.

If there are discrepancies in dates, for instance, you should be suspicious and check carefully. Suppose you find that John Jones, who emigrated to America in 1630 and died in Dorchester, Massachusetts, in 1685, aged eighty years, is stated, in the book before you, to have been the son of Sir William Jones, of Buxton, Hertfordshire, England. In reading the chapter on the English origin of the family, you note that Sir William, reputed father of John, the emigrant, died in 1600 and was buried in Buxton. If you stop to figure John's possible birth date, you will see that there is obviously something wrong, for no man who died in 1600 could be the father of a child born in 1605. This sounds ridiculous, doesn't it? Yet, we have known unheeding ancestor hunters to accept such a statement "because they found it in print." Obviously, anyone who would allow such an error to be printed is careless; therefore, anything you find in a genealogy compiled by such an author should be carefully checked—against the original records, if possible.

Sometimes the genealogist or compiler of the book does not actually make such a statement, but the person using it makes a careless assumption from the documents that the compiler has printed in the genealogy. For instance, many of the descendants of Deacon John Doane of Plymouth and Eastham, Massachusetts, who have used A. A. Doane's book have assumed that the Deacon's wife was named Abigail. This assumption is based on the will that Mr. Doane copied from the Registry of Probate at Barnstable, Massachusetts. John Doane, in his will, dated in 1678 (misprinted 1768 in the book), bequeathed his dwelling house and a certain "upland and meadow" about it to his "loving wife." Since Abigail Doane certified to the truthfulness of the inventory of his estate in 1686, it has been assumed that she was his widow and the mother of his children. Now Mr. Doane also printed a verbatim copy of a deed, dated in 1681, in which John Doane conveyed this same dwelling house and "upland and meadow" about it to his daughter Abigail. Obviously his wife had died between May 18, 1678, the date of his will, and December 2, 1681, the date of this deed. Hence, the Abigail Doane who certified the inventory must have been his daughter, to whom he had deeded the house originally intended for his widow if she survived him. Later research by another genealogist indicates that Deacon John Doane had a wife named Ann in 1648, when they both signed a conveyance, who was dead before 1659 when he and his wife Lydia conveyed some land in Eastham (see Mary Walton Ferris's The Dawes-Gates Ancestral Lines [1931, 1943], vol. 2, pp. 304-5).

We doubt if there is a genealogy that does not contain a typographical error or misprint, and there are very few in which there are not some mistakes made by the compiler in interpreting the records at his or her disposal. You should be alert to catch these, and, whenever you see one, try to check it against the original records. Not infrequently you may find that a genealogist has killed off the child from whom you know you are descended, because he did not find that child mentioned in the father's will, or for some other such reason. In a case of this kind, you must be careful to supply ample proof of your ancestor's life and connection with the parents.

Indexes

Failing a published genealogy of the family in which you are interested, the curator of the collection in which you are working will show you how to find any genealogies of the family that have been printed in periodicals as well as gene-alogies of other families with which yours is connected, and local histories. Or the curator will show you how to get at these "buried" genealogies through such indexes as the ex-cellent *Periodical Source Index*, and Jacobus's, Durrie's, and Munsell's (for a list of such indexes see Appendix A). These indexes vary in completeness. Some are limited but thor-ough in covering the ground they are supposed to cover. (Al-ways read the preface and see what the compiler's intentions were.) Others, although they are supposed to be adequate, are very much out of date. Some libraries have compiled in-dexes to their genealogical collections. For example, the Newberry Library, Chicago, indexed family sketches in all local histories it acquired until about 1917. This index, the *Ge-nealogical Index of the Newberry Library* (1960, 4 vols.), is avail-able in several of the large libraries. The *American Genealogical Index*, conceived by Fremont J. Rider, of Middletown, Con-necticut, is another valuable tool, for it combines in one al-phabetical order all the names in a considerable number of genealogies, thus making it short work to locate a given name (watch, however, for variant spellings). A second series, the *American Genealogical-Biographical Index*, is now being published; it includes all the names in the genealogical department of the *Boston Evening Transcript*, 1906-41, the many lists of Revolutionary War soldiers, and several more genealogies.

Frequently such an index will be very useful to you. Although the library in which you are working may not have the volumes to which it refers, if you can get the names of the authors and the titles of such books, you can make a note to use them in some other library where they are to be found, or perhaps you can ask some friend to consult them for you.

Local Histories

If you do not find a reference to the family in which you are interested, the next thing to do is to locate a history of the town or county in which you know they lived. Even though your family may have been too obscure to warrant a genealogy of it in the history of that town, you may find a valuable clue there. For instance, by studying the history of the town of Fairfield in Abby Maria Hemenway's *Vermont Historical Gazetteer*, we found that many of the settlers of that town came from Connecticut, mainly from Litchfield and Fairfield counties, or from Dutchess County, New York, which borders Connecticut. We noted that many of the grantees of Fairfield, Vermont, were from New Fairfield, Connecticut, and later discovered that New Fairfield was settled by families from around Fairfield, Connecticut. The very names of the towns are indicative of these facts. This led us, first, to Elizabeth Hubbell Schenck's *History of Fairfield, Connecticut*, where Dr. Doane found the clues for his Gilbert line and those cognate to it; and later to Donald Lines Jacobus's *History and Genealogy of the Families of Old Fairfield*, where they were given more accurately and completely.

There is, unfortunately, no comprehensive and up-to-date bibliography of local history, although bibliographies of varying completeness exist for some of the states. A very helpful tool to start your search for books on local history is the five-volume *United States Local Histories in the Library of Congress: A Bibliography* (1975), which includes state and local histories for every state in the union. A word of caution: it does not include a list of all the histories published for a state or town, so you will want to inquire for further information from the local library or historical society in the community of your interest. Recently there has been published under the auspices of the Committee for a New England Bibliography volumes for each of the six states in the region. It is hoped that other states and regions of the United States will follow this example. There are now genealogical guides to many more states. Such bibliographies, when they exist, enable you to learn very quickly whether or not there are any printed records about the locality in which your family lived. Once you have the reference, you can generally obtain access to it and examine it or have it examined for you.

If your library has no such bibliography and is too small to have a genealogical collection, you should secure a copy of Nettie Schreiner-Yantis's *Genealogical & Local History Books in Print* (4th edition). Another useful resource for books in print and out of print is the *Catalogue of Genealogies and Local Histories,* which is issued at intervals of two or three years by Goodspeed's Book Shop, 7 Beacon Street, Boston, MA 02108. There is a small charge for handling and mailing. Although it lists only the books that Goodspeed's has for sale, it is invaluable to the genealogist, for Goodspeed's stock is large and makes a specialty of genealogical books. Other bookshops deal in genealogies, and two, Tuttle Antiquarian Books, P.O. Box 541, Rutland, VT 05701, and the Genealogical Publishing Company, 1001 North Calvert Street, Baltimore, MD 21202, publish catalogs. These catalogs are almost the only inexpensive bibliographies of genealogies and local histories available.

You should become familiar, however, with two extensive printed lists of genealogies, which are arranged under family names. One of these, a very valuable one, is, to give its exact title, *Genealogies in the Library of Congress* (Baltimore, 1976); it has two supplements listing materials received by the library between 1972 and 1976 (1977), and between 1976 and 1986 (1987). Noted are genealogies in a variety of formats — printed, typescripts, and handwritten — which are in the library's collections. Here you will find genealogies from around the world and in many languages: American, English, Canadian, Irish, Welsh, Scottish, Australian, Latin American, Polish, German, Dutch, Scandinavian, French, Spanish, Portuguese, Italian, and Asian. This list has cross-references, so it frequently furnishes a clue to a "buried" genealogy. Another list is that published by the New York Public Library in 1974, the eighteen-volume *Dictionary Catalog of the Local History and Genealogy Division of the Library*.

By looking up your family in these volumes, you can quickly determine whether or not a genealogy of interest to you has been published. You may find one and you may not. If you do, you may find in it what you want; or you may have considerable digging to do before you can connect your line with those given in it.

Journals

In addition to the printed genealogies and local histories, the curator of a genealogical collection will give you an introduction to the genealogical magazines covering the part or parts of the country in which you are interested. The oldest and most comprehensive periodical devoted to genealogy is the *New England Historical and Genealogical Register*, familiarly known as the *Register*, the first number of which was published in January 1847. Genealogies of a great many families have been published in it, so you should not allow the local nature of its title to keep you from looking through its indexes for any material for which you may be looking. Quite naturally the preponderance of the material is about New England families, but many of these families are now scattered throughout the United States. In addition to genealogies, this journal contains many transcripts and abstracts of local records, such as town records, probate records, church records, and copies of cemetery inscriptions from many New England towns. For years the society maintained a Committee on English Research, and published the results of careful and painstaking research on the English origin of American families.

The *New York Genealogical and Biographical Record* is another important periodical for the genealogist. As the title indicates, this is devoted mainly to records pertaining to New York. In it have been published transcripts of the 1800 census for several of the counties in that state, as well as genealogies, cemetery inscriptions, abstracts of wills and deeds, and other valuable contributions. The *American Genealogist* (formerly the *New Haven Genealogical Magazine*) is yet another excellent periodical and is devoted exclusively to New England records before 1800 and to studies of genealogical problems rather than long detailed genealogies. *Tyler's Genealogical Quarterly*, the *William and Mary Quarterly* (2d series), and the *Virginia Magazine of History and Biography* are all devoted mainly to Virginia genealogy. The *Pennsylvania Genealogical Magazine* contains a great deal of genealogy. The *National Genealogical Society Quarterly*, an outstanding periodical published in Arlington, Virginia, has reprinted some of its more general articles in a series entitled "Special Publications," which is very useful. There are many other genealogical magazines (most of them much newer than those mentioned) that are devoted to the interests of special parts of the country or to special fields of research. A complete list of these would be too detailed for our purpose, but you can easily find their names if you begin poking about in a library. There are over several hundred of them!

For a helpful compilation of current publications see the *Bibliography of Genealogy and Local History Periodicals with Union List of Major U.S. Collections* (1990), compiled by Michael B. Clegg of the Allen County Public Library, Fort Wayne, Indiana. In addition to the magazines now being published, there are many that were comparatively short-lived, but that contain material of great importance to the ancestor hunter. Such a magazine as the *Old Northwest Genealogical Quarterly*, which was published between 1898 and 1912, is very valuable, for it contains many records of interest to those who trace their ancestry through the region known as the Old Northwest, particularly the Western Reserve in Ohio. The series of magazines edited by the late Eben Putnam, of Salem, Massachusetts, a capable genealogist, is another valuable lot. The *Newport Historical Magazine* (later called the *Rhode Island Historical Magazine*) is another, for it contains transcripts of many early records of that locality.

All of these magazines have been indexed in the *Periodical Source Index* compiled by the staff of the Genealogy Department of the Allen County Public Library, Fort Wayne, Indiana. Capably edited by Michael B. Clegg and Curt B. Wichter, the first four volumes cover the years from 1847 to 1985 and give access to place, subject, and surname information in out of print and current genealogical and local history periodicals. Since 1986 an annual volume appears that indexes the more than fifteen hundred family history and local history periodicals received by the Allen County Public Library. An excellent reference tool, it should be consulted regularly as you pursue your work. Another useful publication that appears yearly is the *Genealogical Periodical Annual Index*, compiled and published by Laird Towle, of Bowie, Maryland. He indexes about 275 journals.

The late William Wade Hinshaw, of Washington, D.C., devoted the later part of his life to the publication of Quaker records. He compiled the first six large volumes of the *Encyclopedia of American Quaker Genealogy*. Volume 1 covers the North Carolina meetings (remember that many New England Quakers traveled by sea from Nantucket to North Carolina, and others moved to Pennsylvania and thence southward along the Appalachian valleys to North Carolina, then over the mountains and up through Tennessee and Kentucky to southern Ohio and Indiana); volume 2 includes four Philadelphia meetings; volume 3, New York City and Long Island meetings; volumes 4 and 5, the Ohio meetings; and volume 6, the Virginia meetings. Volume 7 contains the records of the Indiana meetings, compiled by Willard Heiss. Others may yet be published. These should never be overlooked, even though you may not be aware that your family once had Quaker affiliations. They may save you hours of searching, a long trip, and many dollars as well.

In all genealogical libraries worthy of the name you will find many other sources of genealogical material—manuscripts that have been deposited there, collections of clippings and other scattered material, and so forth. One of the most important of these supplementary sources is the printed transcript of the 1790 census of the United States, taken in 1790 and 1791 and printed in 1909 by the Bureau of the Census. In a later chapter we shall have more to say about this valuable set of books and the census itself.

Newspapers

While we are discussing printed material, mention must be made of the *Boston Evening Transcript* and its genealogical department. Back in 1876, at the suggestion of Oliver Wendell Holmes, the *Transcript* began a department of notes and queries. By 1894 the genealogical queries had become so numerous that a separate department was devoted to them. As long as the *Transcript* was published (that is, until 1941) this department appeared, sometimes twice a week, at other times daily. A wealth of genealogical material was printed in this newspaper: queries from ancestor hunters, answers from others who had been successful in their quest, copies of gravestone inscriptions from forgotten and overgrown cemeteries (mainly in New England, to be sure), abstracts of probate records and deed books, carefully worked-out genealogies, and so forth. Many notable genealogists contributed to the *Transcript* columns, and many arguments over disputed points were included. Much of the material was excellent, and, though some of it was pure guesswork and must be used with caution, it is worth looking at. Rider's *American Genealogical-Biographical Index*, as noted above includes all names that appeared in the *Transcript*'s columns between 1906 and 1941 (note that the earlier years are still unindexed). Since the pages containing the genealogical department have been reproduced on microcards and are usually available in the larger libraries having genealogical collections, this vast storehouse of data, much of it unavailable elsewhere, is now opened for general use. You may find in it the very records for which you are searching.

The *Hartford Times* had a genealogical department in its Saturday issue for many years, beginning in 1933. Alas, this too has been given up. Another query medium of national scope was *Genealogy & History*, a magazine devoted entirely to queries and answers, which was published by Adrian Ely Mount. The Everton Publishers, P.O. Box 368, Logan, UT 84321, publish the *Genealogical Helper*, which has several special issues each year devoted to directories of libraries, societies, professional genealogists, and family associations. The *Helper* publishes in every issue an extensive queries section.

An important resource available for your use is the national Interlibrary Loan System, a network of public, college, university, and special libraries that lends materials on a request basis to member institutions. The Interlibrary Loan System provides the local library with an enormous additional collection of books available for readers. Your librarian is able to speedily check the system's affiliated computer stations to determine if the particular volume you want to borrow is obtainable from another library in the United States. Usually no more than one or two weeks is required for receipt of a book after you have placed your request.

The National Genealogical Society does lend duplicates from its collection of books to its members under certain conditions. If you want to do much digging at home, even though you may live a thousand miles or more away from Washington, D.C., it may be worth your while to apply for membership in that society. The address of the society is Glebe House, 4527 17th Street North, Arlington, VA 22207. Members receive the *National Genealogical Society Quarterly*, a journal of which we've already spoken, and may borrow duplicate books from the society's library.

While on the subject of societies, we should tell you that there are many hundreds of them established in every state and many communities throughout the United States. A large number of them publish magazines of some sort. They range from purely local organizations that are, sometimes, nothing more than clubs, to statewide groups that meet once a year. The *Genealogical Helper*, mentioned above, has a list of them. See also the most recent edition of Mary K. Meyer's *Directory of Genealogical Societies in the U.S.A. and Canada*, which also lists the numerous independent genealogical periodicals. The American Association for State and Local History publishes a *Directory of Historical Societies and Agencies in the United States and Canada*, which is useful in locating local historical societies. In using libraries, particularly by mail, you must remember that none has the staff to do extensive research for you, and most have a rule limiting the amount of time that may be spent in answering your questions. If it is obvious that much time will be required, you will probably be sent a list of local genealogists so you can make your arrangements directly with one of them. In considering their fees, you must remember that you will be paying for experienced and even expert assistance, which is more efficient than ordinary labor.

CHAPTER 6

Blowing the Dust Off the Town Records

When you have tried to connect the lines that you have worked out from your family papers with those that you find in the books at the library, and perhaps have prodded the memories of your relatives a bit more in the process, you may find that you still lack a generation or two, or must have more information before you can definitely establish your pedigree. Then you will want to get at the records of the town in which your people lived and find out what data can be had there. If you happen to live in the same community in which several generations of your family have lived, you will have many pleasant afternoons examining the records in the office of the town clerk (or whatever the keeper of records happens to be called in your locality).

Town Records Offices

Take your chart and your notebook under your arm and make an expedition to that person's office, use your most ingratiating manner (the one most suited to the person who has charge of the records), and ask if you can see the records covering the period in which you are digging or, if the clerk seems so inclined, ask if he or she could help you find the information that you want.

In some states laws have recently been enacted prohibiting unrestricted use of vital records by anyone other than genealogists or members of historical societies, so it is wise to find out what the law is before you ask for such records. Granted, such laws may have been enacted to prevent scandalmongers from verifying (or using illegally) records of bastardy, bigamy, illegal marriages, and so forth, but this precautionary measure works a hardship on those who have a valid right to see the records of their own people.

Even though in most states public records are public property, and you have a right to use them, some of the officials who keep those records may be very jealous of them and guard them from "alien hands." Others are more than helpful to those who are sufficiently interested in what they contain to take the time to study them and use them. Some town clerks are crotchety and cranky and grumble a lot about the trouble of getting down the big ledgers—we have rarely seen town records kept in a volume that is lightweight and easy to handle! Others appear to be annoyed, when they are really delightful old bears who grumble a bit merely to maintain their dignity but who really enjoy the diversion that you create by coming to them for information. Some insist on a fee (the law in some states provides that a fee shall be paid for copies of old records), and others wave a hand and say "Come again!" It is up to you to size up the person and handle him or her with tact and consideration.

Sometimes such records are actually kept neatly and in repair. Once we had occasion to stop in Belchertown, Massachusetts, and look at the vital records of that town, which we found carefully preserved between layers of Japanese silk and in excellent condition. They were, as well, in the custody of a fine gentleman to whom it was a pleasure to talk. But more frequently the old ledgers are covered with dust and dog-eared, loose in their bindings and falling to pieces. Sometimes they have been thoroughly indexed, but more frequently there may be no index or, what is really worse, a poorly made, inaccurate, and inadequate one. Sometimes they have been carefully kept and are fairly complete, including much more than one would expect. Dr. Doane stopped one time in the town of Bridport, Vermont, to get some records for a case on which he was working, and found a wonderful set of records that included not only the births, deaths, and marriages as they had been entered throughout the century and more of the town's existence, but also a complete transcript of all the cemetery inscriptions in town.

Only in rare instances are the early vital records of a town kept in special volumes devoted exclusively to that purpose. Generally they are interspersed among other records, those of the business affairs and transactions of the town, land records, tax lists, and town accounts. The town clerk should know in which volumes there are to be found vital records, but many times it pays to go poking about yourself, if what you are handed does not contain the records you are searching for—provided, of course, you have gained the clerk's confidence and thus secured permission to enter the sanctum in which the records are kept. After you have been digging a very long time, you will have developed an instinct that seems to telegraph from your subconscious the message: "That's the volume I want!" You begin to have hunches; and when you do, you should play them.

In many towns the records have been destroyed by fire—hard luck in such a case. In others they have been lost. Occasionally lost records are restored, and sometimes records turn up after their existence has been completely forgotten. A few years ago in a certain town where we had done considerable searching, there was a change in the town clerkship, and the offices were cleaned up (we mean really cleaned, not merely swept). The great safe in which the volumes of town records were stored was actually moved out from the wall—for the first time in fifty years, probably. Behind it was the large thin folio volume containing the mid-nineteenth-century records of births, marriages, and deaths. It had slipped down there many years before and had never been missed. What problems it solved, and how eagerly we began to check carefully through it!

Although the date varies in the several states, there were practically no general laws requiring the registration of births, marriages, and deaths before 1850; and in the states in which there were such laws, they were frequently ignored or rather carelessly observed by the town officials. (In some cases they were ignored even after 1850 and up until the twentieth century.) So, you can never be sure that you will find the record you are searching for.

However, we are going on the supposition that the records exist and that you have gained access to them. Let us suppose that you have your chart complete through your Grandfather Merrick, that you have gone to the library and found a Merrick genealogy that does not come down to him, and that, therefore, you must work the line back another generation or two before you can make the connection. Let us suppose that his name was Joseph Merrick and that you know he was born in Derby, New Hampshire, about 1834. You have gone to the town clerk's office and have in your hands the volume covering that period. You begin to search for Merrick records. You find "Joseph, son of Jeremiah and Hannah Merrick, born March 24, 1833." Make a note of it and the page and number of the volume in which it was found—the date is near enough that of your Joseph to warrant an investigation of the record—and continue your search. Now, we'll grant you that your Joseph is the only one in whom you are interested, but for the purposes of proof and identification the names of his brothers and sisters are useful and sometimes essential. So, if you are wise, you will take down the records of the other children of Jeremiah and Hannah Merrick, because someone may remember that Grandfather Merrick had a sister Hannah and a brother

Jerry, or you may find a will at the probate court in which Jeremiah Merrick, Jr., directs that his property be divided between his brother Joseph and his sister Hannah, thus proving that your Joseph was identical with the son of Jeremiah and Hannah Merrick of that name.

Births

But let us assume that in proceeding through the volume you find another Joseph Merrick, born there June 2, 1835, son of John and Mary Merrick; and perhaps even a third Joseph Merrick, son of Henry and Jane, born there May 31, 1834.

Now you have a problem. Which of these three Joseph Merricks was your grandfather? How are you going to prove one of them to be your grandfather? The name seems to be a common one in the Merrick family, and it is quite possible that all three Josephs were the grandsons or great-grandsons of a progenitor named Joseph Merrick.

Marriages

One method of identification is that of eliminating the Josephs who could not have been your grandfather. Perhaps on further search you find that Joseph, son of Henry and Jane Merrick, died in 1835. Thus one of them is eliminated. And possibly, still further on, in another volume of records, you find the marriage of Joseph Merrick and Sarah Jones on December 25, 1857. From your family records you have already learned that your grandfather, Joseph Merrick, married Almira Buck, June 30, 1856. Obviously, this isn't the marriage record of your grandfather, but you still don't know which Joseph Merrick was yours, especially since there was no indication in this record of the parentage of the groom. You seem to be up against a blank wall in your attempt to determine whether Jeremiah or John Merrick was your great-grandfather.

Deaths

The next thing to do is to take a look at the death record of your grandfather. As vital records came to be kept systematically, and especially in the later part of the nineteenth century when special ledgers were provided for them, the parentage of the deceased was noted in his death record (and in marriage records the parentage of both the contracting parties). So, in looking at the official town record of the death of your grandfather you may find his parentage given.

But sometimes these details were overlooked by a careless clerk or by the physician reporting the death. Sometimes a man was so old that he was living with grandchildren who did not know his parents' names and the record was never turned in. For the sake of our problem, let us suppose that this was the case and the death record of your Joseph Merrick gives no indication of his parentage. Thus you are forced to continue your search and must work your problem out by using other records and even circumstantial evidence. That is why we advised taking a complete list of the brothers and sisters of each Joseph, as you came across them.

Probate

The easiest step to take next is to go to the probate office, generally in the county seat, although occasionally the probate district is not identical with the county and the probate office is in another town.

But before you take that journey, look back still further in the vital records while you have access to them. Suppose that you find the marriage record of "Jeremiah Merrick and

Hannah Lyon, May 21, 1828." Suppose that your grandfather named his eldest daughter Hannah Lyon Merrick, and perhaps one of his sons James Lyon Merrick, possibly your father. Here is circumstantial evidence that your grandfather was connected with the Lyon family in some way—otherwise why his or his wife's insistence that the name Lyon be carried on by at least two of his children? It certainly looks reasonable that he named his eldest daughter after his mother, and perhaps his son after his grandfather Lyon—the case is even sounder if you find a record stating that James and Hannah Lyon had a daughter named Hannah, born, say, August 21, 1807 (thus old enough to be the Hannah Lyon who married Jeremiah Merrick in 1828).

Pending further proof from the probate records, or possibly the cemetery inscriptions, you may acccept as probable this parentage of your grandfather, Joseph Merrick, and continue your search for another generation of the Merrick line, the parentage of Jeremiah Merrick, your hypothetical great-grandfather. If he married in 1828, he was probably at least twenty years old, and therefore was born in 1808 or before. But your search through the earlier volumes of records does not produce the birth record of Jeremiah Merrick. He may have been born in another, perhaps a neighboring, town; or possibly his birth was not recorded. You should, however, make note of any other Merricks born during this period. Say you find a single Merrick record, that of the birth of a son to Joseph and Mary Merrick in 1805, no name given. This is tantalizing, for the unnamed son may have been your Jeremiah (or, of course, Henry or John). You find nothing more on further search, not even the marriage of Joseph and Mary.

Land Records

Now ask to see the land records, for they are very valuable to the genealogist. As we get further back into the history of the country and vital records become more and more sketchy, these land records assume paramount importance. Even into the nineteenth century many land records are teeming with genealogical details. A husband and wife may deed land jointly—in many states this was required if the land came into the family through the wife's inheritance. Sometimes a father would transfer land to his son "for love"; sometimes the heirs of an estate would give a joint deed, signed by all of them, and even by the wives and husbands of those who happened to be married—we found one such deed that was signed by nineteen people, all of them descendants of the man who had owned that house and lot when he died; sometimes residence in other localities was indicated (for instance, John Merrick, of Malone, New York, might deed land in Derby, New Hampshire, thus indicating a residence in Derby before he removed to Malone). Sometimes people went back to their original homes to spend their old age, and you will find a deed indicating this—let us say that you find a deed in which Joseph Merrick, of Hannah, Massachusetts, transfers his land in Derby. Sometimes, of course, a man was speculating in land and bought a lot of it in a town to which he never went—a link in Dr. Doane's own ancestry is established by such a deed, for Samuel Hungerford, of New Fairfield, Connecticut, deeded land in Fairfield, Vermont, to his daughter, Eunice Soule, and her husband, Joseph Soule, "for love."

To return to the case of the parentage of your great-grandfather, Jeremiah Merrick: suppose you find a deed in which Joseph Merrick, of Hannah conveys his land in Derby to his son, Jeremiah, in 1830. Here you have pretty definite information that your Jeremiah was identical with the son of Joseph. You can picture the young man, married two years, making a go of it and receiving the farm on which he was living from his father, who had removed to Hannah by 1830. You still lack the birth record of Jeremiah, and perhaps his death record, but you are on the trail and no longer digging blindly. You still have probate records and cemetery records to help you establish your case.

Location of Public Records

About twenty-five years before Social Security made a central repository of vital records important to many people, most of the states had passed laws creating such an office and requiring that copies of all vital records be filed in a specified state office—sometimes the Health Department, sometimes the Department of Vital Records. In many of the older states all vital records contained on the town books have been copied and sent to this central state office. These transcripts are made on cards, one for each individual record. The cards are generally filed in alphabetical order under the surname. See Appendix B of this book for a list of the various state offices of vital statistics, their addresses, and the records under their jurisdiction.

In some states the law was made sufficiently inclusive to require that all cemetery records be included with the vital records from the town books (although in Vermont we find that this law has not been fully observed); and occasionally the law has directed that a transcript of church records be made as well.

By writing to the state office of vital records you can obtain all the information that is on file for, let us say, Jeremiah Merrick. For the official title and address of the appropriate office in each of the several states, get a copy of Thomas J. Kemp's *International Vital Records Handbook* (1990). This useful reference book will indicate how early the records in each state (and more than sixty foreign countries) begin, give you the price for ordinary and certified copies, or, in certain instances, direct you to city or county offices for such records.

No state office can be expected to supply an unlimited number of records—say you want all Merrick entries, births, marriages, and deaths—but will usually send you a list of local searchers. You select one and write for an estimate, which is generally based on the time involved. Some searchers, from sad experience, ask for payment in advance; others may rely on your honesty.

In a few states some of the vital records of the various towns have been printed. Massachusetts has taken the lead in this matter, thanks to the impetus given to the movement by individuals and privately endowed societies interested in genealogical and historical matters. The vital records down to 1850 of most of the towns in eastern Massachusetts, and many of those in the western part of the state, have been printed and are to be found in most genealogical libraries. The records of a few of the towns in Connecticut and Maine have been printed also. The Barbour Collection of Vital Records for Connecticut towns deposited at the Connecticut State Library has been microfilmed and is available for use at the Family History Library and its branch centers. The vital records of scattered towns in other states have been printed in magazines, as appendixes to local histories, and occasionally at the personal expense of some interested individual or society.

The early land records of Suffolk County, Massachusetts, have been printed and, in their black binding labeled "Suffolk Deeds," are familiar to many genealogists. Others have been abstracted and printed in whole or in part. The colonial documents of New York, Rhode Island, Plymouth Colony, and Massachusetts Bay Colony, and the Providence, Rhode Island, and Hartford, Connecticut, land records have been printed, to mention but a few. Most libraries having genealogical or historical collections own these volumes.

Mortgage Records

To return to the town offices, don't overlook the mortgage records, which, although they are not so frequently useful, do sometimes contain valuable clues.

Tax Lists

Then there are tax lists, which provide a sort of census of the town, in that all taxpayers are listed. Since the federal census is taken every ten years, these tax lists frequently serve as an intermediate census, and from them you can determine just when your people moved away from the town, or ceased to pay taxes, at least. You can figure out the size of their farms or how much land they owned and the value of it. Aside from definitely locating your people in that town, they help you to paint a picture of your family's standing and interests.

School Censuses

In some localities in the 1870s there were school censuses taken. In these were records of the heads of families and the names of children of school age in each family. If the vital records were poorly kept, these school censuses are valuable, because the age of each child was specified. They may or may not be valuable to you, but at least they are worth knowing about.

You may think that these various kinds of town records are as dry as the dust that so frequently covers them. But if you are on the watch for anything humorous, you will find many a funny thing in them. After all, these people were human, as even the dry old records show. There is one Connecticut marriage record, solemnly and seriously entered on the books and duly printed in a transcript, in which one John Boughton marries "I Dono Who"! Now it is quite obvious that the clerk did not know the name of the bride, perhaps forgot to ask it or had forgotten it when he came to make the entry on the books. Anyhow, we suspect that many a descendant of this couple has laughed off irritation over this funny entry and searched elsewhere for the bride's name. Sometimes the clerk was not sufficiently interested to ask for such details. Sometimes he entered merely the sex of a child, as "a son" or "a daughter," whose birth he was recording, or the clergyman who performed the baptism forgot to write it down. Sometimes the spelling is quite phonetic, and you get curious names like Febe for Phoebe and Kerrence for Concurrence (we have once seen this spelled Kurrants). Alys and Ellis have been known for Alice. Joll has been used for Joel. Misspellings of surnames are even worse. Apostrophes were almost unknown, so sometimes an *s* was added to a name: for instance, Soule became Sowles, where the reference was to Soule's children or something of the sort. Sometimes the clerk didn't cross his *t* or dot his *i*, and you get unintentional misspellings, such as Merrell for Merritt. The further back you go, the more precarious the art of spelling becomes, so you must be always alert to catch it and never overlook a name because it isn't spelled exactly as you spell it today.

If it is not possible for you to go to the town clerk's office—if you live too far away and find it impossible to go halfway across a continent to consult the records—you have two means of getting at them. You may write to the clerk and ask him or her to find the record that you want and send you a copy of it; or you may employ a private searcher to go and examine the records in person—a relative, perhaps, or a professional genealogist.

Many town clerks are not especially interested in genealogy (all this fuss about ancestors seems trivial to them), so any search they make is bound to be rather perfunctory and unsatisfactory. You must remember that your problem does not seem important to them and may even irritate them because it takes them from some more lucrative or pleasant occupation and makes it necessary to lift down those heavy volumes. A search by such a clerk is bound to be rather haphazard and he or she may easily overlook the record most important to you.

On the other hand, you may be fortunate in finding a clerk who is really interested in the records, has them completely and thoroughly indexed, and can give you accurate information. Such an official will frequently go out of his or her way to assist you and may refuse to accept any fee for services. However, whichever type of clerk you find, my advice is that you should never accept a statement that such and such a record doesn't exist until you have had the opportunity to check it yourself or through another's service. Sometimes one eye will see what another missed. But it doesn't pay to let the clerk know that you doubt his or her word, or to insist too much that the records be checked again. File the letter among your notes and make a mental memorandum, if not a written one, to go there sometime to take a look for yourself. But you might write again and ask whether he or she searched the land records for any evidence bearing on your problem. Generally you can tell by the tone of the reply whether the search has been very thorough. If the tone is brusque and abrupt or if the clerk says that the records "seem" to contain no evidence, you may suspect that he or she merely "seemed" to search them. If the clerk goes into details, you may have more confidence in the thoroughness of the search.

In writing for records, you should always offer to pay any fee that the clerk may charge, and you will find it a good policy to enclose a self-addressed stamped envelope for reply. The fact that you are willing to pay for data will have a good effect upon the clerk. Most people dislike those, particularly strangers, who are trying to get something for nothing, and many officials, particularly those living in small towns, object to being ordered about. Play up to them and make your need seem important to them, and impress them with the fact that you depend upon their goodwill and intelligence to help you solve your problem. It tickles their vanity, even though they may be shrewd enough to see through your ruse.

Moreover, in writing, always state your questions clearly and give all the information you can, which will enable the clerk to make the search as easily as possible. Remember that he or she has many duties and may be very busy, and may have no clerical help. You are more likely to be served if you state your problem clearly and ask for specific information. A demanding letter giving meager information, such as "I want the record of my great-grandfather, who lived in your town; please send it by return mail," will probably go into the wastebasket, for it contains no names, no dates (even approximate), and no indication of what the ancestor's name may have been. Nobody unfamiliar with your problem can pull such information out of thin air. How is the clerk to know even the surname of the man whose birth record you require? He or she is far too busy to take the time to figure back four generations and decide that the man in question must have lived about a hundred years ago. Your chance of success would be much better if you wrote a letter like this:

I am searching for the record of the parentage, birth, and marriage of my great-grandfather, Jeremiah Merrick, who is supposed to have married in your town sometime before 1835, and was probably born there between 1800 and 1810. I will gladly pay any fee you may charge for a search of your records, and I enclose an envelope for your reply, which I hope to have at your convenience.

Don't be discouraged if the results of a search of the town

records are very meager, for the sources of information are not exhausted, and you may yet solve your problem from other records.

For instance, there may be something in the county court records—we do not mean just the records of the probate court, which will be discussed in chapter 8, but the records of guardianship proceedings, and of civil and criminal legal actions. Some lawsuits involve evidence of descent from the original grantee of the property in dispute, others may include testimony from relatives distant in ties of blood as well as in locality. By chance, in the papers accompanying such a case the very data you are looking for may be found, or a locality may be named with which you have never connected any of the family, and in the town clerk's office in that place you may find the records you need to prove your descent. We know of one lawsuit involving right of burial in a cemetery lot—a man sued his second cousin for burying the remains of an aged aunt in her grandfather's lot and tried to get a court order requiring that they be removed. He based his case on the fact that the deceased's mother had married and hence could no longer be considered a member of her father's family, but belonged in her husband's family; therefore, her offspring was not entitled to space in her father's lot. In the evidence submitted there was quite a bit of genealogy of the family, and a copy of the original owner's will, lost in the file of the probate court, was produced. It all made us think of J. P. Marquand's novel *The Late George Apley* and the amusing episode of the burial of Cousin Hannah's remains; if you enjoy a chuckle, look it up and read it.

CHAPTER 7

Inscriptions in Cemeteries

Perhaps nowhere is the transitory nature of the existence of human individuals brought home to us more vividly than in an old country graveyard lying neglected and forgotten on a rural hillside. There are thousands of such burial grounds in the United States, each of them known only to comparatively few people, even among those living in the very town in which it is located. It frequently happens that no descendant of those whose remains are buried in such a cemetery is living near there today. In many other cases descendants living there do not care a tinker's damn about the condition of the almost forgotten graves; or, to be more charitable, they are physically or financially unable to care for them. In some places the entire character of the population has changed and the old families have either died out entirely or moved away, to be replaced by recent immigrants who have no interest in the old burial places. Sometimes brush and brambles have grown so high that not a stone is visible when you first look at the thicket that is supposed to be the cemetery lot. Even a ten-foot obelisk may stand obscured from view by the dense young forest about it. Thus has the local fame of some proud old family been blotted out by nature's luxuriant growth.

Families once prominent in the community are now forgotten, even though their position and influence have been subtly indicated by the quality of the marble or granite marking their graves. In one town in northern Vermont, Dr. Doane found the fine marble table-slab over the grave of the most prominent pioneer settler of the town so weathered by the rains and snows of 130-odd years that the long inscription, which presumably records his standing, has been obliterated beyond recall. Yet the old volume recording the affairs of the first quarter century of that town contains his name on practically every page. Only antiquarians such as Dr. Doane, and one or two others, are aware that he played an important part in the establishment of the town, and it is doubtful whether anyone besides Dr. Doane knows where he was buried. Not a person of his name lives in the town today or has lived in it for 125 years. Probably 95 percent of today's inhabitants of that town would not recognize his name at all. Sic transit gloria mundi!

Such a circumstance is not peculiar to that particular town but is duplicated in hundreds of others throughout the country. We live in an age that has little respect for the past and shows no inclination to profit by the experience of those who have lived successfully and died in peace.

Part of the explanation of this neglect of the old cemeteries is that the elements making up the population of these old towns have changed radically during the last century. Old families have died out, or their descendants have moved away to the cities. New people have come in, bought up the old farms, gained control of the town affairs, and, having no active, intimate interest in the past history of the town, have allowed the burial places of the town fathers to become neglected. These, in the course of time, revert to natural growth, for Nature, always fighting her children, has her way unless there is a continual guard kept against her ruthlessness.

Gravestones sink into the ground or fall down, and get broken by barbarians and vandals. The encroaching sod soon covers them and they are buried beneath grass, dead leaves, and broken twigs. Sometimes unfeeling human beings have picked up these old stones, carried them away, and used them as hearthstones, as doorsteps, or as a part of the foundation of a new barn or outbuilding, or for anything else for which a flat stone may have been needed. Sometimes cows, breaking through an old rail fence surrounding a cemetery or clambering over a crumbling stone wall, have rubbed against the gravestones and knocked them over, and then trampled them into the dirt. Years later there comes along an ancestor hunter, looking for the records that those stones contain. On many occasions he must literally dig the records of his ancestors out of the sod, and sometimes, if he has the means, he may restore the cemetery to some degree of order and have the stones reset. Or, when unable to bear the expense of restoration, he carefully copies the inscriptions and preserves them in one way or another for the use of others searching for the data recorded on them.

In searching the cemeteries for the records of your forebears, the task is made easier if you can take an older relative with you, for frequently your grandfather, your great-uncle, or an old cousin can tell you about the relationships that existed between the individuals buried there. Sitting at home, they may not recall even the names of those who died so many years ago, but when they are confronted with a memorial stone, the little bell rings in their minds and memory is restored.

Dr. Doane recalled trying, several years ago, to get a complete list of the children of his great-great-grandfather from his great-aunt. She knew that her father was one of twelve children, six boys and six girls. She could name eleven of them but could not recall the names of the sixth girl and her husband. They had the dates of birth from the eldest in 1791 to the youngest in 1817. Since the six older children she could remember came along in 1791, 1795, 1797, 1799, 1801, and 1803, they felt confident that the missing girl was born in 1793, because, as his great-aunt remarked, "they had 'em every two years in those days." So, one fine afternoon, Dr. Doane helped Great-Aunt Elizabeth into the car and they drove to the cemetery where most of the family were buried. They began a systematic search of the yard, picking out the stones of all women whose births were indicated as occurring in 1793. They hadn't gone very far before Dr. Doane found a stone on which this inscription stood: "Amanda, wife of Willis Northrop, died March 23rd, 1852, in her 59th yr." Sure enough, his great-aunt recalled her Aunt Mandy immediately, and they had the missing child!

But if you are not fortunate enough to be able to take your relatives to the cemetery and thus refresh their memory, you yourself can figure out (and later prove from other records) many of the relationships that you need for your record of the family. For instance, let us suppose that you are still trying to find the records of your great-grandfather, Jeremiah Merrick, and his wife, Hannah. You find in the cemetery their graves with stones reading like this:

Jeremiah Merrick   Hannah, Wife of
1805-1851   Jeremiah Merrick
1808-1878

In your search of the town records you have already found that she was Hannah Lyon. Beside her here in the cemetery, you find a stone reading:

James Lyon
1770-1841

and on the other side of James, another:

Hannah
Consort of
James Lyon
Died
May 3rd, 1838
In Her 66th Year

And perhaps beyond them, in the same lot, several children
of James and Hannah Lyon, possibly two or three of them
dying in maturity but apparently unmarried.

You would be justified in assuming that James and Hannah Lyon were the parents of Hannah, wife of Jeremiah Merrick. Your record of the marriage of Jeremiah Merrick to Hannah Lyon in 1828, and now the approximate date of her birth
figures from her gravestone, together with the ages of James
and Hannah Lyon at that time, indicate pretty clearly that
they were her parents. This is further substantiated by the
fact that your grandfather named a son James Lyon Merrick.
Moreover, Hannah (Lyon) Merrick was obviously named for
her mother, Hannah, "consort of James Lyon." James Lyon's
will, or the administration of his estate, will probably prove
your contention.

Perhaps in another lot not far away, or in an even older
cemetery in the town, you find this inscription on an old
slate stone:

Mary S., wife of
Joseph Merrick
Died
October 28th, 1805
In The 30th Year
Of Her Age

But you do not find beside her or in any other cemetery in
the town the grave of her husband, Joseph Merrick (who,
you may recall, was living in Hannah, Massachusetts, in

1830, and may have been buried there). However, there are, in the lot with her, three small children, let us say:

Jeremiah
Infant Son of
Joseph & Mary Merrick
Died
May 6th, 1801
Aged 6 w'ks

Mary
Daughter of
Joseph & Mary Merrick
Died
May 8th, 1801
Aged 2 y'rs

John
Son of
Joseph & Mary Merrick
Died
May 1st, 1801
Aged 4 y'rs

Here you get a picture of what happened in that fateful May of 1801—an epidemic of smallpox, diphtheria, or scarlet fever sweeping through the town and hitting the Merrick family pretty hard, for they lost three small children, perhaps their entire family, within a week. Possibly the mother had it too, and survived to die only four years later, probably soon after the birth of your Jeremiah, whom she named for the youngest boy that had died. Probably the John Merrick whose son Joseph was born in 1835 was another son, born in 1803 and named for the John who died in 1801; and perhaps the Henry you found was an elder son who survived the epidemic. Families in those days frequently repeated the names of deceased children, so anxious were they to have those names continued in the family. We know of four sons in one family who were given the same name, each after an older brother who died in infancy.

Search Adjacent Town Cemeteries

Sometimes it is well to examine the cemeteries in towns that border on the town in which your people lived. Boundary lines have changed, and land that was once in their town is now in another. Moreover, families marry back and forth, regardless of boundaries. Again, in northern Vermont, we know of four towns whose borders touch at one point. There is a graveyard in the point of one, within a stone's throw of the other three. In this cemetery are buried members of families who lived in three of those towns. There Dr. Doane found, after years of intermittent searching for his grave, the tombstone of the first husband of his great-great-grandmother. He died at the age of twenty-six—was killed in an accident in the sawmill where he worked. Dying so young and within four years after his marriage, he was buried in his father's lot in that little cemetery. His widow married again, produced a large family with her second husband, and was buried beside that husband, nine miles away. You might assume from the inscription of the first husband's stone, and the absence of any wife beside him, that he died unmarried and childless, and so was buried near his parents. Yet a large family developed through the only child of that early marriage. So it is not safe to assume too much from a single grave. Your genealogical intuition and your knowledge of conditions prevailing at the time in which these individuals lived must lead you to reasonable conclusions.

Private Burial Grounds

A century ago there were many more private cemeteries than there are now. In frontier communities especially, many people were buried on their own land or at the edge of the clearings they had made and were developing. Not many years ago Dr. Doane was prowling about on the back roads of his native town, searching for small cemeteries and isolated graves. He stopped to call on an old friend of his mother's and asked him if he knew about any graveyards or private burial grounds in that part of town. He told him there was a gravestone in a small pasture near the house of his son-in-law, so they went over there and found it at the foot of a decayed apple tree that had long since passed its prime. The inscription read: "Bridget, wife of James H. Hawley, Esq., Died in August, 1791, aged 26 years & 3 months." That farm had originally been part of a large tract of land owned by Mr. Hawley, one of the pioneer settlers, who, together with another wife, was buried beneath an imposing monument in a cemetery in a neighboring town. Bridget, his first wife (she was born a Stanton), with whom he had shared the hardships of pioneering, lies forgotten beneath an old apple tree not far from the spot where they built their first cabin.

Carefully Read the Inscriptions

When working in old cemeteries you must really study the stones. Weathered inscriptions are difficult to read. Sometimes their legibility depends upon the light. If the sun is bright and the day is clear, the shadows may be sharp and easy to read. But if the sun's rays hit the stone at such an angle that no shadows are cast in the incisions on the stones, you must shade the stone, or the inscription, so that you can read the letters. Sometimes, especially when you are attempting to photograph a stone, it is better to trace each letter of the inscription with common white chalk; in photographs the inscription always stands out much more clearly if this is done. Follow carefully the course of the engraving with your chalk so that you may get all the lines, especially the fine lines. Sometimes it is easier to make a rubbing of the face of the stone. Take a large piece of wrapping paper, lay it flat against the stone, and rub over it with a soft lead or a piece of marking crayon, such as shippers use in marking packing cases—just as you, when a child, used to make rubbings of the front of your geography book when you were too bored in school to study.

Many different kinds of stones have been used for grave markers. These fall more or less into periods. Mrs. Harriette Merrifield Forbes's *Gravestones of Early New England and the Men Who Made Them, 1653-1800* (1927); Allan I. Ludwig's book, *Graven Images: New England Stonecarving, 1650-1815* (1966); and Peter Benes's *The Masks of Orthodoxy: Folk Gravestone Carving in Plymouth County, Massachusetts, 1689-1805* (1977), are interesting studies of the types of markers used before 1800. In the late eighteenth and early nineteenth centuries the stone commonly used was a soft, dark slate, which weathered easily and quickly and had a tendency to split off as the snow and ice worked on it in the wintertime or the rain soaked into its crevices in the summer. During this period the engravers used mainly a roman letter, which is easily read if it has not weathered too much.

Between 1800 and 1850 a kind of grayish-blue slate was used. This is a harder stone than the dark slate and takes a better polish. But during this period the engravers used an italic script for their lettering, which is sometimes very difficult to read. The heavy lines of the downstrokes made by the engravers were cut deeply and have survived, but the hairlines of the cross strokes, such as most of the top of a figure 7 and the cross stroke of the elaborate 4, and sometimes the semihorizontal strokes of the 3s, 8s, and 9s, were lightly incised and on many stones these are almost or entirely weathered away. If the light isn't right, or your fingers aren't sensitive in tracing them, they are very difficult to see and read. Not infrequently a novice at reading gravestone inscriptions will misinterpret the figure 4 and read it as 11 or even 21 or 71, especially if the little horizontal stroke is obscured by a tiny bit of lichen or is not plain in the direct light of the sun, and the other figures of the date are illegible. Figures that are often confused are 8 and 3, while 9 in that script looks odd, and if the elongated tail has become obscured the figure may be mistaken for 0. The figure 1 was frequently made with an extended serif that can be read as a 7, thus throwing out calculations appreciably, and 2 is also confused with 7, especially if the lower tail is illegible. On a weathered stone 5 and 6, or 6 and 0 may be confused; and sometimes 3 and 5 are hardly distinguishable. A rubbing will sometimes solve the problem of reading. So in reading the inscriptions on this type of stone and those of the period 1800-1850, you should be unusually careful to get an accurate transcription of the record. If you have any reason to question your interpretation of the figures, you should indicate that uncertainty with a question mark and a note of what the alternative reading might be.

About 1840 or a little later a type of hard marble came into use and with it, perhaps because of its hardness, the use of italic script began to wane and roman lettering came back. Late in the nineteenth century granite came into popular use, and with it raised lettering, which unfortunately is sometimes as difficult to read as incised lettering, especially if the light isn't right or if lichen has grown over the stone. Within the last few years, the art of sandblasting an inscription into the stone has come into use. By this method the wording is cut in very deep, so it bids fair to stand a great deal of weathering and survive much longer than the old hand-chiseled inscriptions.

Before 1850, gravestone inscriptions rarely contained inclusive dates, but generally the date of death followed by a statement of the age of the decedent. Sometimes this was given in years, months, and days: "Aged 87 yr's, 6 m's, & 3 d's." Given such an inscription, following the old rule that you learned in arithmetic, you can figure out the exact date of birth. But if you have an inscription such as "Aged 87 Years" your problem is not so simple. Only in extremely rare cases does a person die on the anniversary of his birth; consequently, whenever you find such an inscription, you may be reasonably sure that the odd months and days of the deceased's age were omitted from the inscription. Generally such an inscription implies that the decedent had passed his eighty-seventh birthday, but he may have been within a few weeks of it. You cannot tell from the inscription. If it reads: "Died April 25th, 1841, aged 87 years," he may have been born in 1753 or 1754, for his eighty-seventh birthday may have occurred some time after April 25, 1840 and before January 1, 1841, and hence he was born in 1753; or the birthday had occurred in 1841 before April 25, or had been about to occur, and hence he was born in 1754. If you fail to find any evidence of the exact date of birth, you should always indicate the approximate date as, in this case, 1753-54.

It is equally difficult to figure birth dates from inscriptions that read like this: "Died May 1st, 1840, in the 26th year of his age." If a man was twenty-five in April 1840, he entered his twenty-sixth year at that time, and thus was born in 1815; on the other hand, if he had his twenty-fifth birthday after May 1, 1839, he was still in his twenty-sixth year when he died, but was born in 1814. So here again, failing other data, you must record the birth as 1814-15.

In copying inscriptions from gravestones it is always wise to copy *verbatim ac litteratim*, word for word and letter for letter, including all punctuation as it is given. This eliminates some of the chances for error. If a stone reads: "consort of," copy it that way, and do not substitute *wife* for *consort*. *Consort* signifies that the husband (or, in rare cases, the wife) was living at the time, whereas *wife* does not necessarily have that meaning. *Relict* always means widow (occasionally, widower); hence, in the absence of other evidence, you know that the wife survived her husband. It is a small point, but sometimes it is very significant. Of course, the introductory phrases "In memory of" and "Sacred to the memory of" add nothing to one's knowledge, and they can be omitted without loss; but there is a difference between "in her 57th year" and "aged 57 years."

In the event of illegible inscriptions or portions of inscriptions, it is a good plan to enclose your interpretation of the illegible part in square brackets when you make your transcription. This is a device used universally to indicate an editor's substitution for the original. Thus, any experienced person reading the following transcription—

[Sacre]d to the Memory of
[Jere]miah Merrick
[Wh]o Died
[Ja]nuary 24th 1841
[in] his 36th
[year]

—would know that the inscription was partially illegible and that the copyist had supplied the portion enclosed in the brackets, probably having made out enough of the worn letters to be reasonably sure of what they were originally. This same device can be used to add a descriptive phrase.

Hannah, Wife of
Jeremiah Merrick,
died
August 1 [remainder of
stone broken away]

While poking about in old cemeteries, you come across many sad things and many amusing things as well. There are those, we know, who feel it is very disrespectful to the dead to find amusement in anything in a cemetery, but we hope that attitude is changing, for many of the dead enjoyed gaiety in life and probably, if they know anything about it, welcome a bit of it over their resting places. Death can be beautiful or ludicrous as well as sad. The lugubriousness of the earlier attitude toward it is amply expressed in the first line of the following epitaph from the gravestone of Eunice, wife of Joseph Soule:

> Corruption, earth and worms
> Shall but refine this flesh
> Till my triumphant spirit comes
> To put it on afresh.

In the same cemetery, Dr. Doane found this epitaph on the stone of Lewis Leach, who died in 1841.

> This modest stone, what few vain marbles can,
> May truly say, Here lies an honest man:
> Calmly he looked on ei'ther life and here
> Saw nothing to regret or there to fear.

There are nice implications in the following verses from the marker of Clarissa Page (Was she a sister of the Cynthia Page whose epitaph we quoted in chapter 1? They rest in different cemeteries in the same town):

> While sculptured marble speaks of fame
> And monuments o'er merit rise
> This stone shall to the world proclaim
> Tomb'd deep in earth here virtue lies.

And this in 1813, before the great Victoria was born!

Many people, some of whom are not even interested in digging for ancestors, collect epitaphs, make rubbings from seventeenth- and eighteenth-century gravestones, and plan their picnics and the spare moments of their vacations to include a cemetery, where they examine the old stones and copy what appeals to them.

In one cemetery we came across an orderly row of tombstones recording the existence of five of the wives of the patriarch who lay beyond them, with room left for the grave of the sixth, who survived him! In another we found, side by side, the graves of three sisters near those of their parents. These "Gilbert girls," as they were called, had a total age of more than 240 years and all died unmarried, carrying on their father's farm to the last. Near them were the "Olmstead girls," each of whom lived into her seventies. A telling indication of the New England tendency to spinsterhood!

Such inscriptions as these from a small remote village are not unusual. They can be duplicated in hundreds of others. Moreover, the discerning ancestor hunter can read the outline of the history of any town in its cemeteries. The changing types of names indicate the changes in the elements of the population. The rise and fall of families can be read in the simplicity and grandeur of the stones over their graves. Even the remnants of slavery can be noted, for we found in a small cemetery overlooking the Missouri River a simple marker of an old slave who was buried, at the end of her own life, at the feet of a young woman whom she had years earlier nursed throughout a fatal illness.

Occasionally one finds a reminder of some very gruesome event. On a back road, in the town of Fairfield, Vermont, there is a pasture in which, some hundred yards from the road, stands a small obelisk about three feet high. It is the memorial to Marrietta N. Ball, who was murdered near that spot in 1874. Sunken into it at one time was a daguerreotype portrait of Miss Ball, and below the identifying inscription was engraved a brief account of the manner in which she was killed: she was attacked while walking home from the school where she was teaching, her body was dismembered, and the torso was found on the spot where the monument stands. One other memorial stone of this kind is known to exist in the United States—somewhere in Rhode Island, we are told—but the type is more frequently found in England.

Although, as a general rule, a gravestone tells very little about the personal characteristics and history of the individual beyond the dates of the two major events in life (birth and death), occasionally a stone gives a glimpse of the person he or she was. In a roadside cemetery within a mile of the eastern shore of Lake Champlain, we found the follow-

ing inscription. It is not necessary to tell in more detail the
story it contains.

> When true friends part
> 'Tis the survivor dies
> This Monument,
> By a Beloved friend is
> Erected to the Memory of
> JOSEPH R. FAY
> Who Died on The 19th of May
> 1803 in the 25th Year
> of His Age.
> Thoughtful yet Smiling
>
> Farewell Bright Soul! A Short Farewell
> Till we shall meet in realms above
> In the sweet grove, where pleasures Dwell
> An Trees of Life bear Fruits of Love
>
> Could twin born Souls walk in hand!
> Thro the dark shades of Death!
> Vain Wish!

CHAPTER 8

Where There's a Will There's a Way

There is scarcely any legal record containing names of individuals that is not of use to a genealogist. The ancestor hunter who proposes to conduct a thorough search and who wants as complete a picture of his or her ascendants as possible should by all means use all the records he or she can find. Some of them are of paramount importance in proving a descent; others are interesting only as they shed light upon the life and activities of the individual whom they concern. An excellent reference guide to the use of various sorts of legal records for genealogical research has recently been published by Noel C. Stevenson: *Genealogical Evidence: A Guide to the Standard of Proof Relating to Pedigrees, Ancestry, Heirship, and Family History.* Using legal cases to teach the procedures of mining genealogical information from the records, he carefully illustrates the significance of the materials for genealogical work.

Probate Court Records

Undoubtedly the most important evidence of the genealogy of a family is a collection of the probate court records that pertain to it. Wills are generally indisputable documents concerning the relationship of individuals, although occasionally the information they give is exasperatingly meager.

Sometimes, on the other hand, they tell too much to suit the pride of the descendants. But the wise person knows that his or her ancestors were human beings with human attributes and shortcomings, and therefore accepts them for what they were and tries to determine his or her heritage from them.

Each state has (and in colonial days each colony had) its own laws of probate. Our knowledge and the space at our disposal are too limited to permit us to discuss here the differences in those laws, as they vary from state to state, or to consider the changes that have been made in them during the successive periods of American history. It is up to you, as an ancestor hunter keen on a find, to study the laws that affect the communities in which your ancestors lived—not only the probate laws, but the land laws and other laws governing the conduct of individuals. Although a great deal of digging can be accomplished without studying such laws, your researches will be more fun and will net you a broader knowledge of the world if you have acquired some such knowledge.

Wills

There are two types of wills: the written will, signed and witnessed; and the spoken will, called the nuncupative will, generally given by the decedent on the deathbed in the presence of witnesses who are later called before the probate judge to swear to the testamentary intentions of the testator. The written will is by far the more common form today. In fact, nuncupative wills are rare in the twentieth century. But in the early colonial days, when writing material was not always at hand and a considerable proportion of the population could not write at all or wrote with difficulty even when in the best of health, nuncupative wills were much more common.

Wills have been known since pre-Christian times, and several truly ancient wills have survived, in tradition at least. The Bible (Genesis 4-9) mentions the will of Jacob, the patriarch. Several wills are mentioned in the surviving records of ancient Greece. But the oldest written will known to be extant today in its original form is that of Sekhenren, an Egyptian. This will, dating from about 2550 B.C., was found by the late Sir William M. F. Petrie, the Egyptologist, among some papyruses he excavated many years ago. It might easily have been drawn within the last century, so curiously modern is the wording. The vocabulary of the law does not change as rapidly as language in everyday use. Sekhenren settled his property upon his wife, Teta, for life, and specified that his buildings should not be destroyed, although she was empowered to give them to any of her children. He even named a guardian for his infant children. This will was witnessed in the form of which our courts approve and contained an attestation clause very much like our modern clause of this sort.

English wills dating from the time of the Norman Conquest are common, and in the cases of many the parchment on which they were written has survived. An interesting study of the wills of our English progenitors and those of our ascendants on this side of the Atlantic might be made, for they shed a great deal of light not only on the ownership and transfer of land but also on the kind of possessions people have valued from time to time and from period to period in history. Old wills, English and American, frequently specified what was to be done with such things as silver and pewter, clothing, household utensils, books, and other truly personal property. Today there is little respect for personal property, but in colonial days, when "hard money" was scarce, possessions were more important. A piece of silver was greatly valued, as it represented money; a gun or a sword was precious and worthy of mention in a will; a book was rare and truly treasured. Speaking of books, the identity of the second wife of one of the colonial ministers, the Reverend John Sherman, of Watertown, Massachusetts, is solved by a clause in the will of her mother, Isabella (d'Arcy) (Launce) Simpson, who bequeathed her "great Bible" to her son-in-law in New England.

In the seventeenth and eighteenth centuries, during the period of the colonization of North America, many wills contained bequests of rings or money for the purchase of a ring—"fifteen shillings for a ring," "ten shillings for a ring," were common phrases in the wills of the well-to-do. This referred to what we call memorial rings. They were finger rings, each to be worn in memory of a deceased friend. Many of these memorial rings have survived. The late Sir Frederick Crispe made a large collection of them and published a descriptive catalog of it. Generally such rings were engraved with the name, date of death, and age of the deceased. Sometimes they were enameled, and coffins, death's-heads, spades, crossbones, and other symbols of death were worked into the designs on them. Generally such a ring was in the form of a band, much like the old-fashioned yellow gold wedding ring, but occasionally they were more elaborate. We have seen one memorial ring, made late in the eighteenth century, in which a bit of the woven hair of the deceased was set under glass, and held in place by pearls. Izaak Walton, the famous fisherman, not only bequeathed several such rings to his friends whom he wished to have remember him, but indicated in his will the inscriptions that were to be engraved on them! Not long ago there was found in Nebraska a memorial ring commemorating Sir Francis Nicholson, one of the colonial governors of Virginia, Maryland, and South Carolina.

This is but an indication of the byways into which you may be led by the study of wills and testamentary bequests. William Hazlitt, the nineteenth-century English essayist, wrote a delightful essay, "On Will-Making," which is to be found in his volume *Table Talk; or, Original Essays*. It will be well worth your time to read it, for Hazlitt, a keen observer of human foibles, points out some of the ridiculous aspects of wills and, incidentally, comments in a pithy manner on human nature.

Seriously, however, the ancestor hunter must make an extensive use of wills as he or she digs. The best plan is to visit in person the probate office of the region in which your people lived, and read thoroughly and with an alert mind all wills that pertain to them, although today photocopies save a lot of trouble. A phrase, an apparently insignificant bequest, or the mention of persons whose relationship to the legator is not specified will frequently serve as the clue to further digging. As a general rule the testator names his wife, his sons in the order of their birth, and his daughters in the order of age. This is especially common in wills made in colonial times. The very wording of the will may indicate clearly just how he felt toward each of them. "Cut off with a shilling" is a popular saying, but it has more than one implication in family history: possibly a previous settlement upon that heir, or a retaliation for some offense committed many years before, or a distrust of the legatee's acumen or capacity to use property wisely. Today, in America, the amount of such a bequest is generally a dollar, or another ridiculously small sum.

We should note here that, historically, married women did not possess the right to dispose of their estate by will. The theory for this dated rule was that husband and wife were one person, and the husband was that person, and he controlled the wife's property. However, a widow was eligible to dispose of her estate by will or some other manner.

Not long ago we read the will of a woman who survived her husband a great many years and managed the property he left her with acumen and sagacity. Her estate was of considerable size, and in her original will she mentioned by name all of her surviving children and grandchildren, bequeathing to each of them a just share of her property. A few years after the will was written, signed, and witnessed, she added a codicil in which she revoked her bequest to the widow of one of her sons and gave explicit reasons for her action. Knowing that any money left to the children of that son (they were all minors) would, by hook or crook, soon be squandered by their mother, she cut off those children as well, and stated that the reason for such unnatural action was the "vile" character of their mother. Such a will arouses wonder, especially when it is known that the testator's reputation for a kindly disposition and a lovable character, albeit companioned by a strong, shrewd mind, has survived her these many years.

Wills are generally considered to be a source of proof of descent rather than of ascent, but occasionally the parentage of the testator, even if he was an old man, is given in the will. Several years ago Dr. Doane was tracing a Randall line back to the immigrant. He was stuck on a Joseph Randall, whose gravestone he had found bearing the information that he "died February 22nd, 1822, aged 67 years." Dr. Doane had found out that he was a Revolutionary soldier, and that he had a pension for his service as such. The pension records in Washington stated that he was born in Canada and enlisted first in 1775 from "Saint Tour" (which is Saint Ours, near Richelieu, Quebec). They also gave the date of his marriage to Judith Bowen in Lebanon, New Hampshire. Finally Dr. Doane did what he should have done earlier—he went to the probate office to search for Joseph Randall's will. To his great pleasure and astonishment, Randall had disposed of any property that might be due him from the estate of his father, Michael Randall, and implied that that estate was in "Lower Canada," as Quebec used to be called. The will was exasperating in another aspect, however, because he mentioned none of his children by name and left all his property to his widow with the request that she divide "equally among our youngest children" anything that should remain at the time of her death.

The Record of Distribution

Wills are not the only records or documents to be found in a probate office that are of use to a genealogist. Next in importance to a will is the distribution of an estate. Such a document shows just what proportion of the estate went to each heir, and each heir is generally named. Frequently the relationship of the heirs to the decedent is shown, as "son John" and "daughter Jane" are assigned their respective shares. When a person has died intestate, that is, without leaving a will, the distribution is made in accordance with the law governing cases of the sort. In such an event, owing to the absence of a will, the record of distribution becomes a very important document to the ancestor hunter. We know of one distribution in which over twenty heirs are named and the amount given to each is specified, although the relationship is not specifically stated. The deceased died intestate without children, so his widow received one-third, and the remaining two-thirds of his estate was divided among the surviving brothers and sisters and the heirs of those who had predeceased him. By carefully adding the amounts received by the several groups of heirs it is possible, with a little trouble, to figure out which were which in relationship to the deceased and to the surviving brothers and sisters. This distribution proved to be of great value in determining the number of children of the deceased's father who grew to maturity, married, and produced offspring, and it helped Dr. Doane considerably in tracing the descendants of one branch of a family whose genealogy he was compiling. A little common sense and a little experience in using such a record will enable you to get a great many clues from a document of this sort.

Appointment of Guardians

In the old days, a guardian for minor children—even though one parent survived—had to be selected and appointed by the judge of probate; in some states this is still true. The records of such appointments not only indicate relationships but sometimes contain a commentary on the conditions existing within the family. In colonial days, and even later, children of fourteen were allowed to signify their acceptance of the guardian chosen by the judge, or, when they reached that age, were permitted, with the consent of the court, to choose a new guardian. Hence, a widow might be appointed guardian of her young children, and one of them, say a son, upon reaching the age of fourteen might choose his uncle or even a friend as his guardian, in lieu of his mother. This frequently happened when the mother had married again.

Guardianship papers are also filed for individuals unable to look after their own affairs and for old people who have passed into senility and are no longer capable of managing their own property. Not a few scandals have arisen over such cases, and sometimes it is necessary to refer to the records of courts other than probate courts (orphans' courts, for instance) for more complete data in connection with them. Jurisdiction over such cases varies in the several states, so you should talk with a lawyer about the legal aspects, or you yourself, in your search for further information, should study the law.

Records of Lawsuits

Most amateurs, and many professional genealogists, completely overlook other types of legal court records in their search for ancestors. However, buried in the files of innumerable courts throughout the country are depositions, records of lawsuits, and other court actions that teem with clues to the identity of those who have lived in the past. There are printed indexes to the "reports" of the several states—the long series of printed volumes of cases that have been tried in the courts and "reported" for the use of other lawyers seeking precedents for their arguments and briefs. As a general rule, the documents cited are not printed in full but merely abstracted or summed up, so from the printed reports you get just the pith of what they contain. An examination of the actual documents in the files of the court in which the case was tried will frequently give you much more information, and you may even obtain certified copies of the original records that were filed with those documents at the time the case was tried. Quite naturally, and as you would expect, lawsuits over the distribution of estates, and contests of wills, are of the most value to the ancestor hunter. But we found valuable data in a suit against an insurance company in Wisconsin and still more in a contest over the ownership of some land in central New York. The records of criminal trials, especially murder cases, frequently produce evidence of a relationship for which other records cannot be found.

These more miscellaneous types of court records should be searched in person, either by yourself or by a competent genealogist whom you have hired to do the searching for you. The clerk of such a court, unaccustomed to this use of the records in his or her custody, will hardly know how to get from them the details that you want, for, as a general rule, the clerk has no knowledge of the data that a genealogist requires.

Clerks of Probate Courts

Probate records and transcripts or abstracts of other documents connected with the settlement of an estate can be secured by correspondence. The clerks of probate courts are accustomed to receiving letters from parts of the country asking for information contained in wills, inventories, and distributions. When a fee established by law is paid, it is, in many states, the duty of the probate clerk to furnish certified copies of wills or other papers pertaining to the settlement of an estate. Many probate clerks will undertake to make abstracts, especially if paid for it, but this is generally a private arrangement between you and the clerk. Usually there is someone in the probate office who is willing to augment a slender salary in this way. If you order a certified copy, it is always wise to find out in advance how much it is going to cost you—some wills are lengthy documents! Also, you should be sure that it will contain what you are looking for, since many testators have been exasperatingly reticent about their children's names. We have found that it is generally wise to word your initial query something like this: "Is there on file in your office the will of John Doe, who died about 1821? Or an agreement of his heirs? Or any other paper that mentions his daughter, Mary Jones? If so, can you supply an abstract, and how much would that cost?" Be sure to give the probate office some idea of the date of the instrument for which you are searching, for there may be two or three or more John Does, all of whom left wills. If you are not at all certain of the date of death, ask the clerk to give you the dates of the wills that are on file under that name in the office—in the light of your other clues they may mean something to you.

Sometimes, when you are trying to determine the parentage of an ancestor, it is feasible to have the clerk examine all the wills made by persons of that surname that are on file in the office. Possibly the clerk can do this at his or her leisure and can tell you whether your ancestor, or anyone of that name, is mentioned in any of these wills. Suppose, for instance, that you know that your great-grandfather was born in Cabell County, West Virginia, and have come upon a tradition that he was ten years old when his father died. You could write to the probate clerk of that county, giving the clues you have, and ask if a child of his name was mentioned in the will of any of the same surname who died about 1808-10, let us say, and offer, of course, to pay for a copy or an abstract of the will in which he was mentioned. Frequently a clerk will go out of his or her way to obtain the data that you want. Once, while examining in person the records of a probate court, we found that the clerk was descended from the individual whose will we were seeking. On the slender claim of cousinship, he practically turned the place upside down in helping us and used his intimate knowledge of the records under his jurisdiction greatly to our advantage. (And, of course, to his own, for whatever he found to aid us gave him so much more data for himself. We have often wondered whether he became thoroughly inoculated with the genealogical virus and went on with his digging.)

Although the names of testators are indexed in the probate court files, the names of persons mentioned in wills are not indexed. Would that every probate court ordered such an index made! It would be of great assistance to us genealogists. Frequently we are searching for the identity of some ancestor's wife whom we know only by her given name. In innumerable cases the will of her father, could we but find it, would prove her identity. But it takes a great deal of time and patience to read through volume after volume of crabbed old handwriting in the hope of finding her mentioned in some will. If we had an index to the legatees, witnesses, and other individuals mentioned in testaments and distributions, our work would be much simpler, although perhaps not quite so thrilling.

It is a good plan to find out just what the probate court is called in the state in which you are searching, particularly if you are working by correspondence, for the names differ in some states. Most states call the repository for wills and other probate records the probate office, or probate court.

But in New York, for instance, it is called the surrogate's court, because it is in the charge of a surrogate. Moreover, in some states the limits of the probate district do not correspond with the county limits, although generally they do; if so, you will find the probate records in the county court house. There are sometimes exceptions even within states. For example, in Vermont, although many of the probate districts correspond with the counties, there are twenty probate offices and only fourteen counties. Occasionally the limits of a probate district have been changed in the course of time, so it becomes necessary to learn something about the history of the district.

Incidentally, many states issue, generally through the office of the secretary of state, a manual in which are listed all state and county officials. In many states this manual can be obtained for the asking. There certainly is no harm done in applying for it. If you do get it, you will have definite information about where and to whom to write for your data.

For instance, there is an unofficial annual publication for Vermont, first issued in 1818 as *Walton's Vermont Register*, now called *The Vermont Year Book* (published by the National Survey, Chester, Vermont). It contains, in alphabetical order, a list of all the towns, cities, and villages in the state. Under each town it gives its location, area, elevation, population, officers, manufacturers, merchants, churches, pastors, lawyers, postmaster, and so on. In the introductory section the state and county officers are listed, as well as schools, colleges, and other institutions and organizations. A folded map of the state is usually included. Such a handbook is useful to the ancestor hunter and should be consulted in your search.

A useful book, compiled with painstaking care by Noel C. Stevenson, of Laguna Hills, California, a Fellow of the American Society of Genealogists, is *Search and Research* (1977), which tells you under the heading "Official Records" where the probate offices are located and gives you many other valuable addresses. It is arranged by states and is easy to use.

CHAPTER 9

What You Can Find in the Church Records

Long before the earliest colonists came to America, it had become the custom in most European countries to keep records of the members of the ecclesiastical parishes. In fact, in England an act of Parliament was passed in 1538, requiring the clerk of each parish to keep a register of all marriages, christenings, and burials that occurred within his jurisdiction. In many of the English and European parishes these records have survived from the sixteenth century to the present day, although innumerable volumes have been destroyed by fire or war or lost by careless custodians.

Although for a while our forebears in this country, particularly in New England, did not recognize as legal the ecclesiastical ceremony of marriage—the colonies of Plymouth and Massachusetts Bay were especially anxious to get away from the authority of the official church, to separate church and state, as it were—the hundreds of volumes of church records extant, dating from the earliest colonial days, are of inestimable value to the ancestor hunter. Buried in them are many records without which the problems inherent to such a search would be even more serious than they are.

It is interesting to note that, religious as the Puritans are reputed to have been, and religious as they were, they considered marriage to be not a religious sacrament but a civil contract. A marriage ceremony was performed before a mag-

istrate. In fact, at one time ministers of the church were forbidden to perform marriages. Hence, although you will find
baptisms and burials in the record books of the old churches,
you will not find the early marriages entered there. But intentions of marriage may be found in church records, since
"publication of banns" in the church preceded the civil ceremony. Sometimes, however, there was a slip; the intention
was not fulfilled and each of the parties married someone
else! Study the baptismal records of the children and note the
mother's name (if both parties are mentioned, as they generally were if both were members of the church). If there is a
change in the mother's name between, say, the fourth and
fifth children, it is an indication of the death of the first wife
and the remarriage of the father, even though the spacing
between the children may not be more than the usual two
years—in those days, when a wife was an economic necessity, they didn't always wait a "respectable" period. Young
children had to be cared for; fields had to be tilled; meals had
to be cooked; wool had to be carded, spun, and woven: a
man could not do everything. So be alert for any change in
marriage partners.

Sometimes a man and his wife were not admitted to the
church until after several children had been born—perhaps
they did not settle in that town until some time after their
marriage, or perhaps they did not realize what it meant to
them spiritually or socially to be members of a church. Re-
spectability in those days was closely allied to church membership and religious belief. Frequently you will find the
baptismal record of a family of two adults and four or five
children on a single page of the church records, perhaps following the record of the admittance of the parents to membership.

Sometimes, especially in pre-Revolutionary records, you
will find children baptized "in the name of" one parent or
the other. This generally means that that parent was a mem-

ber of the church while the other was not, although, if the record of the admittance of both parents to membership has been found, it may simply mean that one parent was absent from church on the day on which the child was presented for baptism. If, however, the record reads: "Admitted to the Ch. Clarissa Smith and baptized for her four children, John, Seth, Sarah, and Clarissa," you may be sure that Clarissa's husband did not become a member at that time, and perhaps never did. In rare instances, when the record of the admittance of both husband and wife to the church is given and then the baptism of a child is recorded in the name of the wife only, it may be an indication that the paternity of the child was in question.

Locating Church Records

Church records, unlike town records, are not always easy to locate. They were generally kept by the minister, or, more recently, by a clerk. Since few churches had offices for the minister in the church building, the record books were kept at the minister's home (or at the home of some other individual) who had charge of them. Sometimes the pastor moved on to another charge and took the records along, perhaps through oversight. Sometimes they got back to his successor, sometimes they didn't. Many of them were destroyed by fire or flood, many of them mislaid or lost, and occasionally some were inadvertently destroyed in other ways. Occasionally they were deposited for safekeeping in some secure place and forgotten. This is especially true of churches that have gone out of existence in older communities. Dr. Doane looked for years for the records of a church in his native town, which once was Methodist and then was Baptist and then became a "union" church. Each person to whom he talked knew there were records, but no one could say just where they were. An excellent and comprehensive handbook that should be consulted before you begin your search for church records for any religious group in any state is E. Kay Kirkham's *Survey of American Church Records.*

Sometimes the state organization of the church or religious society has gathered into its keeping the older records and those of the abandoned churches. In many cases, in the older states, state historical societies have become the custodians of the records of many of the churches, particularly those no longer active, that exist or have existed within their borders. In Connecticut, and undoubtedly in many other states, the state library has gathered into its fireproof vaults many of the ancient church records of the state and stands always ready to accept the custody of more. In Vermont the Vermont State Historical Society has obtained possession of many such records. Some of the church historical societies have actively collected the records of their denominations. For example, at the Colgate-Rochester-Bexley-Crozer Divinity School, Rochester, New York, the American Baptist Historical Library contains many invaluable records—both manuscript and printed—pertaining to the activities of the Baptist church in North America. Incidentally, in this connection it is valuable to know that the Baptists were organized into associations, covering several towns. These associations held annual or biennial meetings, and frequently the proceedings were published and the list of the official delegates was printed with the proceedings. These printed proceedings, collected at Rochester, are truly a source of data for the ancestor hunter—especially the lists of delegates contained in them.

The Drew Theological Seminary in Madison, New Jersey, has a collection of historical material pertaining to the Methodist church.

Those interested in the records of the Roman Catholic church should consult Duane L. C. M. Galles's instructive article "Roman Catholic Church Records and the Genealogist"

(*National Genealogical Society Quarterly*, vol. 74, 271-78) and E. Kay Kirkham's *Survey of American Church Records*. The records of the Episcopal church are retained in the parishes, but the records of abandoned missions and parishes will be found in the diocesan offices. The American Jewish Archives, Cincinnati, Ohio, and the American Jewish Historical Society, Waltham, Massachusetts, have large collections of historical material. One great difficulty in locating church records arises when the church is of the "mission" type; that is, the pastorate is supplied from a neighboring church or congregation. Sometimes there is a clerk who has charge of the records, but quite as often the records are kept by the minister who supplies the pulpit, and who carries them with him or, worse yet, makes the record of a baptism or marriage when he gets home from the service, if he happens to remember to do it.

Ministers' Private Record Books

Some ministers kept private record books and carried them about with them as they served one charge after another. This was especially true of Methodist circuit riders, who traveled constantly from one group of communicants to another. The heirs of these ministers have sometimes preserved such record books; but more frequently, we fear, the records have been destroyed as worthless or lost during the migrations of the family. These are generally nineteenth-century records, but they cover a period that the genealogist has difficulty bridging. It is sometimes much harder to find the records of the generations between 1775 and 1850 than it is to find those covering 1620 to 1775. Moreover, the period between 1800 and 1870 was one of great migration—the West was being opened up for settlement. Pioneer settlements were not organized to keep vital records. Marriage licenses were scarcely known. The itinerant minister sometimes had several ceremonies to perform on one of his rare visits to the community. Hence, his record, if he kept one, is sometimes the only source of data—and it is very difficult to find that marriage book. Whenever you do find such a volume in private hands, you should make every effort possible to secure it for deposit in a historical or genealogical library, or should urge its owner to deposit it. Failing in this, you should attempt to secure a careful and accurate transcript or microfilm of it and publish or deposit that transcript. By doing this you can greatly help other ancestor hunters and save someone else the time you spent in your search for the records.

Family History Library of Salt Lake City

Since its founding in 1894 the Family History Library has become the largest and most important institution of its kind in the world. Established under the auspices of the Church of Jesus Christ of Latter-day Saints, popularly known as the "Mormon church," the library's interest in genealogy is based on the church's theological belief that family relationships are intended to be eternal and not limited to our earthly existence. Accordingly living members have an obligation to search out the records of their ancestors, proving carefully the connections from one generation to another, and to trace these family lines as far back into history as possible. This accounts for the presence of this outstanding library in Salt Lake City. It has a collection of nearly one million seven hundred thousand rolls of microfilmed records, such as vital records, church, cemetery, census, land, and probate records; over two hundred and fifty thousand books; past and present genealogical and historical periodicals; more than eight million family group record forms, and many other resources relating to genealogical and historical research. In 1964 a system of local family history centers was established. Formerly known as branch genealogical libraries, more than fifteen hundred family history centers operate in the United States and about fifty other countries.

The spacious and comfortable library in Salt Lake City and the family history centers are open to the public. You may use the collections of these libraries without charge—except, of course, for duplication fees. Copies of most of the research materials on microfilm or microfiche at the library can be obtained by interlibrary loan at the family history centers. These centers are generally in local church meetinghouses and are staffed by volunteers. A list of locations of centers in your area and their telephone numbers is available from the Family History Library, 35 North West Temple Street, Salt Lake City, UT 84150. Because each center is open different days and hours, you should contact the center before you visit. Prior to visiting the library in Salt Lake City you will want to go to a family history center near your home and acquaint yourself with the basic research materials available for your use.

In addition to the largest collection of genealogical records in the world, the library has several valuable research aids that can help you find your ancestors or records about your family. FamilySearch is a computer system that simplifies searching for your ancestor. The system includes a powerful search and retrieval program and files containing family history information. The files are distributed on compact discs. The program enables you to search for information in the following files: Family History Library Catalog, International Genealogical Index, Ancestral File, Social Security Death File, and Military Burial Records File. FamilySearch is available at the Family History Library and at the larger family history centers in the United States and Canada. The Family History Library Catalog and the International Genealogical Index are also available in microfiche editions at the library and at each family history center.

The Family History Library Catalog describes the records at the library. You can use it to find the book, film, or fiche numbers of the records you want to search. The microfiche edition allows you to search for a surname, locality, subject, author, or title. Written instructions and a brief video about using the microfiche edition of the catalog are available at the library and at family history centers.

The 1988 edition of the International Genealogical Index lists the name of the person, names of parents or spouse, sex, date and place of birth, christening, marriage, death and or burial, as well as will, probate, and census information, and Latter-day Saint temple ordinance dates of more than 150 million deceased persons. The compact disc edition used with FamilySearch enables you to search more than one state or an entire country, and to search by parents' names. Most of the persons listed in the index lived between 1500 and 1875. Entries in the index are for persons born or married in more than ninety countries. It is particularly strong in percentage of records indexed in it for the British Isles; the Scandinavian countries of Sweden, Denmark, Norway, Iceland, and Finland; the Germanic countries; parts of the United States, particularly the New England states; and Mexico. Excellent step-by-step instructions on the screen will guide you.

The Ancestral File, available only on compact disc, is a family-linked file containing genealogies contributed to the Family History Department since 1979. The file contains the names of more than seven million persons. You can search this file to see if anyone has already contributed information about your family.

Quaker Records

The records of the Quaker meetings are being published as the *Encyclopedia of American Quaker Genealogy*, which has already been mentioned. The Friends keep very careful records of all their members, their births, marriages, and deaths, as well as transfers from one meeting to another. When using Quaker records you should remember that they use numbers to refer to months and days of the week. Generally the number representing the month is given first, the day second, and then the year of our era, thus: 1-9-1777 (meaning January 9, 1777). A Friends marriage record, or certificate, will be signed by all those present; hence it has unusual value to the genealogist.

Additional Information

Church records contain more of interest to the ancestor hunter than marriages, baptisms, and burials. Frequently the records of the transference of members, generally by letter, to another congregation serve as valuable clues to migration; and, vice versa, the admittance of new members by letter from another church will enable you to trace a migrating ancestor back to his or her former residence. As an example, one church record book contains this information: "Admitted to this Ch. Lewis Gilbert, by letter from the Ch. in Cornish." This leads the digger to another state and another source of information—the town records and the church records of Cornish. Membership lists are sometimes annotated with data added in a later handwriting. Words, such as "dec'd" (for deceased) or "removed," have been written into the margins, generally by a later clerk who was revising the membership list. Dates are sometimes added to these notes, thus possibly giving you the date of an individual's death, for which you have found no other proof.

Once in a while you will find "excom," or some similar abbreviation, written in. To our astonishment, we found several such notes on the membership list of a certain Congregational church. We had never before known or heard that the Congregational church sometimes excommunicated members, but as we leafed through the records of that church, we found several lengthy accounts of excommunication trials. One man and his wife were tried on several counts, back about 1819, and were finally declared excommunicated from the church for blasphemous language, failing to attend church on Sunday, and nonsupport of the church. Verbatim reports of some of the evidence made very interesting reading, and from these reports we gained a vivid picture of the family life of this couple. The dignified and righteous old deacons reported the names they had heard each call the other, and also the opinion each had expressed of the other. Moreover, the record of this same trial gave us considerable insight into the rivalry existing at that time between the two Protestant churches in the town, for it seems there had been some proselytizing by the other church and its members had told these backsliders what they thought of the tenets of the "society" (Congregational) to which the defendants belonged. One can imagine the gossip at afternoon tea parties on the front porches, that summer of 1819, and the sanctimonious awe with which some of the words and phrases were repeated—in quotation, of course!

Amusement aside, however, church records are far too valuable to be overlooked when you go digging for ancestors. You should make every effort to find them and use them, even if you have to go through them page by page in search of the records of your forebears.

CHAPTER 10

Government Aid in the Search

There is in Washington a great building devoted to the National Archives. Here, where they can be properly housed, listed, cared for, and made available to the public, the older records from the various departments, bureaus, and offices of the national government have been concentrated. The use of these records has been greatly facilitated by the introduction of modern methods of arranging them, and by the many lists, guides, and catalogs compiled by the staff; by microfilm reproduction of many collections; and by the availability of photocopies.

Many records to be found in the archives of the government of the United States are of great value to those who dig for ancestors. From the earliest days of its existence, even during its provisional period, the federal government has been accumulating records that quite naturally pertain to individuals. Among the earliest of this kind are the payrolls of the troops serving in the Continental Army during the Revolutionary War. These are of value to persons who wish to establish membership in the Daughters of the American Revolution, and the other organizations, called "patriotic societies," in which membership is based on a descent from a patriot of that period. Some of the later records are, however, of more general interest. An excellent and detailed description of records of interest to family historians is the *Guide to*

Genealogical Research in the National Archives (1985). You will want to look at it at your nearby public library before undertaking research work with the collections.

Census Records

Probably the most important records in the National Archives in Washington are those gathered by the census takers every ten years. The first federal census was taken in 1790 and was probably ordered by Congress for the purpose of determining the possible military strength of the nation. The returns of this census were published by the Bureau of the Census in 1909, in the twelve volumes known to genealogists as the 1790 census. We quote from the introduction to one of those volumes:

> The First Census of the United States (1790)
> comprised an enumeration of the inhabitants of the
> present states of Connecticut, Delaware, Georgia,
> Kentucky, Maine, Maryland, Massachusetts, New
> Hampshire, New Jersey, New York, North Carolina,
> Pennsylvania, Rhode Island, South Carolina,
> Tennessee, Vermont, and Virginia. . . . A complete set
> of schedules for each state, with a summary for the
> counties, and in many cases for towns, was filed in
> the State Department, but unfortunately they are not
> now complete, the returns for the states of Delaware,
> Georgia, Kentucky, New Jersey, Tennessee, and
> Virginia having been destroyed when the British
> burned the Capitol at Washington during the War
> of 1812.

It was found, however, that partial returns for Virginia were available in the state's own enumerations (called "tax lists") of 1782, 1783, 1784, and 1785; so it was possible to reconstruct for Virginia a list comprising "most of the names of heads of families for nearly half of the state." These lists were printed in 1909 to form the Virginia volume of the set.

Thus we have printed schedules for Connecticut, Maine (originally taken as part of Massachusetts), Massachusetts, Maryland, New York, North Carolina, Pennsylvania, Rhode Island, South Carolina, Vermont, and Virginia, in which are listed the heads of families living in those states in 1790. The returns for South Carolina were not all in until March 1792, because the marshal for that state had difficulty finding enumerators who would work for the salary the government was authorized by Congress to pay. Since Vermont was not admitted until 1791, the actual census in that state was not taken until the period April through September, 1791. For a list of schedules on file, and those missing, see Appendix D.

In addition to those volumes, the Bureau of the Census published, also in 1909, an analysis of this census, called *A Century of Population Growth from the First Census of the United States to the Twelfth, 1790-1900*, which forms a useful supplement frequently overlooked by genealogists and ancestor hunters. There are two particularly valuable features of this supplement. The first is the series of maps showing the development of the country from 1790 to 1900, especially useful because it indicates the boundary lines of the various counties of the several states and the changes that have been made in them from time to time. The second useful feature is the lengthy table of names found in the census schedules in 1790, showing which spellings were used for each name in the different schedules. This list, called "Table 111," is found on pages 227-70, and is worthy of careful study, for only a few names achieved the distinction of uniform spelling in this census. Those are generally monosyllables such as Fox, Gage, and so on, which even a census taker could not help but spell correctly. A complex name like Fitzgerald appears in twenty-four different spellings, including one as strange-looking as Fitsjerald. Even as simple a name as Smith is found in nine different spellings.

The instructions issued to the 650 marshals who took this census directed them to list the heads of families by name and note the number of individuals living in each of the families in the following five classifications: (1) free white males, sixteen years and older, including heads of families; (2) free white males under sixteen years; (3) free white females, including heads of families; (4) all other free persons; and (5) slaves. The "all other free persons" category comprised white people who were not considered heads of families (for instance, in Exeter, New Hampshire, Joel Gill is so listed, but was not considered a "head of a family," although the census, following his name, noted three "free persons"— apparently himself and two others); "free colored persons"; and possibly a few Indians.

The amateur ancestor hunter who has traced his or her lineage back to 1800 or a little before will find these printed volumes of the 1790 census a mine of information and a source of clues that can be followed up in further searching. Let us suppose you are tracing a Pangbourne line, and that Grandfather Pangbourne has told you that his people came from Vermont. You know from the records he has given you that his father, whom we will call John Pangbourne, was born about 1788-89, presumably in Vermont. You are searching for a clue to his parentage, so you consult the 1790 census for Vermont. Here you find that Stephen and Samuel Pangbourn and Timothy Pengborn were heads of families in the town of Addison, Addison County, Vermont, in 1790 (1790 census, Vermont, p. 11); that Samuel and Joseph Pangbone were heads of families in Ferrisburg, Addison County, Vermont (p. 12); and that Jesse Pangbowen was the head of a family in Fairfield, Chittenden County, Vermont (p. 24).

The differences in the spelling of the surname should be ignored, for two reasons. In the first place, spelling was precarious at that time: people even signed their own names with different spellings on different occasions; and clerks frequently spelled names as they heard them pronounced rather than bothering to ask how to spell them. The other reason is that these census records were printed more than 125 years after they were written, so the paper and ink have faded, fine strokes of the pen have worn away as the pages have rubbed against each other in use, and the clerks, expert as they were in reading old documents, have occasionally erred in interpreting the several handwritings in which these records were written. Hence, although the name was printed Pangbowen or Pangbone, an examination of the original record in Washington might show that the name was actually written Pangbourn, and was misinterpreted by the clerk who prepared the copy for the printer. Or, the marshal who made the enumeration in Ferrisburg or the one who made it in Fairfield did not catch the soft Vermont slur of the *r* and understood the name as Pangbone or Pangbowen.

Of these heads of families named Pangbourne (in its several spellings) one, Jesse, can be eliminated immediately, for the time being at least, for his family consisted of but two males over sixteen, no boys and no females. It is possible that he had left his family somewhere else and, with a man to help him, was preparing a home in Fairfield at that time. But we will not consider that possibility in this instance. Thus your search is narrowed down to Stephen, Timothy, and Samuel in Addison, and Joseph and Samuel in Ferrisburg, each of whom had in his family a male or males under sixteen—your hypothetical John Pangbourne would have been in this classification if he had been born in 1788-89.

You will note that, through the use of this census, you have been able to narrow the field of your search to two towns in Addison County, Vermont. So you are in a position to go ahead, searching the vital records in those towns, and the wills and other probate records in that probate district, for evidence that one of these five men was the father of your great-grandfather. In writing to the town and probate clerks you ought to leave nothing to chance, and therefore should mention the various spellings of the name that you have found in the census records.

Possibly the 1800 census might be of further assistance to you. The Vermont Historical Society has published that Vermont census from a photostat copy that has been in its possession some time. From this we learn that there were only two Pangborn families then residing in the state: Reuben Pangborn at Panton, Addison County, with two males under ten, one male between ten and sixteen, one male between twenty-six and forty-five (without question Reuben himself), one female under ten years, one between ten and sixteen, and one between twenty-six and forty-five; and Stephen Pangborn, still in the town of Addison, with one male between sixteen and twenty-six, and one over forty-five (undoubtedly Stephen himself), two females between sixteen and twenty-six, and one female over forty-five (probably Mrs. Stephen). Either your hypothetical John had migrated elsewhere with his father's family or he was the son of Reuben Pangborn. None of the schedules for the censuses after 1790 has been printed by the government, although they are all on file in Washington (a few schedules, such as the Alabama schedule for 1800, have been lost or destroyed). The National Archives has microfilmed all of the available census schedules and the Soundex indexes to them, and positive microfilm copies are available for purchase or through the archives' loan system. These microfilms are arranged alphabetically by state and thereunder alphabetically by county. Usually all of the schedules for one county are on the same roll; some rolls contain records for several counties. The National Archives publications *Federal Population Censuses, 1790-1890; 1900 Federal Population Census; 1910 Federal Population Census;* and *1920 Federal Population Census* contain roll listings. These publications may be purchased at the National Archives or may be ordered by sending a check or money order, payable to the National Archives Trust Fund (NEPS), P.O. Box 100793, Atlanta, GA 30384. You need to specify the exact title being ordered and add the appropriate amount for postage and handling per order. Microfilm copies of the censuses, 1790-1920, and the Soundex indexes may be examined in the National Archives building and in all regional archives centers. Frequently, by searching these later census records, you can trace the progress of a family, either as the children mature, marry, establish families of their own, and come to be listed as heads of families, or as they disappear from the records of one town and appear in those of another. You can determine the approximate date of the death of a man as his name disappears from the census records. If he died young, frequently his widow is listed as the head of the family in the next census—not a few women appear, even in 1790, as heads of families consisting, generally, of minor children.

Incidentally, the National Archives can provide copies of specifically identified pages of federal population schedules ordered by mail. To receive this photocopying service, you must provide (preferably on NATF Form 82, Order for Copies of Census Records) the name of the individual listed, page number, census year, state, and county; and for the 1880 through 1920 censuses, the enumeration district. Frequently it is possible to use a census index to locate this information. In recent years many private firms have produced statewide indexes to census records for specific years. These are available throughout the country in libraries that have genealogical collections. In addition to the printed indexes, there is a microfilm index to the 1900 census and partial indexes to the 1880, 1910, and 1920 censuses. From these printed and microfilm indexes you can determine the exact page upon which a family was enumerated and then place your order with the General Reference Branch (NNRG), National Archives, Washington, DC 20408.

As an example of the use of successive censuses, let us take a bona fide case this time, in which the only records used are those obtained from the censuses themselves. John Castle (or Castel, as his name was spelled in some of the census records) was a resident of Fairfield, Vermont, and first appears there as head of a family in the 1810 census, when his family consisted of one male aged between twenty-six and forty-five, two males under ten, one female between twenty-six and forty-five, and two females under ten. By using our heads and a little arithmetic we can figure out that he was born between 1765 and 1784 (if he was aged between twenty-six and forty-five in 1810); since all the children were under ten, he was probably married about 1799 or 1800, or perhaps a year later than that (allowing a year after marriage before the birth of the first child, and two years between the births of the other three). Since neither he nor any other man of the name of Castle was listed in the 1800 census of Fairfield, we know that he must have settled there some time after 1800 and probably was not married there. So we begin to get a picture of his family.

In 1820 his family, as enumerated in the census of that year, consisted of one male between twenty-six and forty-five, two males between ten and sixteen, three males under ten, one female between twenty-six and forty-five, one female between sixteen and twenty-six, one female between ten and sixteen, and two females under ten. Now we can narrow his birth date down to some time between 1775 and 1784 (he was still under forty-five in 1820); moreover, he now has nine children (unless the female between sixteen and twenty-six was a hired girl helping his wife, or some other dependent, which is unlikely in so clear-cut a case as this).

In 1830, as the census of Fairfield for that year states, his family was made up of one male between fifty and sixty, one male between twenty and thirty, one male between fifteen and twenty, two males between ten and fifteen, one male between five and ten, one female between fifty and sixty, one female between twenty and thirty, two females between ten and fifteen. Taking this additional record we can narrow still further the period in which he must have been born; that is, sometime between 1775 (as determined by the 1820 census) and 1780 (since he was over fifty in 1830)—quite different from the 1765-84 which we got from the 1810 census. The same is true of the birth date of his wife.

This John Castle was still listed as the head of a family in Fairfield in 1840, the family then consisting of one male between sixty and seventy, one female between sixty and seventy, one female between thirty and forty, and one female between twenty and thirty. It is most probable that all the boys had married and established homes of their own, or had moved away or were working somewhere, and that the girls had all married except two who were staying at home with the "old folks." We find Stanley Castle living in the same neighborhood as the head of a family consisting of two males between twenty and thirty, one male under five, two females between twenty and thirty, and one female between fifteen and twenty. From this record and the proximity of the two families, we can assume that Stanley was one of the sons of John Castle, perhaps born about 1810, that he had married some time between 1835 and 1840, since he had a son under five, and possibly that he was working the original farm (his parents having perhaps moved to a smaller house up the road, let us say) or had bought himself a farm near his father's. Possibly the male of his own age in the census was one of his brothers; and possibly the extra females were his sisters, or those of his wife.

Now, using only the data that we have obtained from the successive censuses of Fairfield, Vermont, we can construct a tentative account of John Castle (we should note that no person of the name of Castle appears in the 1850 census of Fair-field), something like this:

John Castle was born between 1775 and 1780; he was living in 1840. He married about 1800, and settled in Fairfield, Vermont, before 1810. He appears as a head of a family there in the United States censuses of 1810 to 1840 inclusive.

He had children.

i. A daughter, b. ca. 1800-4 (under 10 in 1810; 16-26 in 1820; 20-30 in 1830).

ii. A son, b. ca. 1804-10 (under 10 in 1810; 10-16 in 1820; 20-30 in 1830).

iii. A daughter, b. ca. 1804-10 (under 10 in 1810; 10-16 in 1820); married or died before 1830, when she was no longer listed in her father's family.

iv. A son, b. ca. 1804-10 (under 10 in 1810; 10-16 in 1820); away or dead in 1830, when he was no longer listed in his father's family.

v. A son, b. ca. 1810-15 (under 10 in 1820; 15-20 in 1830); perhaps the Stanley Castle of the 1840 census.

vi. A son, b. ca. 1815-20 (under 10 in 1820; 10-15 in 1830).

vii. A daughter, b. ca. 1815-20 (under 10 in 1820; 10-15 in 1830).

viii. A daughter, b. ca. 1815-20 (under 10 in 1820; 10-15 in 1830).

ix. A daughter, b. ca. 1815-20 (under 10 in 1820; 10-15 in 1830).

x. A son, b. ca. 1820 (probably the 3d male under 10 in 1820; 5-10 in 1830).

You will have noticed that only the head of the family is named in these first five censuses, 1790 to 1840, although the classification of the members of the family by age had been extended and was much more close than in the first census. Undoubtedly this increase in the number of classes within the family was due to the government's growing interest in education and the desire to ascertain how many children of school age there were in the United States. The military interest, shown in the first census, was still there, but by 1840 men of military age were more closely classified than they had been in 1790.

The 1850 Federal Census

Beginning with the census of 1850 each individual member of the family or household was listed by name. The age in years, the occupation, the place of birth (that is, the state or the country), and the value of the real estate of each were given. Thus for the first time it was possible, in 1850, to determine from the census records the nationalities making up the population of the United States. From the viewpoint of the genealogist, this census is very valuable because it does list each member of the family by name, and gives the age and state, territory, or country of birth of each free person in a household. Let us take a typical record from the 1850 census of Center Township, Lake County, Indiana:

> David Hungerford, aged 46, farmer, born in Conn.
> Eunice   "   "   44   "   " N.Y.
> Esther   "   "   18   "   " Ohio
> Marian   "   "   14   "   "   "
> Busan D.   " (male) "   12   "   "   "
> Freeman G."   "   10   "   "   "
> Mary A.   "   "   5   "   " Mich.
> Hannah A. "   "   2   "   " Ind.

From this record we get the following story about the family: David Hungerford was born in Connecticut about 1803-4; probably he met his wife, Eunice, somewhere in Ohio and married her there about 1830; their first four children were born in Ohio, and then, between 1840 and 1844, they moved to Michigan, where they lived but a short time; about 1846-47 they moved, probably to Center Township, Lake County, Indiana, where they were living in the summer of 1850. It looks as though they might have lost a child between Esther and Marian, and another between Freeman G. and Mary A. It happens that after obtaining the census record for David Hungerford, we found a record of his family, which proved the suppositions we had made, supplied the names of the two children who had died, and gave the further information that David Hungerford removed to Oakland, Iowa, and died there in 1855.

The records of all the federal censuses from 1800 to 1920, inclusive, may be consulted in the National Archives in Washington; they are also available on microfilm and may be used also at the twelve regional archives centers located in key metropolitan areas throughout the United States. No complete index exists for the 1910 census. A researcher must use other sources to obtain the address of a relative, such as city directories, county landowners atlases, enumeration districts, and page-by-page searches of the complete census schedules. Soundex and Miracode indexes were created by the Bureau of the Census for twenty states (Alabama, Arkansas, California, Florida, Georgia, Illinois, Kentucky, Louisiana, Michigan, Mississippi, Missouri, North Carolina, Ohio, Oklahoma, Pennsylvania, South Carolina, Tennessee, Texas, Virginia, and West Virginia). Both indexing systems give the surname, first name, state and county of residence, city (if valid), race, age, and place of birth of the individuals listed; and volume number and enumeration district number of the census schedule from which the information was obtained.

Incidentally, the 1920 census indexes are arranged by state and by the Soundex system of codes, which uses a letter and three numbers to phonetically spell the family name. Under this system similar family names are indexed together regardless of minor variations in spelling. An index card, which was prepared for each household, notes for each member of the household the following information: name, date of birth, age, place of birth, father's place of birth, mother's place of birth, citizenship, mother tongue, occupation, and education; for the head of the household, the volume, enumeration district, sheet, and line number of the census schedule are listed. Frequently the index card records the family's address in 1920. You can purchase the reel of film that covers the area in which your ancestors lived (see Appendix D); but be sure you have a reading machine that will enable you to enlarge the microfilm copy and project it on a surface from which you can read it. The larger libraries have such reading machines, and those with genealogical collections have some of the microfilm copies, perhaps all of them. The census records since 1920 (the 1890 schedules were burned in a fire) are available in the Kansas depository of the Bureau of the Census but may be used only under certain conditions, for the contents are still considered confidential. Write to the National Archives and Records Administration, Washington, DC 20408, for the earlier records. For the later ones, ask the Bureau of the Census, United States Department of Commerce, Pittsburg, KS 66762, for the "Application for Search of Census Records"; it lists the regulations governing their use and tells you how to obtain copies.

You should not overlook the census records as a source of information in digging for ancestors. Although those who took the censuses (that is, the enumerators) were human beings and liable to error, and sometimes the person who answered the questions didn't know or didn't remember correctly, the records given in the census schedules are valuable and furnish important data that can generally be checked against other documents, such as a Bible record. In using census records, or in having them searched, try to get your ancestor pinned down to a definite locality if you possibly can. It is easier to search the records for Allegany County, New York, in 1850, even though the schedule runs to more than 700 pages, than it is to search those for the entire western end of New York State; and it saves a great deal of time if you know that your ancestor lived in Granger township!

Other Government Records

There are many other types of records in Washington that will be of use to you in your search for ancestors. For instance, there is a great mass of land records; there are petitions to Congress for "relief" for one reason or another (many of these are noted in the Documents Index, which indexes the documents that have been printed; any reference librarian can show you how to use it); and there are pension records.

Searching in Military Records

Nearly every generation of American families has been touched in a direct and personal manner by war: perhaps a husband, brother, or son has served in one of the armed forces and returned home safely or has been wounded or killed in the course of military action. The time line of family history has been punctuated in the twentieth century by the tragic rhythms of the wars in Vietnam and Korea and by World Wars I and II. During the nineteenth century we recall the Spanish-American War, the Civil War, the Mexican-American War, and the War of 1812. The colonial period of America's past was marked by the various colonial wars of the seventeenth and eighteenth centuries and capped by the Revolutionary War. The records that were created as a result of military service throughout America's history are of genealogical and historical interest. Military records are significant for this reason: it was necessary to verify and certify personal information to qualify for the benefits of service. A military file will give us information regarding the serviceman, his family, military experience, and places of residence. Also, when a widow makes application for benefits, she is required to prove her marriage to the serviceman with supporting documents from the clergyperson who married them or from relatives or friends. The same procedure is followed, too, by the heirs of veterans seeking service-related benefits.

How Do I Begin?

Begin your search for genealogical and historical information from military records by gathering those military documents that you may have found in the bottom drawer of the family desk or chest: records such as registration for the draft, enlistment, promotion, transfer, discharge, and, of course, the military units in which the veteran served as well as the wartime career. We should remind you that for seventy-five years after a serviceman's discharge his records are generally restricted by the Department of Defense and not available for your use. Information from the files may be requested on Standard Form 180, Request Pertaining to Military Records, from Military Personnel Records, 9700 Page Boulevard, St. Louis, MO 63132. For information regarding Navy officers separated since 1902, and enlisted men separated since 1885, and Marine Corps officers and enlisted men separated after 1895, inquiries should be made on Standard Form 180, Request Pertaining to Military Records, from Military Personnel Records at the above address.

Draft Records

Certain draft records are available through the National Archives—information that for World War I includes such data as the name, address, age, birthdate, race, citizenship, and nearest relative and address. For copies of World War I draft records, you need to know your relative's address and then send your query to the National Archives Regional Archives, 1557 St. Joseph Avenue, East Point, GA 30344.

Federal draft records for the Civil War are located at the National Archives in Washington, D.C. Arranged by state and Congressional district, these records note the name, residence, age as of July 1, 1863, occupation, marital status, and the state, territory, or country of birth. However, it is essential for you to know the registrant's place of residence at the time of his enrollment to gain access to this information.

We should mention that the archives of the various states should also be consulted for data regarding draft registration. This is particularly so for the Confederate states, since their records were not deposited in the National Archives.

Records of Various Wars

For the several wars that were waged between the close of the Civil War and the inception of World War II—the various Indian wars in the West, the Spanish-American War (1898-99), and the Philippine Insurrection (1899-1902)—inquire at the National Archives, since the records for veterans of these wars are deposited there.

When requesting a search of the military service records at the National Archives for the Civil War, use NATF Form 80, Order for Copies of Veterans' Records, and do be certain to complete as much of the form as possible. Although the National Archives is the depository for Union Army personnel records, remember that it also has some Confederate military records, but that your search should be supplemented by investigating the state archives of former Confederate states, and the Confederate Memorial Building in Richmond, Virginia. An excellent reference book for your search is James C.

Neagles's *Confederate Research Sources: A Guide to Archive Collections* (1986). Since there are several potentially rich sources for you to consider as you search for the Civil War military records of your ancestors, do read the booklets printed by the National Archives relating to military records for guidance. You will want to know how and when to use the Confederate Citizens File, the Union Provost Marshal Citizens File, or amnesty oaths records in the course of your careful research.

Your ancestors may have served in the Mexican War (1846-48), or in one of the several Indian wars before the Civil War, or the War of 1812 (1812-15) and if so you should check the records at the National Archives for assistance. There are three key collections to check for veterans of these wars: first, the service records of the particular war; second, the veterans' records for the appropriate war; and third, the bounty land warrant application files based on service between 1775 and March 3, 1855. An important research tool for veterans of the War of 1812 is Virgil D. White's *Index to War of 1812 Pension Files;* also useful are Virgil D. White's publications, *Index to Old War Pension Files, 1815-1926* (1987), and *Index to Indian Wars Pension Files, 1892-1926* (1987), and *Index to Mexican War Pension Files* (1989). These books have much useful data. Although the National Archives has some Revolutionary War records, the collections are incomplete because fires in Washington, D.C., on November 8, 1800, and August 24, 1814, destroyed many records. It is essential to check both the National Archives and appropriate state archives when looking for Revolutionary War records, since your ancestor may have served either in the Continental Army (in which case the records that survive are at the National Archives), or in the state militia (records at the state archives), or both. A helpful resource is Patricia L. Hatcher's publication *Abstract of Graves of Revolutionary Patriots* (1987-88).

Claims for Pensions and Bounty Land

Since the Revolutionary War period many laws have been adopted awarding money and land to Army, Navy, and Marine veterans and their widows and dependents. Each application for a pension or for bounty land is filed under the name of the veteran on whose service the petitioner based his or her claim. Bounty land warrant application files for service in wartime between 1775 and 1855 and pension application files for service between 1775 and 1916 are deposited at the National Archives. Incidentally, for pensions based on military service for the Confederate States of America, which were authorized by some southern states but not by the federal government until 1959, inquiries should be addressed to the appropriate state archives at the capital of the veteran's state of residence after the war.

The form and content of applications for claims have changed through the years and thus the kind of information recorded has varied. There are, however, certain important distinctions:

1. A veteran's claim will probably show his place and date of birth, place of residence after service, and a brief account of military service.

2. A dependent's claim generally includes the dependent's age and residence, relationship to the veteran, and date of the veteran's death.

3. A widow's application includes her maiden name, the date of her marriage to the veteran, and the names of their children.

You should submit your inquiries about pension and bounty land claims to the General Reference Branch (NNRG), National Archives, Washington, DC 20408, on NATF Form 80, Order for Copies of Veterans' Records. Instructions are printed on the form for its use. When a claim file is found, documents that usually contain information of a personal nature about the veteran and his family will be selected and photocopied and sent to you with a bill for the cost of service. A very helpful tool for access to certain pension records is Virgil D. White's *Genealogical Abstracts of Revolutionary War Pension Files* (1990, 1991, 1992). These volumes are packed with helpful information.

Perhaps your ancestor served in one of the colonial wars: French and Indian War (1754-63), King George's War (1740-48), War of Jenkins' Ear (1739-42), Queen Anne's War (1702-13), or King William's War (1689-97). These wars were fought to protect the colonies and colonists from the intrusions of the French and Spanish, and shaped in an important manner the path to independence from Great Britain. The records of colonial war service are generally deposited in the archives, library, or historical society of the state in which your ancestor resided and served. Many of the records have been published in records series sponsored, say, by the state, a historical society, or the Society of Colonial Wars. These materials are frequently found in libraries with substantial genealogical collections.

Ship Passenger Lists

Since 1819 federal laws required that the customs officials at the several ports of entry give quarterly reports with detailed information about both immigrants and Americans entering the United States. Under the statutes the name of the entrant and his or her age, sex, occupation, country of origin or nationality, and place of intended residence were recorded. During the last two decades of the nineteenth century the records became more detailed. Added were the specific destination within the United States, the name of the relative or employer receiving or sponsoring the immigrant, his or her final destination in the United States, and the name and address of the nearest relative overseas. In the twentieth cen-

tury additional data supplied included the religious affiliation claimed; language spoken; ability to read, write, and
speak English; and country of birth. All records note the last
country from which the ship departed en route to the United
States. A useful resource is Michael Tepper's *American Passenger Arrival Records: A Guide to the Records of Immigrants Arriving at American Ports by Sail and Steam* (1988).

If the name of the port of entry and the approximate arrival date are known, it may be possible to determine the exact date and the name of the vessel from records of vessel en-
trances maintained at the ports. We should note, too, that
family records and traditions may assist research in passenger arrival records. Naturalization records may also aid in locating the appropriate passenger list for an immigrant who
later petitioned for naturalization. Some naturalization
records show each petitioner's full name, and the date and
port of arrival in the United States.

Two valuable reference works for passenger lists are *Adler's Directory: A Compilation of Passenger Steamships Sailing
from European Ports and Arriving in the Eastern Ports of the
United States from 1899-1929* (1940), and the *Morton Allen Directory of European Passenger Steamship Arrivals*, which contains information concerning vessels arriving at the ports of
New York, 1890-1930; and at Baltimore, Boston, and Philadelphia, 1904-26. These books list by year the name of the
steamship company and by exact date the names of the vessels arriving at these ports.

For information about publications concerning early passenger lists, see *Passenger Lists Bibliography*, edited by P.
William Filby (1981), which is a revision and enlargement of
A Bibliography of Ship Passenger Lists by Harold Lancour (3d edition, 1963). Another useful source is the multivolume *Passenger and Immigration Lists Index* (1981—) also edited by P.
William Filby. Excellent studies using the passenger arrival
records have been made, such as Nils William Olsson's *Swed-

ish Passenger Arrivals in New York, 1820-1850 (1967), which lists more than four thousand Swedish immigrants. For a bibliography of such works, see Olga K. Miller's *Migration, Emigration, Immigration* (1974).

If the specific date of arrival or the name of the ship is known, copies of passenger arrival records can be ordered by mail using NATF Form 81, Order for Copies of Ship Passenger Arrival Records. Copies of the form are free from the Reference Services Branch, National Archives, Washington, DC 20408.

Naturalization Records

Naturalization records are an important resource for the family historian. From 1790 until 1867, various federal laws stipulated that free white males twenty-one years of age and older who desired citizenship could apply for admission to citizenship status once they met the residency requirements. Their wives and children were naturalized automatically. The process of obtaining citizenship required two steps: the filing of a declaration of intent after a year's residence in a state or territory and the petitioning to be naturalized after five years of total residency. Statutes enacted after the Civil War allowed for the immediate granting of citizenship to persons who had served at least six months of federal military service and received an honorable discharge. Persons of African descent were allowed to become citizens after the Civil War, and women could be naturalized in their own right after 1922, and in certain other instances prior to that date.

Under the pre-1906 statutes, any court of record, federal, state, or local, could naturalize a person if permitted by state or territorial law. The statutes did not require the two acts to take place in the same court, state, or territory; but as the naturalization act was a legal process, several records were created. The applicant petitioned in writing for citizenship and if successful received a certificate of naturalization. As both actions took place in a court of law and an interrogatory was part of the proceedings, the court should have created a record of the entire proceedings which should have been recorded in the court's minutes. The court docket should indicate the date and disposition of the court's action. If a petition to be naturalized was denied, the petition and a record of the court's rejection should have become a part of the court record.

The information acquired in the processing of a declaration of intent included the applicant's name, age, sex, place of birth, place of residence, and nationality; the name of the country to which the applicant owed allegiance at immigration; the date and place of entry into the United States; the name of the judge presiding over the petition proceedings; the name of the court; and the date of the event. Occasionally the name of the vessel on which the applicant arrived is also noted in the record. In the petition proceedings the information gathered during the declaration proceedings is duplicated in the court record. The proceedings also included the results of an interrogatory made of the two witnesses who avowed the morality and loyalty of the applicant, and also of any other witnesses. A written petition was received that indicated the applicant's current address, and if naturalization was approved, a duplicate of the certificate was issued to the petitioner and was made a part of the court record.

Many court records have been lost, while others have been deposited in a variety of centers. Some states have established facilities for old state and municipal records; in other instances the records remain with the court. Records of naturalization proceedings in federal courts are usually among the records of the district court for the district in which the proceedings took place. These records may still be in the custody of the court, or they may have been transferred to the National Archives and deposited in one of the regional archives branches.

Since 1906 the federal government has centralized records relating to immigrants. These records are with the Department of Justice, Immigration and Naturalization Service, and essentially all such records remain closed to public examination under the Freedom of Information Act. Lists of immigrants, ship passenger lists, duplicate declarations of intent and petitions to be naturalized, passport information, information relating to the naturalization of other family members or to foreign travel, and other information relating to the immigrant may be included in such records. Access to closed immigrant records can be obtained, by those legally entitled to receive such information, through the Immigration and Naturalization Office in one's state of residence only.

Naturalization records are of great assistance in learning the identity of the place from which a person emigrated. They may also help in determining the person's principal permanent residence before arriving at the port of departure, and accordingly in the identification of other members of the immigrant's family. For further assistance see the following helpful books: James C. Neagles's and Lila L. Neagles's *Locating Your Immigrant Ancestor: A Guide to Naturalization Records* (1986), and John J. Newman's *American Naturalization Process and Procedures, 1790-1985* (1985).

Social Security

The records of the Social Security Administration, which was established in 1934, are a rich source of information on deceased family members. It is possible to obtain copies of records from the file of a deceased direct relative. As all applicants for Social Security are required to document their birth to prove their age, the information from the early years of the program's operation includes helpful data on persons born in the 1850s, 1860s, 1870s, and later. Included in this group are naturalized citizens from foreign countries. The essential details on specific birthplaces of these individuals may not be recorded anyplace else. This is particularly true for people naturalized before 1906, when detailed birth information was not required.

Should you have an ancestor who lived past 1935, he or she may have a Social Security file. The Family History Library in Salt Lake City has available for readers' use a computer database of the millions of persons who were on the Social Security rolls between 1937 and 1988 and who have died since 1962. If you provide proof of your deceased relative's death, such as a death certificate, and his or her Social Security number, which is frequently noted on the death certificate, you should be able to obtain a copy of the decedent's original application for a number or his or her claim for benefits. You should write to the Social Security Administration, 6401 Security Boulevard, Baltimore, MD 21235. Describe the information you are seeking and note that it is not available from any other source.

CHAPTER 11

How to Arrange a Genealogy

Now that you have gathered together a mass of notes on your ancestors, you will want to arrange them in some orderly fashion, especially if you propose to print or publish them in some way. You will probably plan to preserve what you have dug out of the various original records and hand it on to your children, and perhaps to your nephews, nieces, cousins, aunts, and uncles. In distributing copies of your genealogy, keep in mind the help you have had from the printed books and genealogies at your favorite library, and deposit a copy of it there and perhaps in one or two other genealogical collections, for others to use.

In using genealogies, especially those found in the *National Genealogical Society Quarterly* or the *New England Historical and Genealogical Register,* you have undoubtedly noted the string of names, each with a superior number attached to it, printed in italic type and enclosed in parentheses, following the name of the head of the family. This is an abbreviated way of showing a descent in the successive generations from the emigrant ancestor or the progenitor of the family, the superior figure indicating the number of the generation, thus: (James^4 John^3 Henry^2 John^1). This, interpreted, means that James was of the fourth generation and a son of John the third generation, who was the son of Henry the second generation, who was the son of John the emigrant, or the progenitor of the family.

Because of this custom of using superior figures to indicate the generations, which has developed through long usage, it is unwise and confusing to use the same device in a genealogy for reference to footnotes or authorities, in the way such numbers are used in histories and other works. For this purpose it is better to use letters of the alphabet, or figures enclosed in parentheses, thus (1), or the customary symbols (*, †, ‡, §, ‖, ¶, etc.).

You should write first the account of the progenitor (or emigrant ancestor) of the family whose genealogy you have been preparing. In the first paragraph should be given the dates of his birth and death, his parentage (if known), and the authorities for these statements. Incidentally, if only one fact is taken from some authority, that source should be cited immediately following the information gained from it; if more than one fact comes from that authority, the reference may be cited at the end of your account of that generation and referred to by a superior letter or figure in parentheses.

The next paragraph should contain the record of the progenitor's marriage, giving the place and date if known (or, if not known, the approximate date and the reasons supporting it), the bride's full name and her parentage, as well as the dates of her birth and death. If she was a widow, the name of her first husband should be given; and if she married a second or a third time, the name or names of her successive husbands should be noted—this is all a part of her history. Interesting details of her life and accomplishments can be reserved for a later paragraph. If this progenitor had two or more wives, we prefer to give a separate paragraph to each marriage and the vital details about each wife. It sets the successive marriages apart in the text and enables anyone using the genealogy to quickly find the data for which he or she is searching.

Following the marriage paragraph (or paragraphs) should come the account of the life, activities, and accomplishments of the head of the family—his military service, the offices he held in civil life, the migrations he made, and all details that will help you or your prospective reader paint a picture of him. In a paragraph by itself should be given an abstract of his will, and that of his wife (or widow) if she made one. In abstracting a will you should note the relationship of the heirs to the testator, as mentioned in it, and any other interesting details you think should be noticed. The date of the will and the date of probate should always be given. In the absence of a will, any details gleaned from the administration of the estate should be given, as well as abstracts of any deeds or conveyances that contain genealogical evidence. Then, beginning a final paragraph with some such phrase as "The children of . . . and . . . " or simply the word "Children" or "Issue," you should list in columnar form all the children of this progenitor or head of a family. There are several models to follow, such as the "Register form," as the style used in the *New England Historical and Genealogical Register* is called, using small roman numerals to indicate the order of birth of the children (even if, in the absence of specific evidence, you have had to arrange them hypothetically), and reserving the arabic numerals for the child (or, in the case of a comprehensive genealogy of all the descendants of the progenitor, the children) whose line is carried on. See also the format practiced by the *National Genealogical Society Quarterly* and the Family History Library at Salt Lake City when you consider the style most useful to you.

Following the account of the children, you can list the general references used in building up the history of this generation of the family. In giving references to books you should always use the author's name and the title of the book as given on its title page, rather than the "binder's title," or the title from the back of the bound volume (binder's titles may vary in different libraries, but the title page is always the same wherever you use the book). If there is a date of publication on the title page, it should be cited in parentheses following the title of the book; if there is no date on the title page, use the copyright date given on the back of the title page, or the date at the end of the preface. Any of these dates not only serves to identify the edition of the book that you have used, but indicates the approximate time when the record you abstract from that book was obtained by its author.

Now let us see what this looks like in printed form. We are writing up, as an example, an imaginary family in which all names, places of residence, and other data are fictitious. We give the "records" of two generations and two families only, but my use of arabic numerals indicates that this is a comprehensive genealogy of all John Jones's descendants.

The Descendants of John Jones

GENERATION I

1. JOHN JONES was born, probably in England, about 1750-51; he died in Pollock, Blank County, New York, April 23, 1833, aged 83 years, according to his gravestone in the Pine Grove Cemetery there. His parentage is unknown, but it has been said that he was the younger son of a prominent English family and that he came to America as an officer in the British Army during the Revolution. Convinced of the righteousness of the American cause, he resigned his commission, assumed the name of Jones, and enlisted in the Continental Army. He never disclosed his real name, and no evidence of it has been found. There can be little doubt of his English origin, for he was referred to as "John the Englishman" in the Pollock Town Records, apparently to distinguish him from another John Jones living in Pollock at that time (Pollock Town Records, Book B, p. 26). He married, May 1, 1783, at Allen, Massachusetts, Mary Smith, daughter of

James and Mary (Hancock) Smith. She was born in Allen, August 3, 1760; she died in Pollock, New York, January 29, 1851, and was buried beside her husband in the Pine Grove Cemetery.

John Jones served in the Massachusetts Line in the Revolutionary War from 1780 to 1783. He claimed a pension in 1820. His pension record in Washington shows his service, but gives no indication of his birth or parentage. His widow received a pension, and her papers give the place and date of their marriage and contain a transcript of the Bible records of their children. (The Bible appears to be lost.)

After his marriage, John Jones and his wife lived in Allen, Massachusetts, for two or three years. About 1786 they removed to New York State, and were living in Pollock by 1790 (U.S. census, 1790, New York, p. 221). He was a miller and is said to have established the first mill in Pollock. He held several town offices, and was a member of the Congregational church in Pollock.

His wife, Mary, is said to have been a woman of considerable ability as a nurse. The obituary notice of her in the Pollock *Messenger*, January 31, 1851, comments on her kindliness and notes the great esteem in which she was held by the community.

John Jones's will was dated March 30, 1833, and probated July 6, 1833. He mentioned his wife, Mary, eldest surviving son, Henry, sons Eugene, George W. (if he is found within two years), and Jonas; and his daughters Mary Martin and Almira Martin (deceased), and her son John Jones Martin. (Surrogate court records, Blank County, New York, Book D, pp. 195-201.)

Issue:
      i. John, Jr., b. in Allen, Mass., June 21, 1784; d. June 22, 1784.
     ii. Mary, b. in Allen, Mass., June 15, 1785; d. young.
2.   iii. Henry, b. in New York, July 5, 1787.

3. iv. James Smith, b. June 28, 1789; removed to Michigan.

4. v. Mary, b. in Pollock, N.Y., July 1, 1791; mar. Henry Martin.

5. vi. Almira, b. in Pollock, N.Y., September 6, 1793; mar. John Martin.

vii. Eugene, b. September 15, 1795; d. unmar. March 29, 1850.

viii. George Washington, b. September 1, 1797; disappeared in the West before 1833.

ix. John (twin), b. April 6, 1800; d. April 15, 1800.

6. x. Jonas (twin), b. April 6, 1800.

References:

Biographical sketch of John Jones in William Johnson's *History of Blank County, N.Y.* (1879), pp. 345-46.

Vital Records of Allen, Massachusetts to 1850 (1910), p. 37.

Pension records of John Jones, No. W. 56,666, Washington, D.C.

Surrogate Court Records, Blank County, New York, Book D, pp. 195-201.

Inscriptions, Pine Grove Cemetery, Pollock, N.Y.

2. HENRY JONES (John[1]), son of John and Mary (Smith) Jones, was born, probably in Pollock, New York, July 5, 1787; he died in Whosset, Iowa, December 31, 1869, and was buried in the Center Cemetery, Buren, Illinois, beside his wife. He married, in Pollock, New York, December 25, 1810, Sarah Allen, daughter of Joseph and Sarah (Smith) Allen, and sister of his brother James's wife. Her mother is supposed to have been a sister of his mother. Sarah Allen was born in Allen, Massachusetts, December 25, 1790; she died in Buren, Illinois, June 3, 1860, and was buried in the Center Cemetery there.

Henry Jones served in the War of 1812 and was present at the Battle of Lake Erie. For this service he received a pension in 1858, which was continued until his death (pension records, Washington D.C.).

As the western country was opened up in the years following the War of 1812, he became interested, and finally moved to Buren, Black County, Illinois, about 1840. He lived there until the death of his wife, and then went to Iowa to live with his son John.

In his will, dated March 16, 1867 and proved January 5, 1870, he mentioned his deceased wife, Sarah, and expressed a desire to be buried beside her. He named also his sons John, Henry, George, and Joseph; his daughter Sarah Martin; his grandchildren Henry and Sarah Griffith, children of his deceased daughter Mary; and his grandson James, son of his son John.

Issue (all born in Pollock, N.Y.):
  7.   i. Mary, b. October 10, 1811, d. June 16, 1849; mar. Jonathan Griffith.
  8.   ii. John, b. March 29, 1815.
      iii. Henry, b. April 4, 1817; living in 1867.
  9.   iv. Sarah, b. March 17, 1819; mar. Joseph Martin.
      v. Hannah, b. October 25, 1821; d. January 3, 1822; bur. in Pine Grove Cemetery, Pollock, N.Y.
     vi. Jane, b. October 13, 1823; d. July 6, 1830; bur. in Pine Grove Cemetery, Pollock, N.Y.
10. vii. George Washington, b. February 9, 1826.
11. viii. Joseph, b. February 29, 1828.

References:
Bible record in possession of Mary Jones, eldest daughter of John Jones, Whosset, Iowa.
Smith, William E., *History of Blank County, Illinois* (1886), p. 801.
Vital Records of Allen, Massachusetts to 1850 (1910), p. 10.
Will of Henry Jones, Blank County Probate Office, Illinois, Book 9, pp. 222-23.

If you want to write up your direct line of descent from, let us say, John Jones, you should give arabic numerals to that child in each successive generation from whom you descend.

Your pedigree blanks form only a skeleton of your pedigree. The complete details of each line of descent should be written up in the style just given. If you want to examine a fine example of this type of genealogy, one in which the ancestry of a man has been worked out in detail, look at Mary Walton Ferris's *The Dawes-Gates Ancestral Lines*, in which she worked out in elaborate detail the ancestry in all lines of Rufus Dawes and his brother, General Charles Dawes. An excellent example of the comprehensive genealogy of the descendants of an immigrant, worked out in detail and noted for its accuracy, is Donald Lines Jacobus's *Bulkeley Genealogy: Rev. Peter Bulkeley, Being an Account of His Career, His Ancestry, the Ancestry of His Two Wives, and His Relatives in England and New England, Together with a Genealogy of His Descendants through the Seventh American Generation.* These books are models you should study and follow in writing up the account of your family, for each has been compiled and written by an accomplished genealogist, whose ability and reputation for accurate, painstaking, documented work is well known.

Descendants of John Jones, of Pollock, N.Y.

1 May 1783

JOHN JONES = MARY SMITH
b. in England, ca. 1750/1   daughter of James and Mary
d. Pollock, N.Y. 23 Apr. 1833,   (Hancock) Smith
age 83; served in the   b. Allen, Mass., 3 Aug. 1760;
Revolution; miller   d. Pollock, N.Y., 29 Jan. 1851

JOHN b. 1784; died young
MARY b. 1785; died young

25 Dec. 1810

HENRY = SARAH ALLEN
b. in N.Y., 5 July 1787   daughter of Joseph
d. Whosset, Ia., 31 Dec. 1869;   and Sarah (Smith)
served in War of 1812;   Allen; b. 25 Dec. 1790;
farmer, Buren, Ill.   d. 3 June, 1860

JAMES
b. 1789, settled
in Michigan
married and
had issue

MARY = HENRY
b. 1791;   MARTIN
had
issue

ALMIRA = JOHN
b. 1793;   MARTIN
had issue

EUGENE
b. 1795;
d. 1850
unmarried

GEORGE WASHINGTON
b. 1797; went West

JOHN (twin)
b. 1800;
d. an infant

JONAS (twin)
b. 1800; married
and had issue

MARY = JONATHAN
b. 1811;   GRIFFITH
had issue

JOHN
b. 1815;
married and
had issue

HENRY
b. 1817;
living 1867

SARAH = JOSEPH
b. 1819;   MARTIN
had issue

HANNAH
b. 1821;
died young

JANE
b. 1823;
died young

GEORGE W.
b. 1826
married and
had issue

JOSEPH
b. 1828
married and
had issue

Form 4. The "English" Type of Pedigree

This is a type of graphic pedigree much used by English genealogists but somewhat less common in America. It presents in greatly condensed form the data given in my genealogy of the hypothetical Jones family in this chapter.

CHAPTER 12

New Tools for Important Tasks: The Computer and the Camcorder

During the last decade two kinds of high-technology equipment—the computer and the camcorder—have become popularly priced, widely available aids in compiling, managing, and presenting family stories. The computer and the camcorder can be very useful in your research efforts.

The Computer

Enormous strides have been taken in improving the computer's capability to control genealogical data. As we all know, it does not take a long time to gather a considerable variety and amount of information regarding family members. Numerous pads of paper, countless file cards, and pencils of every size have been the primary tools for our investigations in the past. Now technological progress allows the computer (technically known as a microprocessor) to assist you in managing your records, graphically producing your charts, processing your words, assisting you in conducting your business with other persons, and providing the basis for telecommunications with a genealogy network or with another individual whose research interests are compatible with yours. Of all of these capabilities the control of your records will account for the most use of your computer.

It will give you the opportunity to begin a draft of your family's story as soon as you begin computerizing your data. You will be able to revise and add to any of the records stored in the computer without having to retype a page already produced, and you can duplicate copies of the material within seconds.

We all encounter computers in our daily lives, and marvel at the ease, speed, and efficiency with which they go about their work. In our kitchens microwave ovens, ranges, and dishwashers today contain small computers that guide them in their tasks. For many of us who have relied on pencils to write down our genealogical notes, the prospective application of the computer seems little more than complex and confusing wizardry. We want first to explore in this chapter how computers and compatible genealogical software programs can assist us in controlling our information and processing data, and save us time in our work.

It is not the purpose of this book to discuss technically how a computer works. Such questions are pursued in detail in articles in the major encyclopedias and numerous books available at your local public library. We should acknowledge that the computer has an accurate, expansive memory and the capability to retrieve again and again the information you enter into its program. The work that previously required several minutes or hours to do manually can be accomplished by the machine in seconds or minutes. A computer helps you to do many tasks you would probably defer, or overlook as too cumbersome, too menial, or too repetitive. Now you can do a variety of tasks—to help you control your information, understand the material, and tell your story— that you would have formerly shelved. The genealogical software programs available for use today on computer relieve you of many labor-intensive jobs. What does a computer do for you? How does it do its job?

Software

The computer is the basic equipment, or hardware, that you see on top of desks or work stations. To make it work after you turn on the power you will need to use software: programs developed to drive the computer as you record the details you have uncovered about family members. You must have a software program to do your job. It is the "operating system" or "disk operating system" for the computer. The software instructs the computer how to operate its disk drives, its memory, its video display, and its printer. The software program is vitally important because it determines what applications programs will run on your particular computer. As software applications programs are written to be compatible with a specific operating system and equipment, you are limited in the choices available. Should you wish to exchange information you have recorded on your disks with another researcher, it is important that your systems are compatible or your data will not be transportable.

The format of your computer genealogical files is entirely based on the design of your software program. Also referred to as the "applications program," the program combines with programming languages and systems programs to tell the computer what you want to do with the information you have compiled. As we have noted earlier, the primary task you want the computer to do is to assist you in managing your family history records. From the pages of your local newspapers, which usually feature articles on computers and software programs every week, you learn that equipment and programs are constantly being advanced and enhanced. There is a stream of new programs being produced addressing various interests and needs; these can be purchased and used with your computer. The informative computer section of the bimonthly publication *The Genealogical Helper* (published in Logan, Utah), describes and discusses recent innovative software programs designed to aid your genealogical research. The number of programs on the market for your consideration seems to grow monthly.

An important task for you is to consider the advantages and disadvantages of the many genealogical software programs available. It is an evaluation process that requires patience and some consideration. You need to gather from the sellers as much information as is available regarding the features of the various programs. Your goal in this investigative process is to identify the two or three programs most suitable for your needs. After that process of selection, closely review the strengths and advantages of these final two or three programs. It is much more prudent to take the time to carry out this important review process at the beginning of your use of computer technology, rather than starting your job and later learning that another software program would more effectively and efficiently serve your interests as you collect, refine, and write your family's story. You will be quickly rewarded for your diligent attention to this information-gathering assignment with an applications program that complements and supplements your persistent efforts.

If you have been involved with your research for some time, you probably have notebooks stuffed from cover to cover with information gathered from interviews with family members; or data retrieved from the pages of public birth, marriage, or death records; or facts from town histories, newspapers, and other sources. Doubtless you have also charts of the family, some completed and others with gaps here and there for ancestors who have not yet been adequately identified or for whom evidence has not turned up to document the events of their lives. Long winter evenings are especially made for reviewing, organizing, and shuffling these raw materials. We are constantly reminded of the many biographical facts we have gathered about family members, and of our need to continue our search for details about even the most obscure relations. There are inevitably many loose ends that need to be carefully and systematically controlled if we are to finish, to the best of our ability, the family's interesting story. While the computer helps us in the compilation, management, and printing of the data we introduce into the machine, it also limits our frustrations in trying to keep such information clear in our heads, precise in our notes, and understandable to our eyes.

Over the years we have been delighted to apply particular technological advances to our work. We think of the various kinds of microfilm machines, photocopying equipment, and tape recorders that have speeded and assisted our efforts. The computer today can also be a part of the family of equipment we use to do our jobs. Compared to the cost of a new refrigerator or bread maker, computers are expensive objects in our homes. We must remind ourselves that we spend a lot of time searching for our ancestors, at home, at libraries, and perhaps on sightseeing trips to their hometowns. The computer will reduce the number of hours we spend processing and managing our data. It is without a doubt a very helpful research assistant! (It is also able to do other work for us besides maintaining our genealogical information. It can be used for filing family financial records, for keeping address lists and favorite recipes, and for playing a variety of games.)

The patience you already have practiced in the process of accumulating data on your family members can be applied to learning how to operate a computer. Your inquiring mind can turn for a while from locating records on individuals to understanding the computer's operating manual and practicing what you learn on the keyboard. Keep in mind that the computer is your assistant and that you must give it directions and data to do its job. It is an extraordinary tool for storing family group charts, pedigree charts, census information, military and educational records, and medical records, as well as all of the other data that must be gathered on a fam-

ily's story. It also can store your records of correspondence to
and from family members and church and civil officials. The
computer becomes the recipient of information on the papers
in the bottom drawer of your desk or in the boxes pushed to
the back of the closet in the guest room or the attic. Moreover, the information can be readily accessed by keywords
such as names, dates, places, family members, and record
groups, in multiple combinations, to help you understand
and write your account.

Computers relieve us, by the use of programmed instructions, of repetitive elementary tasks that must be done again
and again. We are freed of recording laborious details, and
can pursue more complex and demanding assignments. For
example, a genealogy computer program can aid the preparation of a family group sheet. The subject is generally the
male family head and the form includes information about
the birth, marriage, death, and/or burial of the individual.
There are also details about a spouse, parents of both the
subject and the spouse, and any children of the marriage.
The records include supplementary information regarding
sources, places, relationships, religious associations, work,
education, health, and military particulars.

Using Genealogy Programs

The fundamental purpose of a genealogy program is to instruct
the computer to do specific tasks. Arranging your family members alphabetically or by identification number is an example of
such tasks, as are entering data, revising details, and linking
your family. Each of these tasks is programmed as a *routine*. Together, these routines are known as a *genealogy program*.

Computer software programs are the creative work of an
author, as your family history book will be the result of your
patient and persistent efforts. What the computer software
programmer writes is what we have to work with. The au-

thor has identified tasks to be done and has established a program to do the work.

All genealogy software programs require that you enter the names, dates, and places of particular events in the life of each family member. The program requires that you assign an exclusive identification number to each relative or ancestor for whom you are recording information. You can then call up the data for the individual by entering his or her identification number. Incidentally, when you have recorded details regarding several family members into the computer and given them each an identification number, you can instruct the computer program to print in alphabetical or identification number order your lists of family members. You can also instruct the computer program to note the blood and marriage connections among specific persons.

The computer is programmed to locate the full name of an individual, his or her spouse, and his or her parents and children. You need only enter the details for each person once into the computer, as against recording it by hand three times in the preparation of group sheets: as parent in a child's group sheet, as a principal on his or her group sheet, and as a child on his or her parents' form. You now can have access to the data and quickly print a variety of reports based on the information. Should you turn up new information about the subject, either correcting past details or adding to your records, such emendations are easily accomplished.

The laborious task of creating by hand family group charts, or pedigree forms, can now also be done by the computer. Single page or multipage, multigenerational charts for any family member in the computer's records can be generated by entering the individual's identification number. Your ever-ready research assistant provides you promptly with the precise information you request. No longer do you have to spend minutes, or possibly hours, fumbling through the fileboxes or notebooks in which you "know" you last placed the piece of paper recording the important information.

The computer forces us to follow rigorously the format of the genealogical software program, not occasionally, but continuously. Details relating to family members that have been noted in an irregular and incomplete manner on paper must now be regularized during the process of entering the information into the computer. We are forced to present our data in a consistent, programmed manner. While the task may seem to require overmuch discipline, we find that it really aids us in organizing our research work, compiling our notes, and presenting the information. You will wish your earlier efforts had been so systematically and logically arranged. Many hours of research time, many days of compiling and recording the data, could have been saved.

Remember that a computer is easier to use than a typewriter. You can correct mistakes by backspacing and typing over them. After you have entered one record, the computer program recites the procedures for entering additional details. You will find it helpful, rewarding, and enjoyable to have the computer as your workmate. The results are immediate. The data can be viewed on the screen and printed on paper. Multiple copies can be sent to family members for their review, comments, and suggestions. Should you receive new information or need to make corrections in the text, you can address the task when you next use the computer.

We should note that while there are variations in procedures from one genealogical software program to another, the basic functions are essentially the same. You have the option to add to, change, or print the information on your family members, individually or as a whole, at your convenience.

As you go about the task of compiling your family history gathering names, dates, and places, as well as consulting statistical data, historical and biographical books, you must also note the sources of your information. The strength of your book is anchored in the accuracy of your information and the evidence you have marshaled from a variety of sources to prove your story. The validity of your book is firmly based on the foundation of evidence you have brought together relating to the life and work of each family member. You will learn along the way that evidence, the irrefutable facts you accumulate regarding an individual, may partially or completely revise a family tradition cherished and polished for decades. You may indeed find that a revered ancestor served in a distinguished way in the Revolutionary War on the battlefield of Princeton, but that, on the basis of investigation and evidence, he was not an aide-de-camp to General Washington during the New Jersey campaign or any other campaign.

For every serious researcher there will be encounters with gaps in the family's story—an ancestor, perhaps a father or mother of a spouse, who despite repeated and persistent searches remains elusive and unidentifiable. It is possible to place an advertisement in a periodical such as the *Genealogical Helper* in the hope of finding another researcher who may have found information regarding your family member. With the advancement of technology during the past ten years, and with an increased number of men and women using computers and genealogical software in their work, it is possible to quickly exchange research information. The computerization of records provides a new medium of exchange of machine-readable data. Information may be sent from one computer to another by a telephone line equipped with the proper attachment or by exchanging disks by mail. Assuming that both researchers have placed their families' data on a computer database, the resource is a new, simple, and speedy means for finding and merging another person's information. A word of caution, however, is appropriate at this point to save you disappointment or frustration. It is essential for you to feel certain that the evidence the contributing researcher has brought you about your family member meets the same high standards you have set for your work. You do not want to assimilate questionable or unfounded data into your permanent records. The purpose of your demanding genealogical investigations would be eroded.

Planning for Desired Program Features

There are two or three features of software programs that should be on your checklist so that you may perform essential applications. One of these is database management. When computer specialists speak of a database, they mean a collection of records. For us it means all of the information we have gathered relating, for instance, to the births, marriages, deaths, and burials of our family members. We may now have this information in a notebook, on loose pieces of paper, or on family group charts. Our immediate task is to transfer this raw material to the computer file. Besides the new database of names, you may want right away to establish a list of the names, addresses, and telephone numbers of current family members from whom you can both solicit and share information regarding your family's story. Quickly you have established an important file for your future research work. For each person you will want to enter the date and place of birth, the name of the spouse, the type of work he or she does, educational background, military experience, and so on. Another database you will want to set up is a comparatively simple genealogy file that records surnames and first and middle names. You will enter such details as date of birth, place of birth, date of marriage, place of marriage, date of death, place of death, place of burial, spouse's surname, spouse's given name, names of parents, and reference notes regarding the sources of your information. The more powerful your computer system, the more powerful the database management, the more records that can be entered and managed, the more fields that can be included, and the longer these fields can be.

You will want to do some planning about the kinds of information you need to store in the computer before you begin the task. This is valuable strategic and tactical planning that will pay dividends many times over in the efficient use of your most precious commodity, time. The process will also help you to manage systematically and logically various categories of records. Your goal is to decide the number and type of fields you want to establish for your records and the length of each file. All applications programs require this information to assign memory and disk space and to instruct the program exactly where to find the particular field sought.

When you are investigating the advantages and disadvantages of computer software programs you want to know of their "relational" features. It is common for programs to establish relationships between bits of information in the file. Some software programs allow you to relate information between several files. You recognize immediately that the capability of relating one piece of information to another is a significant and useful tool. We want to carefully understand the procedures we must follow to instruct the computer to relate our pieces of information in a way that is helpful to us. It should be noted at this point that the use of "relational" in this way does not mean that you can identify family connections between particular members in a database created with a software program.

It is important to understand how the applications program reports its information. Most genealogical programs have designed record forms on which your data is printed. There are a few programs available that will allow you to create your own reporting system, but we caution you that this requires a complicated and time-consuming effort.

Word-Processing Programs

Another system you should evaluate and consider is a word-processing program, which has many special features to help you with your records management. Information categories created by a word-processing program are called text files, and do not require any complicated planning for their establishment. Enter your data on a free form, using as few words as necessary to do the work. Later you can merge, rearrange, or change their contents or formats; search them; print them; or refile them. It all can be done by your directions and a few fingerstrokes on the keyboard. Your word-processing files can be arranged in any manner you wish, and can be changed with ease. You can set up disks labeled according to the information you store on them. One disk might contain the names of your ancestors on your paternal or maternal line to the progenitor. Other disks may contain blank group forms or pedigree charts, or research notes, or details on your sources. One of the advantages of the word-processing program is that you can design your own family record form, see it on the monitor, and add to it and change it with speed and ease.

An attractive characteristic of a word-processing program is that it allows the user to enter information in a free rather than a structured way. For a family historian there are other benefits too: you can write letters; compose biographical accounts; create other narrative text for your family genealogy; establish source documentation files, research notes files, a "missing ancestors" file, and much more. Each database set up can be saved for later changes, use, and printing. When you want to remind yourself of biographical details of a family member you need only enter the name into the computer and the information appears on the monitor or the printer. A word-processing program is very valuable to a family genealogist, so you will want to select a computer that will support an excellent application.

Today there are many word-processing programs available on the market. They range from valuable to excellent; you will want to evaluate their features and decide which program is most useful for your work. As you investigate and compare, there are a number of questions you will want to raise. Does the program operate on your computer? Does it operate under the system you use for genealogy file maintenance? Will it support your printer? Does the video display have the required screen width? Are the editing commands easy to use and easy to remember? See Paul Andereck's and Richard A. Pence's helpful book *Computer Genealogy: A Guide to Research through High Technology* for additional questions.

There are two or three supplementary features you should consider acquiring. Doubtless the software program you select will do well the various tasks it is designed to accomplish. Nonetheless, there may be programs that will complement your basic application and that take over the information at different times or for different tasks. For example, a typical integration of software programs in genealogy occurs when you have created the family records with a program and have placed in those records the footnote numbers without having entered the actual references, which you have in your word-processing files. Or a genealogy program may provide for a paragraph or two of source material or a brief statement on a person's life. You may have appropriate text relating to a family member's World War II experience, or the narrative of a last will and testament that illuminates family relationships or family property, recorded under your word-processing program. Having used your word-processing program to create complementary and supplementary text files, they can be called up and printed under the control of your genealogy program. Frequently we will gather data on family members that run for several pages—say, entries from diaries, journals, letters, or account books. The texts may be expansive and rambling, yet give us important insights into the character, temperament, and experience of an ancestor. These should be stored in word-processing files rather than within the confines of your expanding genealogical file. Keep in mind that your genealogical and word-processing software programs were created to serve certain purposes. You want to fully use the distinctive features of each program and integrate the information they have separately compiled.

Briefly, we want to call your attention to the contribution that graphics software can make to the visual understanding of your family history. A map of the family farm or hometown with the house lot identified is instructive material for your story. Some computers can store photographs, which you can later draw from the file to provide illustrations for your book. Explore your graphic opportunities with care before launching this aspect of your project, as the process is complex and demanding.

Modems

One piece of equipment you may want to put to work is a modem, the telephone-connecting device that allows you to transmit family data from your computer to another or the reverse. You need communications software to make the modem operate. This software application allows you to "download" programs and files from the computer you are remotely operating. You can also "upload" programs from your smart-terminal—your personal computer—to the remotely located other computer, and store them in that computer's external memory disk files. The files you download can be sent to your own computer's external memory device, to be recorded on disk, during the link-up. When you finish this task, those records are in your computer and you can now use them without further connection with the remote computer. Also, when the telephone connection is ended, the distant computer you have been operating possesses disk copies of your files or transmitted software programs. Right away you can see that any two family historians can exchange information by telephone link-up. While not a necessity for undertaking the computerization of your records and notes, telecommunications software is a tool you may want to consider later when you are prepared to exchange the results of your research efforts.

Keeping Up

Constantly genealogy software is improving. New programs appear in the marketplace frequently. To keep track of the rapid developments in this field you will want to consult *Genealogical Computing* (Ancestry, P.O. Box 476, Salt Lake City, UT 84110), which publishes a directory to genealogical software and its vendors in each bimonthly issue. You can write to or telephone vendors who issue operating manuals, demonstration disks, brochures, and printout specimens, usually at little or no cost, from various genealogy software specialists.

A genealogy program is a specially written database program. It is unlike the database management program that controls the nearby supermarket's inventory, or that runs membership lists for your church organization. Genealogy files have management requirements much more complex than most small-business database needs. When you examine various genealogy programs you will want to note their similarities and differences in terms of programmer competencies, program adequacy, and value for dollars spent. You need to raise particular questions regarding software programs to determine if they fulfill your research and records management requirements. You should keep in mind that no one program will probably contain all of the features you would like to have at your fingertips. You must aim to identify those programs that most nearly fulfill your research requirements. The following are a few of the questions that should be raised: Will the program work on your computer? Does the number of disk drives required match your computer's drives? Is the disk operating system required the same as your computer's? Does the program require use of a printer which is like your printer? Are the instructions in the operator's manual easily understandable? Does the program vendor give buyers helpful after-sale assistance? Do many other genealogists use this program? Can the program handle unlimited family size? Is the program genealogically adequate? Are the charts, indexes, and reports generated by the program satisfactory? Is there room for footnotes and brief comments for any field and in any record? Is it possible to integrate files made with your word-processing program with files from this software program? Does the program allow you to designate a subject and then create an automatic search of ascending and descending bloodlines? Is a field easy to edit during or after the record-entry process? Can you return the software and manual with a reasonable or total refund if it does not satisfy your needs? Additional questions posed to help you in your investigation and evaluation of genealogy software programs are presented in Andereck and Pence, *Computer Genealogy* (pp. 91-98).

The Camcorder

Another recent development, the camcorder, offers the family historian an additional opportunity to supplement and complement his or her research work. Despite a rather high price, the camcorder, a combination TV camera and video recorder, is fast becoming the most prevalent means of recording family milestones and, for that matter, any family occasion. Camcorders are easy to operate and inexpensive to use. Two hours' worth of videotape costs only a few dollars. It is delightful to visually recall family members at special events such as birthday parties, Fourth of July picnics, marriages, anniversary parties, or Thanksgiving or Christmas dinners. Unlike film, video can be used, erased, and used again. The camcorder is a hybrid of a camera and a portable tape recorder. It is small, light, and simple to use. Camcorders come in a variety of body shapes, feature loads, and tape formats. There are several types of camcorders to choose from and we would recommend you do some comparative shopping before making a purchase. Consult your local public library for current publications discussing the technical specifics of camcorders and how they operate. Recent issues of *Consumer Reports* or the annual publication, *Consumer Reports Buying Guide Issue*, usually have articles on the advantages and disadvantages of comparative models. You will want to also investigate which film format is best for you.

There are a number of fundamental requirements to consider while using a camcorder. Is the light satisfactory? Is the camera steady so you do not film a shaky picture? Are there ways to move the camera to give variety to the film-making process? Can camera angles be varied?

What to Tape

The desire to tape family events is the most common reason for camcorder purchases: birthday parties, weddings, baby's first steps, are the reason that most videotapes are made. Some persons enjoy videotaping their summer vacation at the lake cottage, or the antics of their children, and then mailing the videotape to family members like a letter.

As you do your family history research you are documenting your family's story. You also can create a documentary film of your family's story. While methodical recording of significant formal events gives important skeletal and symbolic structure to a family video record, you also need the flesh of the rhythms of daily life. Family life changes slowly with the passage of years, and you do not realize how much until you see an old photograph. Children grow; neighborhoods change; shrubs planted as seedlings eventually mask the sides of the house; styles of dress, furnishings, and grooming change; pets come and go. You do not want to live in the past, but remembering how things were puts the present and the future into perspective. There is much to record in everyday events: the preparation of meals, tending the garden, the rooms of your house, and children and pets playing.

Rituals and celebrations are the stuff of home movies. Every family with a camera records birthdays, Christmas morning, Passover seders, baptisms and bar mitzvahs, and sports events. Conceptualize in advance the distinctive elements of the event and be certain to include them in the coverage. Some features are instantly identifiable—decorations, clothing, a birthday cake, a Christmas tree—incorporate these early in the tape so that there is no question of setting. There are many important events in the lives of children and families: first communions, baptisms, weddings, first days of school. Each one marks the passage of time and can serve as a subject for videotape.

Your oldest relatives have direct experience of things that disappeared before you were born. Travel before the days of jet airplanes, communication before radio and television, shoveling snow onto covered bridges so sleighs could travel across, the terrors of childhood diseases before antibiotics. The document you make today about yourself and your family will be a treasure for children and grandchildren seeking clues to how their ancestors lived, how they looked, talked, and felt in that past world—it will be as distant and strange to them as the world of your grandparents is to you today.

Recording Family History

The easiest way to begin documenting your family history on

videotape is through interviews with family members. But taping good talk requires careful preparation, in addition to the selection of an interesting subject. You cannot point a camera at people and expect them to speak poetically and from the heart while you manipulate the camera like a robot. In their minds they are speaking to the interviewer, not to the camera, or the potential audience it represents. You should know what your subjects are likely to talk about and arm yourself with key questions to guide the conversation. A conversation makes the best interview.

Pick a comfortable but interesting location, preferably one with some meaning to your subject, and sit on a chair or stool with casters so you can slide around to change angles. Props are useful in keeping conversations going and providing something else for the camera to look at. Old photographs can be invaluable in discussing other family members. They give a visual element to what is being talked about. They may also stimulate memories and elicit emotions that straight talk will not. Time lines are another useful graphic element. Using a long roll of paper fixed on the wall, significant dates in the history of the family are written on it at appropriate intervals. Photographs, plaques, awards, and other relevant artifacts can be attached above and below the corresponding dates. Reaching further back, you can chart the migrations of family members. This can be handled effectively by using a large map; the speaker stands beside the map and draws on the migrations with a broad marker while describing them. Photographs are not the only prop to stimulate good talk. Collections, such as artwork, crystal, china, books, hobbies, or other objects related to your interviewee will bring forth easy and valuable conversation.

Assembling and researching props and graphics should be a cooperative effort between the family media specialist and the rest of the family. In that way, everyone has more of a stake in the venture and greater eagerness to participate. Not all family history is ancient: children should be included too. A group conversation can be more fun to watch and easier to tape than a monologue. People stimulate each other, argue, reinforce, become enthusiastic—and ignore the camera.

Another approach, rather than recording family history, is to make family history on videotape. During the year a cassette can be used as a journal, with important events and thoughts added to it periodically. Then at the end of the year, the last part can sum up the year's activity. This can be an individual effort, or can be treated, more rewardingly, as a group effort in which all family members contribute to the archive. An ongoing journal or an end-of-the-year report should involve the whole family in both the planning and the execution. All members should have input concerning what they want to present about themselves and the others. Each family member can be responsible for different stories, thinking them up, planning them, and executing them. There is no limit to the type of subject covered, and the form is limited only by imagination. Make a family portrait, to see how people change from year to year: hair gets longer and shorter, beards come and go, and styles of dress change dramatically. For comparative purposes, the annual video can be taken in the same place each year, with each person in the same position. Make individual portraits of each family member. The toasts at a celebratory dinner, the stories on a car trip, or the lullabies before bed are unparalleled subjects for home video.

Interviewing Family Elders

You will find it of interest to do a series of audio or videotaped personal interviews with older members of the family. For many persons it is much easier to talk about the family's story than to sit down at a desk, put pen to paper, and write the account for many hours or days. Besides, the legacy of hearing an older family member's voice or seeing their face on the television screen establishes a link with the past at once memorable and informative. The development of audio and film technology permits us to establish a family archive that builds a bridge between the life experiences of the older members and the need in younger members to hear and learn about the family's past and the continuity of its experience.

As you undertake an oral or videotaped interview with a parent, grandparent, or other relative, be guided by the same principles of inquiry we outlined in chapter 2. Tact, thoughtfulness, and patience are all elements that make for productive and effective interview sessions. You do not want to create an intimidating or threatening atmosphere between interviewer and interviewee. A relaxed and easy manner for all parties will lead to rich results: to more descriptive and intimate accounts of the family members and their experiences.

Preparation is an important aspect of successful interviews. You want to be certain that any equipment is in operating order and that you have a list of questions to ask that will provide structure to the session and help you do your job. It is always valuable to share your list of questions with the interviewee in advance of the taping sessions. You want the family member to feel as relaxed as possible before the video camera or microphone, and to provide the questions in advance will reduce anxiety about the process and contribute to stimulating your subject's memory.

There are three main segments of your family's story on which you will want to gather as much information as possible. The first section can be called "family history." You will want to raise such questions as "Where were you born? When? Where were your parents and grandparents born? When? Did you know any of them? What were they like? What kind of work did they do? Did they have special talents or skills? What were they? Where did they live? What church did they attend? What did they look like? What was their height, weight, and color of eyes? Does anyone in the family

look like these family members, or have similar tempera-
ments? Did they suffer any physical or medical disabilities?
Do any family heirlooms survive? What about their educa-
tions, courtships, and marriages? Any tragedies in their
lives?" These are merely suggestions of the kinds of questions you can ask brothers and sisters, aunts and uncles,
cousins as well as parents and grandparents. You will want
to capture as much detail as possible about the family's experience, as detail will give life to your work.

Give attention to prompting interviewees to talk about
their childhoods, the neighborhoods where they lived,
schools attended, diseases encountered, roles of brothers
and sisters in their lives, family vacations, celebrations on
the Fourth of July, at Thanksgiving, Christmas, and other
holidays. Their adolescent and young adult years should be
explored too: memories of high school, dating, courtship,
college, military experience, the first job, and marriage. The
latter half of a person's life, from middle age on, is rich in
another kind of information, details that are reflective, in-
sightful, and spiritual in character. Ask "What was it like
when you turned forty, fifty, or sixty? Did you have a midlife
crisis in your marriage, or your job?" The elder years, too,
prompt questions: about health, problems, understanding
the young people, regrets, and advice. Ask parents, "What
was it like being a parent? What was the cost of childbirth
and rearing a child? Any differences between your children?
How were the children named?" Questions should be raised,
too, with grandparents: "What were your feelings when you
became a grandparent? What are your impressions of your
grandchildren? What is your role as a grandparent?"

Besides asking biographical questions of your family
members, you will want to raise with them questions on
what their responses were to larger experiences in the world
during their lifetimes—perhaps the impact of the Great Depression on their lives on the farm, or in the small town or

big city. What were the consequences of the various twentieth-century wars on the family? What was life like in the
1920s, 1930s, 1940s, and 1950s? What was it like emigrating
to America? Did they pass through Ellis Island? Are there
any heirlooms of the removal from the Old World to the
United States? What were first automobiles like? In which
elections did they first vote? What changes occurred as a result of the Depression or the various wars? Where were they
when Presidents Roosevelt and Kennedy died? When did
they buy their first TV set?

These questions are the outline of the kinds of information
you could attempt to obtain from family members to assist
your research efforts. A valuable guide that describes in detail the process of effective oral and videotaped interviews is
William Fletcher's *Talking Your Roots: A Family Guide to Tape-
Recording and Videotaping Oral History.* Interviews will prove
to be one of your most valuable resources for writing your
family's story, and certainly the most memorable. They will
constitute a permanent legacy passed from the older generation to the younger.

The computer and the camcorder have been created by
people, to work for people, and to be operated by people.
The computer is able to help you manage, process, and
present your family's story in an orderly and effective manner. The camcorder focuses on family events, recording the
physical features and voices of family members attending
festive and ceremonial occasions, special moments marking
every family's life. These two pieces of technology can complement and supplement your research efforts.

PART II

Special Searches

CHAPTER 13

Searching for Your Ancestors in North America

Native Americans

During the past decade persons of Native American ancestry have become interested in searching for their ancestors. Their interest is reflected in the broader interest taken by members of many ethnic groups in defining and recovering their family heritage—a heritage eroded by three and a half centuries of mistreatment and injustice, in the case of Native Americans. Many Indian groups in the past few years—the Penobscots in Maine and the Mashpees on Cape Cod in Massachusetts, for example—have sought legal action in hopes of reclaiming a portion of their ancestral lands or a share of any financial settlement. Accordingly, there is a need to define Indian ancestry, and also to determine what is a tribe and who comprises it. Incidentally, should one wish to establish tribal membership, it is necessary to file papers with the Secretary of the Interior—in particular with the Tribal Enrollment Section of the Bureau of Indian Affairs in Washington, D.C.

A first step in launching your search for Native American ancestors is to consult E. Kay Kirkham's helpful two volumes, *Our Native Americans and Their Records of Genealogical Value*. For families associated with North American Indian tribes the *Journal of American Indian Family Research* provides valuable guidance and information.

The constant conflict that shaded relations between the Native Americans and the whites from the earliest settlement at Jamestown, Virginia, in 1607 to the massacre at Wounded Knee, South Dakota, in 1890 made the accumulation and care of records difficult indeed. You may find some information on Indian ancestry in the records that have survived for the Indians in the eastern United States, particularly eighteenth- and nineteenth-century records. However, should your ancestors have been converted to Christianity at one of the Franciscan missions in the Southwest, or at one of the missions in New England sponsored by the Society for the Propagation of the Gospel among the Indians, or at a Jesuit mission in the Great Lakes region, there may be church records to assist you in your search.

During the years between 1830 and 1850 the United States government pursued an active policy of removing Indians on lands east of the Mississippi River and settling them on lands west of the river. At the National Archives in Washington, D.C., there are two helpful sets of records for this period: an 1832 Census of the Creek Nation and an 1835 Census of the Cherokee Nation, and the muster lists. These censuses were taken before the Indians of these two tribes were uprooted from their ancestral lands and sent west. The removal muster rolls are arranged chronologically, list individuals, and are indexed. The records vary in usefulness; some show only the names of heads of families. Others show, in addition, the number of persons, by age group and sex, in each family, and for some tribes that moved westward, the original place of residence of each head of family.

We should indicate that because the policy of the United States government was to isolate Indians on tribal reservations, especially west of the Mississippi River, and to exclude them from the privileges of the Fourteenth Amendment to the Constitution, no reference was made to Indians until the federal census of 1860. It was not until 1890 that there was an effort to include all Indians in the census.

America has not proved to be a melting pot for American Indians because tribal Indians have continued to live apart from American life. Nonetheless, there are government records to aid you in pursuing your ancestors. For the Indians who became a part of the non-Indian community, information may be sought in the usual public and private records sources.

Our cardinal principle, to learn as much about our families as possible from our relatives, is important for Indians. Moreover, since Indians frequently used several Indian names during their lifetime and may also have used an English name in their contact with federal officials, you must try to learn all the names, Indian and English, of your various ancestors as you chat with your older relatives.

The Indian tribal records at the National Archives in Washington, D.C., are significant because they contain such materials as lists of Indians removed from the eastern sections of the United States, especially for the Cherokees of the southeast, and several Indian censuses. These records are open for research on your ancestry, and if you provide certain basic information, such as your ancestor's name, the name of his tribe, and the approximate date of this tribal association, a staff member at the National Archives will undertake a search for you. You will want to consult the useful *Guide to Records in the National Archives of the United States Relating to American Indians* (1982), compiled by Edward E. Hill, before undertaking extensive research. The volume will provide a useful understanding of the administrative structure of the Bureau of Indian Affairs, and guidance for extensive genealogical research in Indian records.

At regional National Archives field branches you will find the records of the Bureau of Indian Affairs for the area in which your ancestor lived. Covering the years between 1850 and 1952, the records include birth, marriage, and death data as well as educational records and censuses of tribes. Should you be unsuccessful in locating information on your ancestors at either the National Archives or at the various field branches, you should check the office of the federal agency in charge of your tribe's records. Write to the Bureau of Indian Affairs, 1951 Constitution Avenue NW, Washington, DC 20245, and ask for the name and location of the agency responsible for your tribe.

There are two sorts of census records that you must consult at the National Archives. First, the United States censuses beginning in 1860 for those persons in the category of "Indians taxed, that is living off the reservation and among the white population," should be searched. Second, beginning in 1885, the federal government took an annual census of Indians living on reservations, and since most Indians did live in those communities, the returns are helpful. These records continue for most reservations until 1940 and are perhaps the most useful single series for Indian genealogy. They are available on microfilm as Indian Census Rolls, 1885-1940.

The census rolls are arranged alphabetically by name of Indian agency, thereunder by name of tribe, and thereunder by year. A tribe may have been successively under the jurisdiction of several Indian agencies, so it is important to learn which agency had responsibility for a particular tribe during the life of the subject of the research. The names of individual Indians on the rolls before about 1916 are not arranged alphabetically; locating a particular name may require scanning all entries for the tribe. After 1916 most agents alphabetized the names of individuals on the annual census lists.

Also at the National Archives is a four-volume Special Census of Indians Not Taxed undertaken in 1880 for particular tribes in the territories of North and South Dakota and

Washington and the state of California. There are scattered earlier censuses, too, which should be studied at the National Archives if your ancestors were of the Creek or Cherokee nations.

Do not overlook the valuable records called annuity rolls, which the government maintained for the period between 1850 and 1887. These records, which relate to several tribes, note the annual payment of money or goods to heads of Indian families. Occasionally the sex and age of each member of the family are recorded. Beginning in the 1870s, several school censuses of Indian children were taken from time to time by the Bureau of Indian Affairs. These should be checked, since they do list the students, their ages, where they were born, and frequently the names of their parents.

Another significant source for genealogical data is the Allotment Registers. The federal government, by the terms of the General Allotment Act, began in 1887 to convey to Indians, who proved they were able to supervise their own affairs, tracts of land. When an Indian died, all of his or her heirs had to be identified and their relationship to the deceased described. The registers were used during the period between 1905 and 1930, although some of the family information is carried back to the early decades of the nineteenth century. Here you will find the Indian and English names of the allotted person as well as age and birth date, and the names, ages, and relationships of the other members of the family. You should inspect, too, at the National Archives the Sanitary Records of Sick, Injured, Births, Deaths, etc., maintained by the Bureau of Indian Affairs. Beginning late in the nineteenth century the bureau's medical service listed those persons who had been treated for physical or mental illnesses. For births, you will find the date noted and the names of the parents; for deaths, usually the date is indicated.

After 1910, with approval of the commissioner of Indian affairs, an Indian could prepare and file a will. These too will

be found at the National Archives, along with other supporting papers, and they do detail such information as name,
tribe, residence, date of death, age at death, name of spouse,
date of marriage, names and dates of marriage of parents,
and the names of brothers, sisters, and children.

Canada

The first permanent settlement in Canada was established in
1608 at Quebec City by the Frenchman Samuel Champlain.
For the next 155 years the French strengthened and advanced their claims in Canada, although it is a story punctuated by the various colonial wars against the British. European imperial politics, commercial rivalries, and maritime
power were mirrored in North America in the geographical
areas of present-day Canada and the United States. Following the French and Indian War, France's stake in the New
World ended under the terms of the Treaty of Paris of 1763.
Under British control, Quebec province was divided into Upper and Lower Canada by the Constitutional Act of 1791.
Fifty years later, in 1841, following the Rebellion in 1837-38,
the two Canadas were reunited as the Province of Canada. In
1867 Parliament approved the British North America Act,
which created the Dominion of Canada, a confederation of
provinces consisting of Nova Scotia, New Brunswick, and
Lower and Upper Canada. The remaining provinces of
present-day Canada joined the confederation on various
later dates.

For an understanding of the history of Canada and its
people, look at the following books: Kenneth McNaught's
Penguin History of Canada (1988), and George Woodcock's *The
Canadians* (1979). Both books will lead you to other books related to your special areas of interest in Canada's past.

Genealogical research in Canada has been significantly
aided by the publication of Angus Baxter's book *In Search of*

Your Canadian Roots (1989). It is an informative guide to the materials that are available at the local, provincial, and national levels to assist the researcher who is studying his or her family's history.

The maintenance of civil registration for births, marriages, and deaths did not begin until 1869 in the province of Ontario. Unlike European countries, Canada has no central national registry office for civil registration; it is a procedure managed by each of the provincial governments. Such records are kept at the vital statistics offices in each of the ten provinces and two territories. The correct addresses are listed in Thomas J. Kemp's *International Vital Records Handbook* (1990).

Church records throughout Canada generally remain in the hands of ministers or clerks of local congregations. Again, we must emphasize that should you wish to use this sort of record to identify a particular event in an ancestor's life, it is essential to determine the religious affiliation of the ancestor and then locate the records of the particular church of which he or she was a member. The Roman Catholic church, the first religious group to come to what is today Canada, was established in Quebec City as early as 1614. Today nearly half the population of twenty-six million people is attached to the Roman Catholic church. The second largest denomination in the country is the United Church of Canada, composed by union during the past fifty years of the Congregational, Presbyterian, and Evangelical United Brethren churches. For aid in finding church records helpful to you in your research, address your inquiry to the United Church of Canada, Committee on Archives, Victoria University, Queen's Park Crescent East, Toronto, Ontario M5S 1K7. The Anglican Church of Canada is the oldest Protestant church and the third largest religious group in the nation. Records remain in the hands of the local parish or diocesan offices. For information about the addresses of local diocesan offices, write to the Anglican Church of Canada, 600 Jarvis Street, Toronto, Ontario, M4Y 2J6. In this brief overview of Canadian resources for the study of family history, we can direct you only to the several provincial archives and libraries throughout the country that hold materials relating to the development of the various regions and their peoples. We do wish, however, to bring to your attention the excellent resources of the Public Archives of Canada, since it is the largest repository of historical, governmental, and genealogical records in the country. Here you will find census and military records helpful to you, as well as emigration materials and records relating to the many ethnic groups that have settled in Canada. An excellent feature of the Public Archives system for researchers who live at a distance from the headquarters in Ottawa is the interlibrary loan of microfilm. Generally, any material that has been microfilmed at the Public Archives is available for use at your local library, so do ask your librarian about the procedures to be followed to use this service. Make your inquiries to Public Archives of Canada, 395 Wellington Street, Ottawa, Ontario, K1A 0N3.

The publications program of the Public Archives has provided several helpful guides to its collections: Maureen Hoogenroad's pamphlet "Genealogical Sources at the Public Archives of Canada," and the booklet "Tracing Your Ancestors in Canada." For information regarding the purchase of these and other publications, write to the Publications Division, Public Archives of Canada, Postal Station B, 59 Sparks and Elgin, 6th Floor, Ottawa, Ontario K1A 0N3.

Mexico, Puerto Rico, and Cuba

The opportunities are rich for pursuing the study of family history in Central and South America and the Caribbean islands. In particular, after family records, the researcher will find the civil, church, and notarial records of most assistance. Since the greatest number of United States residents with Latin American backgrounds have come from Mexico, Puerto Rico, and Cuba, we will focus our attention on the records in these three countries. Indispensable guides for use in our survey, as well as for all of the other Latin American states, are Lyman De Platt's comprehensive *Genealogical and Historical Guide to Latin America* (1978), and George R. Ryskamp's *Tracing Your Hispanic Heritage* (1984). You will want to be familiar with the valuable contents of both works before you launch your search further afield.

Mexico

The empire of the Aztecs was conquered by the Spaniard Hernando Cortez in 1517, and the viceroyalty of New Spain was established in 1535. The territory of New Spain included Florida, Texas, New Mexico, Arizona, California, Mexico, and most of Central America. Although settlements in all of these areas were established in the sixteenth century, it was not until the late eighteenth century that there were significant numbers of settlers throughout all these areas. California's settlement was particularly late. Mexico's political history has at times been turbulent, not only before gaining independence in 1821 but since then as well. Nonetheless, Mexico is a country with rich collections of genealogical and historical materials.

Civil registration of births, marriages, deaths, divorces, annulments, fetal deaths, adoptions, and acknowledgment by fathers of illegitimate children is maintained at the municipal level of government in Mexico. The procedure began in 1859, although in some places it started earlier and in other communities it was initiated later. It has been the key source for doing genealogical research for the past hundred years.

These materials compiled by the state should be used to supplement and complement church records. Since between

90 and 100 percent of the population of Mexico (or any other country in Latin America) before 1900 was Roman Catholic, it is to the registers of Catholic parishes we must look for assistance. Many parish registers have been lost or destroyed through the decades, but those that do survive will give you information regarding the baptisms, confirmations, marriages, and dates of burial of your family members.

We should mention that the Genealogical Society of Utah, an organization of the Church of Jesus Christ of Latter-day Saints, in Salt Lake City, Utah, has microfilmed many of the civil records and church registers in Mexico and throughout Latin America. These microfilms are available for public use at any of the Mormon family history centers throughout the United States and Canada—indeed, the world.

In the Latin world, both in Europe and in Central and South America, another important source for genealogical information, especially before the keeping of civil records, are the notarial records. This sort of record is based on Roman law and was translated to Latin America from Spain. The registers kept by the notaries public contain several sorts of legal transactions: wills, buying and selling of land, letters of indebtedness, and so forth. These records are deposited in nearly eight hundred notarial archives located throughout Mexico, although many states have brought the materials within their jurisdiction under the supervision of the state archives or in special notarial archives. Although each state in Mexico has its own major archives, the most important archives in the country for genealogical research is the Archivo General de la Naçion (national archives), Palacio Naçional, Mexico 1, D.F.

Puerto Rico

Attached to the viceroyalty of New Spain between 1534 and 1821, Puerto Rico became a dependency of Spain from 1821 until the Spanish-American War in 1898. After that war, Puerto Rico became a protectorate of the United States, which in 1952 declared it a free territory under its jurisdiction. During the years since the end of World War II there has been a substantial emigration of Puerto Ricans to the United States.

Vital statistics since July 22, 1931, are filed at the Division of Demographic Registry, Department of Health, P.O. Box 11854, Fernandez Juncos Station, San Juan, Puerto Rico 00910. Earlier records, dating from about 1880, are kept at the office of vital statistics in the particular municipalities.

Parish registers in Puerto Rico, should they survive, will be either in the hands of the local parish priests or at the Ecclesiastical Archive of San Juan (the Archbishop's Archive). A complete guide to the available parish registers has been compiled by the Family History Library, Salt Lake City.

A major center for genealogical and historical resources is the Archivo General de Puerto Rico (national archives), Avenida Ponce de Leon 500, Puerta de Tierra, San Juan, Puerto Rico 00905. The notarial records are of special interest, as is the alphabetical card index to the names of Puerto Ricans found in the records deposited in institutions in Spain. The index notes the name, document, and source of the information, and new information is constantly added to it.

Cuba

The viceroyalty of New Spain supervised Cuba from 1535 until 1821, save for an interlude in 1762 and 1763 when the British controlled the island. Under Spanish rule until the Spanish-American War, it became an economic and political protectorate of the United States in 1899. Since 1934 dictatorial rule of one fashion or another has governed the fortunes of the country. Many Cubans emigrated to the United States, especially to Florida—particularly, before and immediately after the revolution led by Fidel Castro in 1959. During the past thirty years, with an interruption of cultural and diplomatic relations between the United States and Cuba, our knowledge of Cuban affairs has been restricted, too. This is certainly true regarding our understanding today of genealogical and historical materials available in Cuba for the researcher's use. We can note only that civil registration began July 31, 1889, and that these records, should they have survived the various military uprisings, are in the hands of the civil registry of the town in which the birth, marriage, or death occurred. Parish registers, where they exist, are in the hands of local parish priests. The notarial records are preserved in the archives of the notarial districts and generally note materials dating from the early eighteenth century on. The Archivo Nacional (national archives), Compostela y San Isidro, Havana 1, Cuba, has such genealogical and historical materials of interest as census returns, military records, and land petitions.

CHAPTER 14

Searching for Your Ancestors Overseas

"How do I go about finding my ancestors in the old country?" This question is asked frequently by those who have traced their American ancestors back several generations and who have found the immigrant ancestor.

All we can do to help you with this problem is to suggest what you can do before you initiate any research overseas, and call your attention to several sources of more specific direction that will tell you better than we can what to do when you are ready to start searching overseas. In other words, there is a certain amount of hunting that you must do right here in the United States, and there are places to which you can write for records once you have gathered as many facts as you can.

Your very first step, regardless of the nationality of your immigrant progenitor, is to marshal all the facts and traditions you can collect from your relatives, whether by personal interview or by correspondence. You may find that you should do a little traveling in the United States before you plan to cross the seas; and, if you are able to get to Salt Lake City, you may be able to do a considerable amount of digging right there, where the Family History Library has microfilm copies of many overseas records and genealogists who are trained to read them. It also has publications on genealogical research in many countries, giving the location of the archives office and other repositories, if any.

From your own family records, you need to assemble all the facts you can and arrange them in clear and logical order. From your own knowledge, or perhaps from your grandfather or great-aunt, you know or learn that your progenitor was English, Swedish, or Italian. Perhaps there is a vague recollection that your grandfather, before he died, said that this ancestor came from northern England, but beyond that, when you commence your search, about all you know is that his name was Thomas Ackroyd. That much has been handed down!

Interview as many of the older relatives as you can, and quiz them about any old letters or papers they may have. If they won't let you take that bundle of old letters home to read or copy at your leisure, go through them then and there and note carefully the names of all persons and places mentioned in each letter, the date of the letter itself, and the names of the writer and recipient. One of your older cousins, perhaps, adds a piece to the puzzle when she tells you that her mother said the family came from Yorkshire; but another cousin tells you that his father said they came from Liverpool. As you poke around you find that many of the nineteenth-century emigrants from England sailed from Liverpool, so both of these cousins may have been right, and Thomas Ackroyd was a Yorkshireman who sailed from that port. Then you pick up the story that he landed in New York on the Fourth of July and was "rather" surprised at the celebration he found in progress. But as yet you know nothing about his age when he came, or even the year in which he arrived.

But you do know that the family has lived in Wisconsin for four or five generations, so you begin to search for records of them. You find in the State Historical Society there the 1850 census, and a card index to it that tells you that in the township of Vienna, Dane County, there was, in 1850, a Thomas Ackroyd who was the head of a family, and another Thomas Ackroyd who was younger and single and working as a laborer on a farm. One of your problems now is to distinguish between these two.

As a hypothesis you settle on the head of the family and begin to analyze the record. You note that Thomas and his wife Mary and the two eldest children in their family were born in England before 1840, and that the next five children were born in Wisconsin between 1840 and 1850. The significant fact is that sometime between 1838, when the younger of the two older children was born, and 1840, when the first child born in Wisconsin arrived, the family must have come to the state. As you look at the records of other families in the township, you find that there are several of English origin, and the same pattern prevails in some of them—sometime between 1838 or 1839 and 1840 or 1841 each came to Wisconsin. So it appears that there was a group of English immigrants that probably came together. Note the names (at least the surnames) of these, for they may be useful to you in identifying the ship on which they came and even the community in England from which they came.

Then some fine day you drive out from Milwaukee, where your family has lived for two generations, and see what you can find in Norway Grove, the most central village in the township of Vienna. At least you will visit the cemeteries and perhaps you can find the gravestone of Thomas Ackroyd. At the grocery store in the small village you find a man who tells you that there are still descendants of some of the English families left there and that old Miss Green up the road a half mile knows more about them than anyone else, because she was related to some of them. You go and talk with her, and she gives you an earful indeed! The main facts you glean from her are that there was a "shipload" of Englishmen and their families who came to Vienna in the summer of 1840, for they landed in New York on the Fourth of July and came straight out to Wisconsin. She recollects that her grandmother told her the ship was called the *Aniseed*, which always struck her as odd, naming a ship after a plant seed. She, too, thought that the ship sailed from Liverpool, but her own people were from Yorkshire. You ask her about cemeteries, and she tells you where most of the English families were buried and that you will find some of the Ackroyds there, although most of the family left Vienna before she was born.

In the cemetery you are somewhat disappointed. But you do find the gravestones of Thomas Ackroyd and his wife Mary and two or three other Ackroyds whose names you recognize from the census records, and you carefully copy the inscriptions. You look at the other stones of the same general period, and you find more names you have seen in the census records. One of them, quite near the Ackroyd stones, is that of John Darcy, who was born in York, England, February 16, 1818, and died August 6, 1885. Some of the others have the words "born in England" on them, but Thomas Ackroyd's gives merely the date of his death and his age at that time, so you can figure about when he was born, say 1810.

Your next step, now that you have some definite dates, is to search the newspapers of that area—the county weeklies are more likely to carry obituary notices of the inhabitants of the countryside and the small villages and towns than the city dailies are. In one of these you find an obituary notice of Thomas Ackroyd that states that he came to the county in 1840, bringing with him his wife and two children, his nephew Thomas, and his wife's brother, John Darcy. His age checks pretty closely with that given in the 1850 census. So you have him pretty well pinpointed.

You may summarize the facts you have gathered: You have your ancestor's name and age, his wife's name, the names of the children who were born in England, and you may assume that his wife was a Darcy, since her brother, John Darcy, came with them. You may assume also that the ship on which they came was named something that sounds like *Aniseed*, and that it sailed from Liverpool, and arrived in New York about July 4, 1840.

The last you should verify by writing to the National Archives and Record Administration, Washington, DC 20408, and asking if such a ship arrived at that time, and if so, was Thomas Ackroyd a passenger? If your date is correct and there was such a ship, an assistant in the National Archives will check the record for you. But suppose that he writes back that they were unable to find such a ship listed, or it didn't arrive that week. You can employ a professional searcher to check the lists of passengers on ships that did arrive about that time and he may find the ship's name was the *Anglesea*—the old lady probably never knew how its name was spelled and remembered only that it sounded like *anise seed*. Moreover, the *Anglesea* docked on July 2, 1840, having sailed from Liverpool with Captain So-and-So as the master.

Even with as much information as this, and it is more than some have been able to gather, you should continue your search on this side of the water. Look for old family letters, the family Bible—it may be in some cousin's hands in California or Texas. Look at any other old books that may have names written on the flyleaves or letters or clippings tucked between their pages. Sometimes a battered old prayer book will turn up and indicate that even though the groups of English families that settled in Vienna in 1840 were Methodists (or Wesleyans), the Ackroyds may originally have been members of the Church of England, as this old prayer book indicates. Say it has the name Roger Ackroyd, 1776, written on one of its leaves. Could he have been the father of Thomas? Or the grandfather? You recall that one of Thomas's sons, as given in the census, was R. Ackroyd. His name could have been Roger, rather than Richard, as you guessed it was. This Roger may be an important clue when you get your English genealogist to work for you.

There is another important source we have overlooked. Just as you think you have gotten about everything you can find and have wearied all your relatives in pumping them for details, you suddenly think of naturalization. Was Thomas Ackroyd ever naturalized? A news item in the evening paper telling about the swearing in of some new citizens at the county courthouse suggests that you find out where the old records of naturalization are. So you get on the trail. You have four names: Thomas Ackroyd and his nephew Thomas, Roger Ackroyd, relationship unknown, but a possible clue, and John Darcy. Perhaps one of these will produce information that will lead you to a specific spot in England somewhere in Yorkshire, possibly the city of York. Even if the clerk of the court is discouraging, try to find someone who can tell you where the old records are. One of our friends had to use a little "influence" and asked a lawyer friend of her husband's to prod one of the officials; she then learned that what she wanted was in Chicago. More influence was needed to get at it, but she finally found the record and it gave her some valuable information about date and place of birth.

Once you have pinned an ancestor down to a specific parish in England, you can write to the vicar and make arrangements to have the parish register searched for baptisms, marriages, and burials—*Crockford's Clerical Directory* will give you the vicar's name. Remember, by English law, he is entitled to a fee for searching his register, which forms part of his income.

Let us summarize what you should do before you think of writing overseas for information. The principles are the same for all countries. You must have names and dates, even though the latter are only approximate. You must try to associate the name with some particular locality, or it will be like finding a needle in a haystack. You should have some idea of when your ancestor migrated. If you can find the names of contemporary relatives, it will aid greatly in the search. Put all your facts into a logical order (see chapter 11 for an example of how to arrange your data about your immigrant ancestor).

Tools for Your Search

Before you go any further, we suggest that you look at Timothy Field Beard's very helpful book, *How to Find Your Family Roots* (1977) and Arlene Eakle's and Johni Cerny's *The Source: A Guidebook of American Genealogy*. In particular, become familiar with their valuable suggestions regarding genealogical sources in each state of the United States and for each country in the world. Note carefully their suggestions about books and articles that may be of assistance to you for the region in which you are searching for your ancestors. Another helpful feature of these books is that the authors have carefully noted the names and addresses of the key archives, libraries, and historical and genealogical societies here and overseas. Beard's book will give you some idea how to proceed in hunting for the records you want in a particular country, or how to get in touch with the proper authorities or a genealogist there. Some knowledge of the language of the country is a great asset, but it is not impossible to accomplish a great deal without it. Another useful book in this line is *Genealogical Research: Methods and Sources*, by the American Society of Genealogists (revised edition, vol. 1, 1980, vol. 2, 1983), which has several important chapters on resources available for pursuing your research in England, Scotland, Wales, Ireland, and European countries.

Some overseas countries have published leaflets that give considerable information about research in these particular countries: the British Tourist Authority, 40 West 57th Street, New York, NY 10019, has published "Tracing Your Ancestors in Britain." The Royal Norwegian Ministry of Foreign Affairs, Office of Cultural Relations, Oslo, Norway, has a booklet called "How to Trace Your Ancestors in Norway" (written in English). The Royal Ministry for Foreign Affairs, Press and Information Service, Stockholm, Sweden, has a brochure entitled "Finding Your Forefathers: Some Hints for Americans of Swedish Origin." Recently a similar booklet was issued for the Netherlands. It is possible that other countries have issued such booklets as well. There may be a small charge for some of these. You might try writing to the embassy of the country in which you are interested and asking for information—they all have offices in Washington, D.C., which will at least refer your request to the proper official.

African-American Ancestors

Alex Haley has charted the course for black persons searching for their ancestors. He systematically read the census records of Alamance County, North Carolina, available to him at the National Archives in Washington, D.C., and reconstructed the family's oral history that he had heard and learned from his grandmother as a boy, supplementing and complementing the story whenever possible with evidence from printed or authentic sources. Finally he traveled to Africa, visited the village of his ancestors, and confirmed the lesson he had learned as a child from a family member who had kept alive the ancient custom of committing to memory the history of the family.

Another inspiring, thoughtful, and dramatic account of a black American's search for her ancestors is Dorothy Spruill Redford's *Somerset Homecoming: Recovering a Lost Heritage* (1988). I urge you to read her book before you begin your research and turn to it for heartfelt encouragement when you feel you have hit a dry patch in your efforts. The book is about the slaves who lived and worked at Somerset Place, an antebellum plantation in Washington County, North Carolina. The chronicle was built on the family recollections of Mrs. Redford's mother and other relatives. The resources of the public library of Norfolk, Virginia, census records, and the inscriptions on gravestones all contributed to the story. The reader feels the author's pride when she finds and reads the bill of sale for her great-great-grandmother. More than 2,000 descendants of slaves of Somerset Place met in 1986 and several times since then to learn about and share their heritage, lost until they rediscovered it.

Recall that wave after wave of immigrants stepped on the shores of the New World from 1607 to 1920. Recall too that black people had been captured in Africa, transported in bondage across the Atlantic, and sold into slavery in America. Families had been broken forever, husbands and wives, parents and children, children and children, never to see each other again. For blacks the New World meant not only slavery but also utter strangeness—the loss of everything familiar.

The search for African ancestors can be very difficult due to the abruptness of the rupture between Africa and America, and the lack of any later communications, but the increasing sense of black history fostered by the civil rights movement during the past few years should make for greater resources for finding African relatives. The study of African languages, offered in black studies departments on college and university campuses throughout the United States, can provide clues to black Americans' pasts.

Fortunately there are now several very instructive books for the study of black genealogy: Alex Haley's inspirational account of his search for his ancestors, *Roots*; a guide to printed and manuscript sources and government records by James Rose and Alice Eicholz that is helpful in the study of black family history entitled *Black Genesis* (1978); Charles L. Blockson's and Ron Fry's instructive handbook, *Black Genealogy* (1977); Tommie M. Young's *Afro-American Genealogy Sourcebook* (1987); *Generations Past: A Selected List of Sources for Afro-American Genealogical Research* (1988), compiled by Sandra M. Lawson and published by the Library of Congress; and the *Journal of the Afro-American Historical and Genealogical Society*. *Black Genesis* calls our attention to the genealogical collections at the Schomburg Center for Research in Black Culture at 135th Street and Lenox Avenue in New York City and the Southern Historical Collection at the University of North Carolina in Chapel Hill. The Schomburg Center has material on black life not only in the United States but also in Africa; the resources in the Southern Historical Collection are particularly strong for those southern states in which slavery was practiced.

For the past hundred or so years, back to 1870, you can use such sources as vital records, church records, cemetery inscriptions, and census records to solve genealogical questions. You should also check the city directories for the towns in which your families lived for the surname you are tracing. Your nearby public library may have copies or be able to direct you to a collection. The city directories published before the Civil War may tell you if a person was black or may have a special code to denote a black person.

During the nineteenth century, in northern cities such as Philadelphia, New York, and Boston, beneficial societies were established by the black community for black people. The purpose of the societies was to provide such benefits as assistance to the poor, sick, and aged as well as burial insurance. Regrettably, many of the records of these societies have been lost; however, it would be useful to check the central public library in each major city for such material. The key local historical societies should also be checked: in Philadelphia, the Historical Society of Pennsylvania; in New York, the New York Historical Society; and in Boston, the Massachusetts Historical Society. Furthermore, black newspapers, usually published in the larger cities and towns, should be searched for family names and information—perhaps news of a birth, a wedding, or a death.

Census records, available at the National Archives in Washington, D.C., or at one of the regional archives branches across the country, should be searched, too. The first federal census was undertaken in 1790, and there is available for use at the National Archives a useful *List of Free Black Heads of Families in the First Census of the United States, 1790*. There was no special procedure for noting free blacks in the first census, so they were frequently recorded in the "other" category, which also included American Indians. Furthermore, the census enumerators freely noted of some families that they were Negro, mulatto, or free, but some received no racial designation at all. Until 1850 only the heads of households were identified by name. For every state, until 1860, slave schedules were prepared on a county basis, with slaves recorded under the owner's name.

Incidentally, for the 1830 census you may find it helpful to consult two books prepared by the distinguished black historian Carter G. Woodson: *Free Negro Heads of Families in the United States in 1830* (1925) and *Free Negro Owners of Slaves in the United States in 1830* (1924).

The National Archives, or its regional centers, should also be consulted for black military records. Since the Revolutionary War, black soldiers have distinguished themselves in battle. There are several key reference tools you should look at in this regard: *List of Black Servicemen Compiled from the War Department Collection of Revolutionary War Records; The Negro in the Military Service of the United States, 1639-1886* (1974); and a microfilm *Index to Compiled Service Records of Volunteer Union Soldiers Who Served with United States Colored Troops*. The payroll records of the Continental Army, also at the National Archives, should be checked, too, for military service during the

Revolutionary War. You should not overlook the records of the hereditary society, Negro Descendants of the American Revolutionary War, which may be useful in your search for an ancestor. Black persons participated in the War of 1812 (1812-15), although by the time of the Mexican-American War (1846-48) army regulations had been revised to exclude blacks except as stewards, cooks, or servants. During the Civil War, more than 186,000 black soldiers served in the Union and Confederate forces. For records of such service you should check not only the materials at the National Archives in Washington, D.C., but also at the state archives, or state library, or state historical society of the state in which the black soldier was a resident.

In the Spanish-American War blacks served in the armed forces, and in World War I more than 350,000 blacks served. More than one million blacks were in the various branches of the armed forces during World War II, and thousands served in both the Korean and Vietnam wars. Again, your first step in searching for the military records of your ancestors should be the National Archives.

Slavery in the New World altered the family life black people had known in Africa. On the wretched sea journey in prison ships, death separated many black families. Ashore in America, in Charleston, Mobile, or New Orleans, the auction block dramatically separated spouses and children from one another. Black men and women, boys and girls, were bought and sold in business transactions. Family life was maintained with great difficulty by slaves at work on plantations. Blacks were not equal under the federal Constitution adopted in 1789. Not until Articles XIII, XIV, and XV were approved between 1865 and 1870 did black people receive equality under the law. Marriage was not legally binding for slaves, and family records of, for example, births, marriages, and deaths were of little interest to slave owners.

We talk about the need to provide proof of a family's past. This is very difficult to do for the families of slaves. Many of the detailed records of the southern plantations were lost or destroyed in the course of the Civil War. Some may remain in private hands, held by the descendants of slave owners. You will find some records in the state libraries, archives, and historical societies of each of the former Confederate states. However, it requires much time, patience, and not a little serendipity to find a clue or two, or more important, some evidence. In any event, before you begin your search, you must know the name of the relevant slave owner and the location of the plantation. Should you know the names of the slaves, you will be greatly aided when consulting the plantation record books. Also, since slaves were considered property, and were passed from one generation to another through wills, do look at the wills, estate inventories, and tax records of the slave owners and their children; you may find important information. For an engaging and instructive account of a black family history research project see Johni Cerny's article in the *National Genealogical Society Quarterly* (1987), "From Maria to Bill Cosby: A Case Study in Tracing Black Slave Ancestry." The author systematically recounts her patient and persistent efforts to establish the family ties of the distinguished entertainer.

There are a variety of other sources for you to pursue when attempting to establish proof of your ancestry. First is the manumission record, a formal statement that the slave master gave to a former slave declaring his or her freedom. Such documents may be part of a will or other legal document. These papers, although occasionally in the hands of families, are frequently found in the collections of research libraries. Second, newspapers of the day published advertisements of runaway slaves, vital information for you since each ad gave such important information as the name of the slave owner and details of the physical features and vocational skills of the slave. However, because newspapers are seldom indexed, you will need to carefully review each issue in your search for clues. Generally, back runs of newspapers can be found at university libraries or at historical societies. Third, the station keepers of the Underground Railroad network occasionally left records of the names of those persons whom they helped to freedom. Although certain northern cities, such as New York, Philadelphia, and Pittsburgh, had antiblack riots during the 1840s and 1850s, many slaves traveled north to them on the Underground Railroad network; some went to towns in Canada, particularly in southern Ontario. Blacks settled in towns such as Wilberforce, St. Catherines, and London. If you know the town in which your relative settled, you should write to the local historical society for information.

Mixed black and white ancestry presents special problems and opportunities for ancestor hunters. Such liaisons were a feature of plantation life until the end of the Civil War and in the South during the years afterward. Nearly all black families in America have some white ancestry. The genealogies of white families that may form part of your background can be helpful to you in turning up information about all your ancestors.

Bridging the Atlantic from the United States to Africa is the last, and most difficult, step. You need to know three important facts: First, you must identify the precise point of entry of the slave ship to the United States. Was it Savannah, Georgia; Charleston, South Carolina; the Chesapeake Bay region of Virginia; Baltimore, Maryland; Philadelphia, Pennsylvania; New York; Newport, Rhode Island; or Boston, Massachusetts? Second, you must identify the slave ship and the ports it called at on its voyage from Africa to the United States. Most of the ships stopped at ports in the West Indies, Cuba, Jamaica, Brazil, and other Latin American countries. Third, locate the port from which the ship sailed in Africa.

We recognize at the outset that connecting the family from America to Africa will be difficult. A leading scholar of the Atlantic slave trade, Professor Philip D. Curtin, has observed that possibly less than 10 percent of the slaves from Africa arrived in the United States. Many died at sea and many were sold at ports in the Caribbean and in South America. Accordingly, black family members were separated from one another at every stage of their captive journey.

To make your family's connection to the other side of the Atlantic, you will need to know the general area from which your ancestor came. Since most slaves came to the Americas from West Africa, your search should focus on the nations and tribes of that region. Several of the key peoples of that area are the Guro, who live in the backcountry of the Ivory Coast; the Hausa, who populate the northwestern region of Nigeria and the eastern section of Niger; the Ibo, in the eastern region of Nigeria; the Senufo, who inhabit the west coast of Africa; and the Yoruba, who live in southwestern Nigeria and in southeastern and central Benin.

A trip to Africa may be necessary. Do consult the appropriate African embassies in Washington, D.C., and at United Nations headquarters in New York for help in directing you to archives and records centers in Africa.

The family tree is central to African cultural and religious life. The family, or clan, is determined entirely by kinship, from descent from a common ancestor. The small village was the stage for clan life, while the tribe, which claimed for itself descent from the same ancestor, was spread over a broader geographical area. Within the tribe, members learn the same customs and language, and learn of the several groups that compose the tribe. Tribes may be organized in two ways: ancestry may be traced through the father's line or the mother's. These ancestral systems have been significant in African cultural life, since they influence education, profession, and class.

Alex Haley had the good fortune during his trip to Africa to meet a person in his ancestral village whose vocation is to commit to memory and recount orally the history of a clan or village. Although today these persons, called *griots*, work at other jobs, too, they are really walking and talking libraries.

Jewish Family History

Interest in Jewish ancestry has enjoyed the same kind of dynamic development in recent years as has that for all other national and ethnic groups. One person whose knowledge, energy, and enthusiasm have shaped in a large way the present-day curiosity about Jewish family history is Rabbi Malcolm H. Stern. By lecturing to audiences from Boston to Los Angeles and taking pen to paper to inform readers through the printed pages of various genealogical journals, he has shared with many people, both Jewish and not, the fruits of his persistent and broad research efforts. His most recent contribution to our understanding of Jewish ancestry is the compendium *First American Jewish Families: 600 Genealogies, 1654-1977* (1978). A massive project, Rabbi Stern's book treats in alphabetical order by surname nearly forty thousand individuals, generally Sephardic Jews, whose ancestors settled in what is today the United States between 1654 and 1840. He notes such details as dates and places of births, marriages, and deaths, and military service. It is an important work not only for Jews but also for non-Jews, since during the past 340 years there have been many marriages between the groups.

Persons of Jewish ancestry must accomplish the basic research tasks facing all family historians before they can direct their attention to special problems: talking with a family member who has kept alive the family's history; gathering copies of birth, marriage, and death records in the United States; searching synagogue and cemetery records; as well as checking for information regarding the immigration and naturalization of family members. You should not overlook federal census and military records for details, as well as ships' passenger lists, city directories, and obituaries.

Another important book on Jewish genealogy that has appeared in recent years is *The Unbroken Chain: Biographical Sketches and the Genealogy of Illustrious Jewish Families from the 15th-20th Century*, by Neil Rosenstein (1976). Beginning with Rabbi Meir, the Talmudic scholar of fifteenth-century Padua, Italy, the author records the many lines of the Katzenellenbogen family descendants to the present day. The account bridges not only the centuries but also national boundaries and the seas as the author examines four hundred years of genealogical history.

Because of the forced conversions of Jews under the Inquisition in Spain beginning in the late fourteenth century and the expulsion of all Jews from Spain in 1492, many Spanish Jews practiced their faith in secret. Many of these hidden Jews, who were known as *Marranos* (crypto-Jews), later emigrated to the New World.

Jewish emigration from Europe to the western hemisphere began in the sixteenth century, with destinations in the Spanish and Portuguese territories of Latin America. By 1641 a Jewish congregation was organized in the Dutch city of Recife in Brazil. The Portuguese forced the Dutch out of their South American colony in 1654, prompting many Jews to return to Holland while others settled in the West Indies and one small group moved to New Amsterdam. Four years later a Jewish community was established in Newport, Rhode Island, and in the years from 1730 to 1760 Jewish settlements were founded in Savannah, Philadelphia, Charleston, and Montreal. Although the earliest of the Jewish colonists were of Spanish or Portuguese origin, Jews of German origin were represented, too. There were major waves of Jewish immigration to America during the 1840s and 1850s from German states and Austria in the wake of revolution in those countries, and from eastern Europe, particularly Poland and Russia, between 1880 and 1920. The movement of America's frontier westward also found Jewish families moving to and settling in inland cities during the nineteenth century, cities such as Cincinnati, Chicago, St. Paul, St. Louis, and San Francisco. Emigration was nearly brought to a halt after 1924, as the United States Immigration Law set quotas on the number of immigrants from each country who could enter the United States.

Special exceptions have been made during the last half century to the number of Jews allowed to enter and settle in America. Greater numbers were permitted to immigrate during the 1930s because of Hitler's attempt to exterminate Jews in Germany; following the Hungarian revolt of 1956; and during the 1960s, 1970s, and 1980s in response to Russia's harassment and persecution of Jews.

Before striking out on your own, read the very valuable book *Finding Our Fathers: A Guidebook to Jewish Genealogy* (1977) by Dan Rottenberg. Prompted by the study of his own family's history, this manual is indispensable for the study of your Jewish ancestors. He identifies the libraries and archives throughout the United States and in key countries overseas that have materials in their collections relating to Jewish families. Rottenberg calls attention to the microfilm collections of the Family History Library in Salt Lake City, which are of help not only to Mormons but to many people seeking to compile their families' stories. He notes the strengths of the American Jewish Archives, 3101 Clifton Avenue, Cincinnati, OH 45220; the American Jewish Historical Society, 2 Thornton Road, Waltham, MA 02154; and the YIVO Institute for Jewish Research, 1048 Fifth Avenue, New York, NY 10028, whose collections are strongest for families with origins in East European Jewish communities. The resources of the Leo Baeck Institute, 129 East 73rd Street, New

York, NY 10021, which focus on German-speaking Jews and their European cultural ties, are recognized, too.

Overseas, the Central Archives for the History of the Jewish People, Sprinzak Building, Hebrew University (Givat Ram Campus), P.O. Box 1149, Jerusalem, Israel, has gathered from around the world registers and records relating to Jewish history in the Diaspora from the twelfth century to the present. It is a very important collection of family histories—town-by-town registration of Jewish births, marriages, and deaths in Germany between 1800 and 1876. The bulk of the materials in the Central Archives comes from Germany, Austria, France, and Italy. The Yad Vashem Archives Har Hazikaron, P.O. Box 3477, Jerusalem, gathers materials on Jewish persons and communities that were destroyed during the Nazi Holocaust. It is especially rich with materials on Eastern European Jews, in particular the *yizkor* (memory books), books for some six hundred East European towns.

Jewish naming practices do present some difficulties in compiling your family story. It was uncommon for Jews in Germany and Europe to have a surname until early in the nineteenth century, although some Jews in Spain, Portugal, and Italy had family names since the tenth and eleventh centuries. Also after family names were introduced, people frequently modified or changed their names when they moved from one country to another. Some Jews, having fled Europe, anglicized their name upon arrival in America, making it very difficult now to trace their origins. Do look at the section of Dan Rottenberg's book entitled "Alphabetical List of Family Names" for a more comprehensive discussion of this matter, as well as the fascinating and valuable book by Rabbi Benzion C. Kaganoff, *A Dictionary of Jewish Names and Their History* (1977). We must call your attention to several additional books you will want to consult as you begin compiling your family's story. Based on his own years of research,

Arthur Kurzweil has written an excellent guide, *From Generation to Generation: How to Trace Your Jewish Genealogy and Personal History* (1980); Janice M. Regenstein has produced the helpful volume *American Jewish Genealogy: An Annotated Bibliography of Books on Jewish Local History, and Other Subjects of Use to Genealogists* (1981); and the useful book by David S. Zubatsky, *Jewish Genealogy: A Sourcebook of Family Histories and Genealogies* (1984). Another helpful tool is the *Encyclopedia of Jewish Genealogy*, edited by Arthur Kurzweil and Miriam Weiner (1991).

Before we leave this part of our discussion about researching family stories, we should urge you to look at two periodicals that publish articles of interest to people with Jewish ancestry. The first publication, the *American Jewish Historical Quarterly*, has appeared since 1892 and has printed on its pages many genealogies, biographies, and vital records. Two periodicals that are vital reference works in the field are *Toledot: The Journal of Jewish Genealogy* and *Avotaynu*.

England

The era of Henry VIII in England (1509-47) witnessed the introduction of a systematic effort to maintain public records. Beginning in 1538 Thomas Cromwell, vicar general to Henry VIII, ordered that parish records should be kept in the churches of England and Wales. The local clergy were to keep records of births, marriages, and burials within their parishes. For information from before 1837, when civil registration was introduced in England, it is essential for you to search parish registers. The records of baptisms, marriages, and deaths remain in the hands today of the clergyman of the particular Church of England parish. Should you know the name of the particular parish in which your ancestor lived, write to the vicar in charge of the church. Incidentally, sometimes the early parish registers have been deposited in the diocesan headquarters or the local or county record offices. However, the parish vicar is responsible for the materials and should be able to answer your questions.

We have mentioned here only the records kept by the priests of the established church, but, you ask, "Where will I find the records of Baptist, Presbyterian, and Methodist churches?" The records may be found in two places. First, beginning in 1695 it was required by all persons in England under the terms of the Registration Act—except for Quakers, Jews, and many Roman Catholics—to register their family's births, marriages, and deaths with the Anglican minister in charge of the local parish. Thus you should also check this source for family information. Second, many of the records of non-Church of England churches can be found at the Public Record Office in Chancery Lane in London. For Baptist records you should also check the famous Dr. Williams Library, 14 Gordon Square, London, WC1H 0AG. The Society of Friends maintains records in the library at its headquarters, Friends House, Euston Road, London, NW1 2BJ. A number of Catholic records have been published by the Catholic Record Society through the years; inquiries should be sent to the Secretary, Catholic Record Society, 5-24 Lennox Gardens, Westminster, London, SW1X 0DQ.

Since there are no Jewish registers deposited in the Public Record Office, you may find it helpful to seek assistance from the Archives of the United Synagogue, Office of the Chief Rabbi, Adler House, Tavistock Square, London, WC1 9HN, which has the registers for the Great Synagogue, the Hambro' Synagogue, and the New Synagogue.

For information about your ancestor who was born, married, or died since July 1, 1837, you should pursue your research at St. Catherine's House, London. The required records for civil registrations of England and Wales are kept there. The address to which you write is: Registrar General,

General Register Office, St. Catherine's House, 10 Kingsway, London, WC2B 6JP.

When requesting information from this office, or from any civil registration office in any country for that matter, supply as many of the basic details as you can about your ancestor. For example, when seeking a copy of a birth certificate, you should give the first and middle names, the family (surname) at birth (since it may have been changed for one reason or another later), day, month, year, and place of birth, full name and family name of father, father's occupation, and mother's maiden name. You may not have in hand all of this information, but provide as much as possible. We hasten to add that in England it is possible to obtain two kinds of birth certificates: a complete one, which states all the data we have just noted, and a short certificate, which is nearly useless to a genealogist because of its key purpose of protecting the illegitimate from knowledge of their parents.

When seeking copies of marriage certificates, do try to give the first name and family name of the groom as well as the bride's first name and family name, and, of course, the date and place of the wedding. The certificates include additional helpful information, such as noting whether it was a second marriage for either party, and the current addresses, occupations, names, and family names of the fathers of the bride and groom.

For copies of death certificates, it is most helpful if you can supply the first name, family name at death, date and place of death (which, incidentally, need not be the deceased's residence), age, occupation, and marital status. Should you have all the necessary particulars regarding your ancestor's birth, marriage, or death in England or Wales you can request a copy of the appropriate documents by mail at the following address: General Register Office, Smedley Hydro, Merseyside, PR8 2HH, England.

The first census in England and Wales that is useful for genealogical purposes was taken in 1841. The 1851 census records the full names of household members and the relationship of each member of the household to the head. Also recorded was the sex, occupation, and birthplace of each person recorded in the return. Microfilm copies of the census returns for 1861 and 1871 are also available for research, and they may be consulted at the Public Record Office in London. Although there is no charge for examining the microfilm records in person, a fee is required if searches are requested by correspondence.

We all know of the assistance that wills provide us in researching our family history. Since January 1, 1858, a copy of every will proved in England and Wales has been deposited at the Principal Registry of the Family Division, Somerset House, Strand, London, WC2R 4LB. A photocopy of a will can be requested at a modest cost. Before 1858 our problems in locating wills are somewhat more complicated, since wills were generally proved in church and manor courts. These records are now deposited either in county or local records offices, or in the Lambeth Palace Library in London, or in the Public Record Office. Before undertaking your search for an ancestor's English will, read Anthony J. Camp's important book *Wills and Their Whereabouts*.

Several reference books that no doubt would be of help to you as you plan and pursue your investigation of ancestors in England are Anthony Camp's *Genealogists' Handbook* (London, 1969) and his *Tracing Your Ancestors* (London, 1972), or his *Everyone Has Roots* (London, 1978), as well as Angus Baxter's useful work *In Search of Your British and Irish Roots: A Complete Guide to Tracing Your English, Welsh, Scottish, and Irish Ancestors* (1986). For students who have advanced experience with materials in libraries and county records offices, I suggest Sir Anthony R. Wagner's excellent study *English Genealogy* (second edition, Oxford, 1972). We are indebted to

Joy Wade Moulton for her valuable and comprehensive guide, *Genealogical Resources in English Repositories* (1988). It provides the reader with the addresses of the 175 key record offices and libraries in England, and also of the depositories in the United States that have either printed or microfilm copies of English materials from these collections.

As in the United States and Canada, numerous genealogical and family history societies have been established throughout England during the past ten or fifteen years. The flagship of these organizations is the Society of Genealogists, which maintains its headquarters and library at 14 Charterhouse Buildings, Goswell Road, London, EC1M 7BA, and publishes the excellent periodical *Genealogists' Magazine*, which is devoted to special problems of genealogy, genealogical methods, as well as extracts from various kinds of source material. The Society of Genealogists has focused its work on developing a collection of typescript and manuscript copies of parish registers and indexes of these for its readers' use.

Wales

A comment or two about Wales and Welsh records is in order. Since 1535 England and Wales have been administratively united, and, accordingly, Welsh records and family papers have found their way into libraries and records offices in both Wales and England. An excellent guide to introduce you to Welsh genealogical research is G. K. S. Hamilton-Edwards's book, *In Search of Welsh Ancestry* (1986). The National Library of Wales at Aberystwyth has received through the years many important genealogical collections, including court records and parish registers. The British Library at Kew in London and the Public Record Office, also in London, should be consulted, too, for resources. Do keep in mind that you must cover the same sort of ground and sources pursuing your Welsh ancestors as you do for your English family members: search parish registers; check for civil registrations, censuses, wills, and land records, naval and military records. An especially useful book on naming practices, by T. J. Morgan and Morgan Prys, *Welsh Surnames* (1985), will ease your way through this fascinating subject.

Scotland

The history of a country, region, or town complements and supplements our genealogical research. It is always essential for us to acquaint ourselves with the history of the area and times in which our ancestors lived in hopes of understanding the rhythms and events that shaped or bruised their lives. The history of Scotland is at once complex, dramatic, and colorful: a nation formed politically and culturally by its many clans at home and by early Norse invasions and English wars triggered from abroad. A useful introduction to the social history of this great country and its people is T. Christopher Smout's book, *A History of the Scottish People, 1560-1830* (London, 1969). A more detailed account is the multivolume work, *The Edinburgh History of Scotland*, sponsored by Edinburgh University and under the general editorship of the distinguished historian Gordon Donaldson.

There are several tools to use in finding one's way to and through the various records in Scotland as one compiles information about the family's past. Before you launch your research efforts, be sure to consult Margaret Stuart's book *Scottish Family History*. It is a very helpful guide to many reference works on the history and genealogy of Scottish families. Do not overlook Joan P. S. Ferguson's volume, *Scottish Family Histories Held in Scottish Libraries;* she lists existing books and the libraries in Scotland where they may be found. Another particularly useful introduction to research in Scotland is G. K. S. Hamilton-Edwards's, *In Search of Scot-*

tish Ancestry (1984). His account on resources in Scotland for the study of family history is at once comprehensive and suggestive. Another valuable guidebook in your search for Scottish ancestors is Donald J. Steel's *Sources for Scottish Genealogy and Family History* (London, 1970).

Generally, parish registers in Scotland do not record baptisms, marriages, or burials earlier than 1700. The registers are of the parishes of the Kirk of Scotland, the Established Presbyterian church. We should call to your attention the fact that unlike England, Scotland has no county records offices and only a handful of the large cities maintain archivists to look after their records; consequently, there has been a considerable centralization of local records in the Scottish Record Office. At the New Register House in Edinburgh, the registers from the more than nine hundred parishes in Scotland have been gathered for safekeeping and research use. Another possibly important source of information about your family may be the Kirk Session Papers. Maintained by the local church minister, these records list the names and dates persons received letters of permission to leave the parish to move to another village or town, or perhaps to the United States or Nova Scotia.

Since 1855 Scotland has required the civil registration of births, marriages, and deaths, and you may request copies of these records from the General Register Office, New Register House, Edinburgh, EH1 3YT. Census records are available for use in Scotland after seventy years, which means you can use the materials on your ancestors in the 1921, 1911, and earlier decennial censuses. These also may be consulted at the New Register House.

Scottish law and legal terms are somewhat different from the procedures and language used in, say, England or the United States. You will want to be aware of such differences when you consult land records or wills and estate papers. Before 1836 Scottish wills were proved before the Commissary Courts, an old ecclesiastical court that operated in a fashion similar to those in England until 1858. After 1830 jurisdiction in matters relating to marriage, divorce, and legitimacy was transferred to the Court of Sessions from the Commissary Court. Should you wish to check on a will relating to one of your ancestors, again, make inquiry at the New Register House. Registers of land sales and transfers since the early seventeenth century exist and are available at the Scottish Record Office, H. M. General Register House, Princes Street, Edinburgh, EH1 3YY.

The role of Scottish emigration to the New World—to Nova Scotia and Prince Edward Island in Canada, and to Virginia, the Carolinas, New York, and elsewhere in what is today the United States—is a story of hope and tragedy, of achievement and disillusionment in new places overseas and in familiar neighborhoods in Scotland. Our understanding of this migration is greatly aided by several books: David Dobson's compilation. *The Original Scots Colonists of Early America, 1617-1783* (1989); Gordon Donaldson's book *The Scots Overseas* (London, 1966), and the excellent volume by Charles W. Dunn of Harvard University, *Highland Settler: A Portrait of the Scottish Gael in Nova Scotia* (Toronto, 1953).

Ireland

Republic of Ireland

Immediately we must acknowledge that the turbulent course of Irish history, crowned by the burning of the Public Record Office in Dublin on April 13, 1922, has created irreparable gaps in our knowledge of Irish genealogy. Not all of Ireland's records were burned in the wake of the civil war, since many records had not been sent to Dublin but remained in the hands of local authorities. The fire in 1922 destroyed about one thousand Protestant parish registers, bishops' transcripts, civil registrations, census returns, wills, and estate papers—records that were not available in any other depository either in Ireland or in London. Consequently, searching for your Irish ancestors is a difficult task. It is important for you to have a basic understanding of the civil and ecclesiastical organization of Ireland before and after the division of the country in 1922. You may find on the United States immigration records that your ancestor noted his birthplace in Ireland, or stated the province, county, parish, or diocese in which he was born or had lived before coming to the United States. At the Office of the Registrar General, 8-11 Lombard Street East, Dublin, 2, you will find arranged on a county basis births, marriages, and death records since 1864, because such information had to be registered. Protestant marriages were registered from April 1, 1845.

Because England governed Ireland until 1922, the favored religious denomination was the Church of Ireland, which practiced the liturgy and doctrine of the Anglican tradition; parish registers for Roman Catholic churches are sparse. Records for Catholic and Church of Ireland parishes are generally in the hands of the particular parish priest, and you should make inquiries to the priest in charge of the congregation of which your ancestor was a member. The Public Record Office of Ireland (Oifig Iris Puibli), Four Courts, Dublin, 7, has microfilm copies of church registers, both Catholic and Protestant, and some manuscript collections of genealogical interest such as the abstracts compiled from wills by Sir William Betham, Ulster King of Arms; extracts from parish registers; and many collections of family papers. Also, the National Library of Ireland, Kildare Street, Dublin, 2, has a substantial collection of printed and manuscript materials relating to Irish family history.

An excellent reference guide to assist you in your research work in the Republic of Ireland (and in Northern Ireland) is Margaret Dickson Falley's two-volume *Irish and Scotch-Irish Ancestral Research: A Guide to the Genealogical Records, Methods and Sources in Ireland.* It is an indispensable survey of the public records, church records, printed books, and manuscript collections available throughout Ireland and Northern Ireland. In particular, we urge you to read Mrs. Falley's instructive chapter "Preliminary Research in the United States" before attempting research efforts anywhere in Ireland; her suggestions will provide you with the necessary framework to build your story. Additional readable handbooks are the volumes prepared by James G. Ryan—*Irish Records: Sources for Family and Local History* (1988)—and Donal F. Begley—*Handbook on Irish Genealogy: How to Trace Your Ancestors and Relatives in Ireland* (1984). If you know the county of your ancestor's origin you will want to write to the county Research Centres for information. During the past few years the Irish Family History Cooperative, comprised of county Research Centres throughout the nation, has been entering into a computer database information gleaned from the pages of parish registers and other sources on local names. The Research Centres can often provide more detailed information on your family and the territory from which they came, and also arrange personal itineraries in the locality of your ancestors. These Centres may be able to prepare personalized reports on your family name—genealogy combined with local history and folklore. For a list of the addresses and telephone numbers of the Research Centres write to the Irish Tourist Board, 757 Third Avenue, New York, NY 10017.

Further assistance may be obtained from the Genealogical Office, which is under Irish control and directed by a chief herald. Located at 2 Kildare Street, Dublin, 2, the Genealogical Office provides, for a modest fee, a consulting service on ancestry. A Clans of Ireland office has been established in Dublin to help organize gatherings of the 243 Irish clan names so far researched. Information on the Clan Association is available from Clans of Ireland, care of the Genealogical Office.

Northern Ireland

Until December 6, 1921, the six northern counties that are a part of the United Kingdom were a part of Ireland, and the public records were at the General Register Office in Dublin. Since 1922 such records for Northern Ireland are kept at the General Register Office, Oxford House, 49-55 Chichester Street, Belfast, BT1 4HF.

The registration of marriages, except Roman Catholic marriages, began on April 1, 1845, and of births, deaths, and Roman Catholic marriages on January 1, 1864. These records are in the hands of local registrars and clergymen. The Public Record Office in Belfast has some materials before 1922 of genealogical interest: wills and probate records, tithe apportionment books, poll tax records, militia yeomanry and muster rolls, parish registers for the Church of Ireland, Roman Catholic, Methodist, and other churches, voters poll, and some census records.

Scandinavia: Sweden, Norway, Denmark, Iceland, and Finland

Many Americans, particularly in the farming and urban communities of the Midwest and West, have ancestral roots in one or more of the Scandinavian countries. Indeed, during the nineteenth century 1,228,000 Swedes migrated to the New World, as did 814,000 Norwegians, 340,000 Danes, and 22,000 Finns. The figure for Finland is somewhat misleading, since immigrants from that country were included with the statistics for Sweden before 1918. Because Iceland was a dependency of Denmark until 1944, the figures for immigrants from that country are included in the category for Danes.

We should note that all Scandinavian countries share the use of patronymics, a naming procedure that identifies the child as the son or daughter of a particular man. For example, a son of a man named Peter would have the surname Petersson (Swedish) or Peterssen (Danish and Norwegian). Women kept their maiden names after they married, a custom that flourished until about 1900. The patronymic plan existed until around 1875, when the children in a family began taking their father's surname. Today Iceland continues the patronymic system and women also keep their maiden names.

Sweden

Research in the Scandinavian countries is a pleasure because the public records have been so efficiently maintained through the centuries. If you know the name of your Swedish ancestor and the place in Sweden where he or she lived before traveling to America, you will find numerous sources to assist you in your hunt.

Since 1686 ministers have been required by law to maintain parish records. Occasionally you will find useful church records before 1686. The pages of the church registers, when they were earnestly kept, include much information of genealogical interest. You will find not only records of births, marriages, and deaths, but also communion records and notes regarding the movements of persons in and out of the parish. Since about 1686 the household examination rolls contain records of the households in the parish, including all their members. These important records, sometimes called clerical survey records, were kept by the Lutheran parish ministers until about 1895, and delineate a family's movement from one parish to another. The records are most complete for the years between 1800 and 1895. The clergy visited every household in their parish and were required to "examine" each member regarding his or her knowledge of the scriptures and reading ability. The survey was done once a year and the new information was recorded in the parish book. The data is indeed important, as it provides information about all members of a household, including husband, wife, children, servants, farmhands, and parents. The details recorded were generally names, including maiden names of women, dates of birth or ages, places of birth, occupations, relationships, marriage data, dates of death, former places of residency, arrival dates in the parish and from where, removal dates and to where, legitimacy of children, marital status, and rating of religious knowledge. After World War II, in 1946, certain revisions were introduced into the system of keeping parish records: a record of each individual is completed in the parish, and when he or she moves, it is sent to the parish where he or she now lives. If he or she dies or emigrates, the record is deposited in the Central Bureau of Statistics in Stockholm. When the parish records do not contain the information you need to locate, pursue your research at the regional district and city archives. The national archive, Riksarkivet, located in Stockholm, may be useful, although it is primarily a depository for papers of the central government and its various agencies, the parliament, courts, and certain notable families. Census materials and real estate books are also included in the collections of the Riksarkivet.

Two other kinds of materials, emigration and probate records, are useful for the family historian. The major ports of departure from Sweden for emigrés were Göteborg, Malmö, and Stockholm. Many Swedish persons also crossed Norway's borders and sailed from Oslo and Trondheim. During the period of first Denmark's, then Sweden's, control of Norway (1624-1905) towns and cities were renamed. Oslo, for example, was known as Christiania from 1624 to 1925. You will want to check a gazetteer for the appropriate names of Norwegian ports during the period your ancestor sailed for America, as records will be filed under the name in use at the time. The immigration lists of each city have been indexed and are available on microfilm at the Family History Library in Salt Lake City. Probate records generally began to be kept about 1725, although some date as early as 1660. The material is useful for several reasons: it provides the name of the deceased, date of death, last residence of the deceased, names of heirs, their ages, their residences, their relationship to the deceased, the inventory of the property, date it was performed and by whom, and the distribution of the decedent's real and personal property.

Norway

In Norway church records should be consulted as noted. They hold the usual information about baptisms, marriages, and deaths, as well as confirmation dates and the movements of people in and out of the parish. For births and christenings the records note the name of the child, dates, parents, their occupations, witnesses at the christening, and places of residences. After 1830 the fathers' ages, place of birth, and place of residence was also required. The death and/or burial records provide the name of the deceased, age, cause of death, date of death, place of death, occupation, and, after the late nineteenth century, place of birth. After 1814 parish registers also noted names of persons who had arrived in the parish, their names, ages, occupations, and former residences. For those persons who left the parish, their new place of residence and place of destination were chronicled. The parishes were ordered to keep registers beginning in 1687, although they were not kept on a regular basis until about 1700. The registers are now under the supervision of the Central Bureau of Statistics in Oslo.

The head-tax list of 1664-66 lists all men and boys over the age of twelve living in the rural districts, the farm names, names and ages of owners, including widows, and names and ages of persons living in cottages on the farms. The 1701 military census lists only males in the rural districts who were over one year old. It includes the farm names, the names and ages of the owners, names of sons and servants, and the residences of all unmarried males living away from home. The 1801 census records name, position in the household, relationship, age, marital status, and occupation. The records are arranged by county, clerical district, parish, and farm; or by county, city section, and street number under county heading. The census records at the national archives (Riksarkivet) are particularly useful after 1865 because the place of birth of the individual was first recorded by the census-taker for the census of that year. Norway has undertaken a census of its population nearly every tenth year since 1801 and without interruption since 1890.

Emigration records were kept for several Norwegian cities: Alesund in More og Romsdal, Bergen, Oslo, Kristiansand in Vest-Aeder, Kristiansand in More og Romsdal, and Trondheim. These materials list the names of the emigrant, the emigration number, age, occupation, year and place of birth, residence, destination, sometimes marital status, ship sailed on, date it sailed, and which state in the United States was the emigrant's destination.

Regional state archives are located in seven cities of Norway and preserve wills that have been proved in the courts of the district, as well as the records of the probate court. The oldest registers of the probate court date from 1660. These records usually give the name of the deceased, heirs, guardians, relationships, places of residence, inventory of property, land tenure rights, and the division of property.

For further assistance we suggest you contact the Norwegian-American Historical Association, St. Olaf College, Northfield, MN 55057, which has published a number of books about Norwegian ancestry. If you get a list of publications from the association you will be able to borrow them through your local library. The Supreme Lodge of the Sons of Norway, 1312 West Lake Street, Minneapolis, MN 55408, also has produced books of genealogical interest.

Denmark

Like Sweden and Norway, parish registers are the most important tool for research in Denmark. The clergy were required by law in 1645 to keep records of the vital statistics of the parish, although frequently you will find that parish registers were kept as early as 1600. The records usually note the following information: given name of child, sex, date of birth and christening, legitimacy, names of parents, mother's age, names of witnesses at the christening, their places of residences, occupations, and relationships. For marriages the names are given, ages, dates of birth, residences, occupations, personal or marital status, witnesses, date of marriage. Death and burial entries provide the name of the deceased, dates of death and burial, residence at the time of death, occupation, marital status, age, and cause of death. After 1814 the state ordered that two copies of parish registers should be kept, one by the clergyman of the parish and the second by the local teacher. Parish registers before 1891 are collected in four regional register offices: Copenhagen, Aabenraa, Viborg, and Odense. Since 1831 the procedure has been to deposit one copy of the registers for the past thirty years in the archives after it is completed.

The Danish state archives department in Copenhagen—the Riksarkivet—is the key national archives. Founded in 1889, it maintains the records of the various departments and agencies of the government, including census, passport, and emigration records.

Danish census returns began in 1787 and provide the full

names of each person in the household, including servants and persons who were staying with the family. Maiden surnames of all women are given, as are relationship, age, title or profession, marital status, and residence by parish, street name, and number. Children, including illegitimate children and stepchildren, are listed by birth order. The 1845 census was the first enumeration to include the place of birth.

In your search for your Danish ancestors you will want to check the passport records for the period 1780-1920, which note the name of the person receiving the passport, occupation, former place of residence, destination, and the date of issue. The emigration records cover the period from 1868 to 1940, and include the name of the emigrant, occupation, place of residence, age, destination, and date of embarkation.

Iceland

From 1380 to 1944, Iceland was a possession of Denmark. Now an independent nation, its records are marked by the style and procedures practiced in Denmark. The records of births, confirmations, marriages, and deaths were kept by the clergy by royal decree since 1746. The format is the same as that followed by parishes in Denmark. The clergy are required to file an annual report with the Statistical Bureau of Iceland, and all parish records are deposited with the national archives, Thjodskjalasfn Islands, Hver Fisgate 17, in Reykjavik. Copies of wills are also deposited in the archives. In 1703 a census of Iceland was undertaken to record the name, occupation, residence, relationships, marital status, and age of every person in Iceland. The 1816 census return was the first to note place of birth. Besides the census records—Iceland undertook a census nearly every ten years between 1703 and 1960—you should also check church records for information. A useful book for families of Icelandic descent in the United States and Canada is Olafur S.

Thorgeisson's *Almanach Fyrir*. Published in 1895, it notes genealogical and historical information for many of the nineteenth-century Icelandic settlers. Eric Jonasson's *Tracing Your Icelandic Family Tree* (1975) is also helpful.

Finland

Finland has historical ties to both eastern Europe and Sweden. Finland was conquered by Sweden in 1157, and the Swedish language, religion, and civilization have markedly influenced cultural development in Finland. Until 1809 Finland was under Swedish control; then control passed to Russia. After World War I and a brief military regency, Finland received its independence.

Church registers are important tools for undertaking Finnish genealogical research. Following the pattern of record-keeping throughout Scandinavia, the parish registers record in chronological order the births, marriages, deaths, and moves in and out of the parish. Dating from about 1650, the national archives —Valtionarkisto/Riksarkivet PL274, SF-00171, Helsinki, 17— has in its collections copies of all pre-1850 church registers.

Civil records date back only to 1918 and they are not compulsory. Citizens can choose either civil or church registrations for births, marriages, and deaths, but not both procedures.

Finnish names are unlike other Scandinavian names. Patronymics were only used among the Swedish settlers. The father's given name is frequently used as the child's middle name and family names are often taken from locations, descriptions, and occupations. An interesting guide for Finnish genealogical research is Alf Brenner's book *Slaktforskning: Praktisk Handbok for Finland*.

The Netherlands

Since the settlement of New Netherland (New York) in 1624,

there has been a close relationship between the Dutch and Americans. As elsewhere on the European continent, the churches in the Netherlands, Protestant and Catholic, maintained registers, and these have been placed in the various national archives offices located in each of the provincial capitals. The Roman Catholic church generally predominated in the south of the country while the Dutch Reformed church's major strength was in the north. Church registers began before 1600 and are the major sources for Dutch research on the time before civil registration began in 1795 for the southern provinces, and 1811 for the northern regions. After the conquest of the Netherlands by Napoleon in 1811, civil registration was introduced. These records are preserved in several locations: the central archives of the state, Algemeen Rijksarchief, Bleijenburg 7, The Hague, and at eleven excellent and helpful provincial archives. With the aid of excellent register indexes you are able to put your hand on much genealogical information, at least back to 1811, in a speedy manner. Another key aid is the Bevolking register (population register), which notes the ancestry in all directions of the entire population of Holland as far back as 1811. Write to the central archives for information and you will be directed, when necessary, to the appropriate provincial or town archive. Beginning in 1850 each town kept a register noting details about the persons who lived in the community. It is a very useful resource for information on family members, since the period of heavy Dutch immigration occurred after that date.

In the 1830s the Dutch began to maintain emigration lists on a provincial basis, and in 1847, nationally. These lists note the emigrant's name, age, marital status, previous residence, and destination. A useful aid for your Dutch family research is Robert P. Swierenga's *Dutch Immigrants in the United States: Ship Passenger Manifests, 1820-1880* (1983).

A word of caution: one of the difficulties in Dutch genealogy is that before 1811 there were few real surnames. Patronymics were in use, but not surnames. Napoleon's decree that all should take names and register them has produced to the present nearly 87,000 family names in Holland. By careful analysis of the names you can determine the region of origin, which may give you a clue to the area of your family's residence.

Belgium

During the period between 1500 and 1830 Belgium was at one time or another under Spanish, Austrian, French, and Dutch rule, and, accordingly, Belgian records were removed to other lands. Before 1795 the local Catholic parish priests maintained registers of baptisms, marriages, and burials, and these are now deposited either in the state archives or in town or commune halls and are indexed parish by parish to easily assist your work. More recent parish registers remain in the hands of the local priests. The French introduced civil registration in 1795, and these records are kept at the town and commune halls throughout the country. The Archives Générales du Royaume, rue de Ruysbroeck 2-6 1000, Brussels, has many materials of genealogical interest. Included in its collections are some parish registers, many family archives, and a variety of state judicial and administrative papers of assistance in family research.

France

One of the benefits of the French Revolution for genealogists was the introduction in France in 1789 of civil registration for births, marriages, deaths, and divorces. The records have been preserved in the communes, and you may write to the office of the mayor of the appropriate town for copies of your ancestor's birth and marriage records.

The Catholic church maintained parish registers for baptisms, marriages, and burials before the French Revolution. The local parish priest was required to keep such a record of his parishioners since the sixteenth century. Parish registers from before 1789 have been deposited in the archives of each municipality. Since 1789 the parish priests have continued their practice of maintaining records, but they now keep one record in the parish and forward another to the headquarters of the bishop of the diocese. In searching for your ancestors in France, as in any other country, it is important to know the province (*département*) of origin to aid the archivist in informing you of your relative's commune of origin. The Archives Nationale de France, 60 rue des Francs-Bourgeois, 75141 Paris Cedex 03, should be consulted for such information as immigration records (including ships' passenger lists), military records, and some property and probate records.

There are many publications available to assist you in your French genealogical research. The following are of particular interest: *Bibliographie généalogique heraldique et nobiliaire de la France,* by Gaston Saffroy (3 vols., 1970, 1974), and Pierre Durye's *Genealogy: An Introduction to Continental Concepts,* translated into English by Wilson O. Clough.

Switzerland

Before 1848 civil registration in Switzerland was in the hands of each of the political units, the twenty cantons and six half-cantons. The Catholic and Protestant churches actually carried out the responsibility until 1876, when the duty was taken over by the civil authorities. Birth, marriage, and death records for the period between 1834 and 1875 were deposited in the registry office of each canton.

Censuses of families living in particular parish areas have been listed in *Haushaltungsregisters,* which provide such data as the names, dates, and places of birth of family members: parents, grandparents, brothers, and sisters. This source of information should be supplemented by checking for related family certificates (*Familienschein*) at the Zivilstandesamt— the office of citizenship. There, family details are recorded, and have been maintained with varying completeness for two to three hundred years. An important research tool in helping to determine the place of origin of a family is the *Familiennamembuch der Schweiz, Repertoire des names de famille suisses, Repertorio dei nomi de famiglia svizzeri* (6 vols., 1968-71). The volumes, in German, French, and Italian, list alphabetically all surnames of families that maintained rights of citizenship in any Swiss community as of December 31, 1962. Families that have become extinct are not included. The book allows the researcher to limit to the specific communities listed the search for family members, rather than having to investigate in all of the communities in a canton.

A valuable handbook to assist your efforts searching for ancestors in Switzerland is Paul Anton Nielson's *Swiss Genealogical Research: An Introductory Guide* (1979).

Spain

The genealogical resources in Spain are indeed rich. The Catholic parish registers are acknowledged to be the oldest in Europe. Beginning in 1570 the parish priests were charged to note the baptisms, marriages, and burials in their parishes. In fact, more than 1,600 of the 19,000 Spanish parishes have registers that record information before 1570. A useful handbook about the Spanish Catholic church, *The Guidebook of the Spanish Church* (14 vols.), published by the General Office of Information and Statistics of the Church, lists all the parishes in Spain, noting their dioceses and the date of the earliest register for baptisms, marriages, and burials. You may inquire at the public library or a Spanish consul's office to learn if they have a copy of the book.

In 1870 civil registrations began in Spain under the supervision of the justices of municipalities, of districts, and of the peace. The municipalities maintain the records today, and you will want to make your inquiries to the town office in the particular town in which your ancestor resided.

For assistance on Spanish family research, there is a very useful institution in Madrid which you should consult either by correspondence or during a visit to Spain. It is the Instituto Internacional de Genealogiá y Heraldica, y Federación de Corporaciones Afines (the International Institute of Genealogy and Heraldry and Federation of Similar Corporations). You should address your correspondence to Apartado Postal 12, 079, Madrid. For Spanish American families, that is, Latin American families, you should consult the *Enciclopedia Heraldica y Genealogica: Hispano-Americana* by Alberto and Arturo Garcia Caraffa. It is a significant compilation of the histories of many families in Spain and Latin America.

Portugal

Like Spain, Portugal has much material that is helpful in the preparation of a family history. Parish registers in many instances date back to at least 1570. During the past century, the registers were to be kept in the civil registry office, or in the central archives in Lisbon, or in the district archives. However, not all the parish registers have been so neatly deposited, and the best course to follow would be to send an inquiry to the central archives. The address is Arquivo dos Registos Paroquiais, Rua dos Prazeres 41-r/c, Lisbon, 2. Civil registration began in 1878 and the registers are under the supervision of local officials. Since there was a form of civil registration in Portugal between 1832 and 1878, you should send inquiries to the Inspector Superior of Libraries and Archives; there is one in every county for information regarding records for this forty-five-year period. For details regarding birth, filial descent, marriage, prenuptial contracts, deaths, emancipation, and care or guardianship of minors, write to the Direccâo-General do Registo e Notariodo do Ministerio da Justiçia, Lisbon. Incidentally, records are available both for Portuguese citizens and for foreigners residing in Portuguese territory.

The Arquivo Nacional da Torre do Tombo (national archives) has in its collections materials of genealogical interest. You will find not only early Portuguese parish registers but also wills. We hasten to add that many old registers were lost in the Lisbon earthquake of 1755, but some survived and others have been deposited since that disaster.

Italy

More than 4,775,000 Italians migrated to the United States between 1820 and 1920. Italian-Americans who seek to locate information about their families in Italy will find that genealogical research is, at best, difficult. Until 1870 when it was united under King Victor Emmanuel II, Italy was composed of many separate states. Consequently, for our purposes, the keeping of records was fragmented. The first national census was undertaken in 1861 and has been repeated at ten-year intervals. Since 1851 there has been civil registration of births, marriages, and deaths, but the records are best kept for the period since 1870. For information on a civil registration, write to the vital statistics office of the particular town where your ancestor's birth, marriage, or death took place. For census information you should write to the Istituto Centrale di Statistica, Via Cesare Balbo 16 00100, Rome.

Before 1870 and civil registration, church registers are our best source. Many of the parish record books remain to this day in the hands of local parish priests. Some registers have been transferred to the custody of the local bishop and the diocesan archives.

Incidentally, do not overlook the collections at the town libraries or offices of the state archives located in many towns throughout the nation, since both institutions may have information relating to the history of local families.

Germany

More than 6,250,000 Germans have migrated to America since the mid-eighteenth century. However, the peak period for immigration was the eighty-year period between 1820 and 1900, when more than five million Germans made their way to the United States to establish new homes. The difficult path to follow to do research in Germany has been made considerably easier with the publication of Clifford Neal Smith and Anna Piszczan-Czaja Smith's *Encyclopedia of German-American Research* (1976) and *American Genealogical Resources in German Archives* (1977). Begin by reading the final section in the *Encyclopedia of German-American Research* entitled "German-American Genealogy." These two books should be consulted before pursuing serious research in Germany either in person or by correspondence.

Divided for more than four centuries by religion, Catholic and Protestant, and until 1871 by numerous political borders, today Germany is reunited, after its forty-five-year division following the close of World War II into two geographical and political areas: the Federal Republic of Germany (with its capital in Bonn) and the Democratic Republic of Germany (with its capital in East Berlin). A researcher should be acquainted with the contours of the country's history.

It is best to know if your ancestor was a Protestant or a Catholic. Parish records begin to be numerous about 1550 and remain in the hands of either the local parish or the bishop of the diocese. The baptismal or christening registers usually note the dates, names of the parents, children, and godparents, who frequently are close relatives. By 1750 the marriage registers record the full names of the bride and groom, the occupation of the groom, his place of residence if different from the parish where the ceremony is taking place, the names of the parents, and often the names of the bride's parents. Death records generally list the name of the decedent, age, occupation, and cause of death.

Family historians have been active for many years compiling and publishing genealogies, lineage books, and periodicals: consult the useful *German Lineage Book: Genealogical Handbook of Bourgeois Families* (vol. 192 appeared in 1986), and for periodicals devoted to German and German-American genealogy see *Familiengeschichtliche Bibliographie*, edited by Johannes Hohfeld, Friedrich Wecken, et al., which covers the years between 1897 and 1977.

A major index to German periodicals is edited by Oswald Spohr—*Familiengeschichtliche Quellen*, which covers over thirty million surnames (not all different: Hoff may appear 1,500 times). Finally, do look at *Der Schlüssel: Gesamtsinhaltsverzeichnisse mit Ortsquellennachweis für genealogische, heraldische, und historiche Zeitschriftenreichen* (The key: Comprehensive index including place names to genealogical, heraldic, and historical periodicals; 1950-65).

Civil registration was begun on January 1, 1876, and each community in Germany had to have its own registry office (Standesamt). Births, marriages, and deaths are recorded at these offices. Each town has its own archives, as does every German province, and you will want to search both repositories to find information useful to you in your quest for genealogical records.

A few researchers are fortunate enough to have the name of their emigrant ancestor's village, province, and state of origin. For most persons the search is not so easy. If you do have a place name, consult a gazetteer and appropriate parish register directories. You need to identify which state, province, and county the town in question is a part of or belonged to at the time your ancestor lived in it. Keep in mind, too, that you want to learn if the village had its own Catholic or Protestant parish. You can then search the parish registers.

Emigration records are the most productive resources for searching for ancestors from Germany and the states of Central Europe. The Hamburg passenger lists are the most important. Bremen, whose lists were almost completely destroyed, and Hamburg were the two principal ports of embarkation for emigrants from this region in the nineteenth century.

The Hamburg passenger lists contain the names of nearly all the persons who sailed from the port between 1850 and 1934. The records provide such information as the name of the ship's captain, name of the ship, the flag under which it sailed, and the port of destination. Also listed for individual passengers are the name, sex, age, last place of residence, occupation, number of accompanying family members, and destination. The Wuerttemberg Emigration Registers are helpful, too, and indexes have begun to appear, compiled by Trudy Schenk and Ruth Froelke as the *Wuerttemberg Emigration Index* (1986), which aid the researcher.

Austria

Before 1918 Austria, Czechoslovakia, and Hungary formed the core of the once vast Austro-Hungarian Empire. Millions of emigrants left the empire for the United States. Your first task is to determine where your ancestors came from. There are the usual variety of resources to assist you: church records, census records, passenger lists, naturalization papers, and obituaries. As for Germany, the Hamburg passenger lists should be checked for emigrants from the Austro-Hungarian Empire. If your ancestor came from Vienna the passport register for that city (covering 1792-1918) is useful. Police authorities in Austria require residents to report when arriving in and leaving Vienna. These reports contain such information as names of adults and children, places and dates of birth, last place of residence, current address, and intended place of residence. If your ancestor resided in Vienna for a time before emigrating to America these records would be of assistance in identifying the village of origin.

Military records may be helpful in your work. For the period between 1740 and 1820 the records provide the name of the soldier or officer, his place of birth, age, religion, occupation or profession, and marital status. A word of caution: you need to know the name of his regiment to find the records of an enlisted man. An index exists to aid the search for officers. The Austrian war records, 1820-1918, give enlistment orders, the birthdate of the soldier, and the names of his parents.

Until 1938 the parishes in Austria registered births, marriages, and deaths. Record-keeping dates from about 1550, although occasionally you will find earlier baptismal registers. To locate the numerous parishes in the country, consult the *Austrian Official Calendar,* a printed book that is available in key libraries and at the Austrian consulates. For Protestant church records (some do exist) send a letter of inquiry to the High Church Council, Vienna I, Schellinggasse 12. It is the administrative agency for several Protestant denominations.

For civil registrations since 1938, write to the appropriate town registry office for your information.

Hungary

Most of the records are arranged by locality; accordingly, you must identify the precise location of your ancestor's origin. As for Germany and Austria, the Hamburg passenger lists are a major resource for determining the last residence of emigrants from Hungary.

Roman Catholic and Reformed parish registers, which in some instances were kept as early as the seventeenth century, are generally most helpful for the period from 1700 to 1895.

The civil registration of vital statistics began in 1895. Certificates of births, marriages, and deaths can be obtained from the Republic of Hungary Embassy, 3910 Shoemaker Street NW, Washington, DC 20008.

The census returns should be consulted. The 1857 census recorded complete households, each member and their relationship to the head of house, birth dates, religion, and sometimes place of origin. The 1869 census also includes places of birth for each member of the household. A helpful reference work to aid your work is Daniel Schlyter's *Hungarian Census Returns* (1981).

As Hungary was an important element of the Austro-Hungarian Empire until 1918, the war records in Vienna should also be consulted for officers and enlisted men.

Poland

During the period between 1572 and 1795, Poland fell prey to the political designs of her powerful neighbors—Russia, Prussia, and Austria. In fact, after 1795 and until 1918 Poland disappeared from the map of Europe. After World War I and the establishment of the Treaty of Versailles, Poland became an independent state. For our purposes it is important to acknowledge that Polish record-keeping varied according to the interests of the occupying nation. In brief, before 1918 the clergy maintained the vital records in the area ruled by Russia; in the Austrian-dominated territory, the parish clergy were treated as state officials; in the Prussian section, the records were kept by public officials. To find our way through the maze of political interests to the necessary records, it is essential to know the voivodship (*wojewodzkie*), meaning, roughly, county, in which your ancestor resided. Looking at a map of Poland, we can recognize that the Prussian-governed area included the western and northern voivodships and the northern section of the Katowice voivodship; the Russian territory covered the eastern voivodships and the eastern area of Bialystok voivodship; and the Austrians dominated the central and Silesian voivodships. Parish records may exist for a period before 1795, but little is known about that material.

It was not until after World War II, in 1946, that civil registration was introduced for the entire nation. However, should your ancestors have lived in Warsaw, where civil records were introduced about 1870, you may request a copy of the records of births or marriages from either the vital statistics office for Central Warsaw (Urzad Stanu Cyivilnego, Warszawa-Strodmiescie) or from the vital statistics office for Praga (Urzad Stanu Cyivilnego, Warszawa-Praga), depending on the area in which the birth or marriage occurred. If your ancestor was born or married in a city outside of Warsaw, you should request a copy of the appropriate record from the local vital statistics office. For other communities in Poland a copy of the records can be obtained from the communal vital statistics office (Urzad Stanu Cyivilnego, Gminnej Rady Narodowej) established for the town or village.

Polish emigration increased steadily during the nineteenth century when, during the last decades, many left for the United States. There seems to have been no systematic method of recording emigration; no passport records exist. As the largest number of emigrants left through the German port of Hamburg, the departure lists for this port, which are available, should be consulted. The records detail the years between 1850 and 1936, and include the emigrant's last residence or place of birth.

A valuable resource for Polish research is the *Polish Genealogical Society Newsletter*, which has appeared for about ten years. See the annual list of genealogical publications in the *Genealogical Helper* for the current address of the editorial and subscription office.

Albania, Bulgaria, Greece, and Romania

Albania

Turkish domination of the Balkan peninsula between 1460 and 1912 resulted in an unevenness in the public records of use for genealogical information. Before Albania's independence from the Turks was declared in 1912, the vital records were maintained by the clergy of the parishes of the Roman Catholic and Orthodox churches. The Muslims are a sizable minority of the Albanian population, but their records were not as carefully maintained as those of the Christian churches. This procedure was followed until 1929, when civil registration was set up in each municipality. Unfortunately, many church records have been destroyed by the Communists, making it exceedingly difficult to search for one's ancestors.

Bulgaria

Bulgaria reached partial independence in 1878 at the close of the Russo-Turkish Wars, and full independence in 1908 under the rule of Prince Ferdinand of Saxe-Coburg-Gotha. In 1860 the Bulgarian Orthodox church became independent of the Greek church, and parish registers were introduced. Certificates of baptisms and marriages can be obtained from the church where the ceremony occurred. The maintenance of civil vital records did not begin until 1893, and these records, of births and marriages, are filed in the office of the appropriate district people's council where the event took place.

Greece

Parish registers of the Greek Orthodox church provide the genealogical researcher in Greece with some helpful information. Only since 1912 has it been required by law for registers to be maintained in all of the parishes: they record baptisms, marriages, and deaths. Earlier church records, should there be any, will probably be incomplete at best. Civil registration began in 1925, and births are recorded in special registration offices in each city and town. Marriage certificates are issued by the metropolitan (a church official) in the area in which the wedding took place. For assistance regarding civil registrations of your family members, write to the Civil Registration Division, Ministry of the Interior, 57 Panepistimiou Street, Athens; and for inquiries relating to church records, write to the Greek Orthodox Archdiocese, 21 Aghias Filotheis Street, Athens.

Romania

In 1831 civil registration was established in Romania and the registers were kept by the clergy of the parishes of the Orthodox church. Until 1865 the clergy recorded the births, marriages, and deaths in their neighborhoods; then the duty was passed on to offices in the city or town government. However, the clergy were required to continue to maintain registers in their churches of baptisms, marriages, and burials. Before it became compulsory to keep these registers, the churches had maintained their own records of births, marriages, and deaths. In Transylvania, civil registration was introduced in 1895. Before that date civil records were listed in the parish registers. You may request copies of civil records from the office of vital statistics (Oficiul Staru Civile) of the people's council (Sfatul Popular) of the particular community in which your ancestor was born, married, or died.

Yugoslavia

As elsewhere on the European continent, parish registers were kept in Catholic and Protestant churches. Beginning in 1895 civil registration was established in the territory of Voivodina, and since 1946 it has been the law throughout Yugoslavia. The State Secretariat for Internal Affairs compiles the information provided by persons concerning births, marriages, deaths, adoptions, and so on. Birth certificates are issued by the registrar of the people's committee in the appropriate village, town, or city.

Czechoslovakia

Composed of the former countries of Bohemia, Moravia, Slovakia, Ruthenia, and Silesia, the Czechoslovakia we know today was formed by the Treaty of Versailles following World War I. Again, as for every other European nation, parish registers, both Catholic and Protestant, are important resources in Czechoslovakia. It was not until after World War I, in 1918, that civil registration was introduced in a limited way, "limited" because it was not required of church members. The state in 1950 took over the duty of recording vital statistics, and copies of records of births and marriages may be obtained from the office of the Local National Committee in the community in which the event occurred. Incidentally, when the state took over the parish registers in 1950, they were deposited in the various district archives. Should you seek information from a parish register, make a request to central state archives (Státní Ustřední Archiv, Karmelitská 2 Prague I). The embassy of the Czech and Slovak Federative Republic, 3900 Linnaean Avenue NW, Washington, D.C., undertakes to issue documents regarding the birth, marriage, or death of a Czech ancestor. Write to the embassy inquiring about this service and the fees charged, and any other genealogical research with which they may be able to assist you.

An exceedingly helpful tool for genealogical research in Czechoslovakia is Olga K. Mitler's book *Genealogical Research for Czech and Slovak Americans* (1978). The author identifies a variety of sources for research in Czechoslovakia, such as land records, census materials, and military records, as well as directing the reader to the location of the many county and state archives.

Russia

The age of *glasnost* and *perestroika* in Russia and the several independent states has also witnessed the birth of interest in family history by persons at home and around the globe. An eloquent testimony to this fact was the epic gathering of the Tolstoys in the spring of 1991. Scattered across the globe by the 1917 Bolshevik Revolution and kept apart by the East-West divide, the direct descendants of Lev Nikolaevich Tolstoy returned home for an extraordinary family reunion. Three generations of Tolstoys gathered at the family estate, Yasnaya Polyana, 150 miles south of Moscow, where Russia's greatest writer was born and spent much of his adult life.

Granddaughter Vera, the doyenne of the family at age 87, crossed the ocean from Florida to reminisce about what it was like to bounce on Tolstoy's knee. Grandson Serge, a prosperous Parisian doctor, arrived with copies of his genealogical book *Tolstoy and the Tolstoys*. Great-grandson Pyotr, who speaks scarcely a word of Russian, left his farm in Sweden. Great-grandson Luigi flew in from Italy and a busload of Russian Tolstoys drove down from Moscow.

The story of what happened to the Tolstoy family after the old man's death in 1910 is itself an epic on the scale of *War and Peace* and *Anna Karenina*. The Tolstoys have been directly affected by the great social and political upheavals of the twentieth century: war, revolution, and the ideological contest between capitalism and communism. At the same time, they have experienced their own private joys and tragedies, births and deaths, marriages and divorces. A family tree prepared by the former curator of Yasnaya Polyana records 187 direct descendants of Lev Nikolaevich, dispersed across four continents.

Since the ninth century Russia has played a key military and political role in eastern Europe and in the Balkan countries. Millions of persons have come under Russian jurisdiction in their daily lives, and that influence has been stamped both within and outside Russia's boundaries.

Peter the Great, czar of Russia between 1689 and 1725, introduced many "westernizing" features during his reign. One of the innovations was the keeping of civil records by the ministers of religion. Begun in 1722, the system required that the established Orthodox clergy keep records relating to the baptisms, marriages, and burials within their parishes. Outside the Orthodox church, clergymen of other denominations, such as Roman Catholic and Lutheran as well as Muslim and Jewish, were also required to keep such records for their congregations. Both originals and copies of parish registers are found in state and regional archives.

Civil registration of births, marriages, and deaths was introduced by the new Soviet government in 1918. It was at this time, during the formative months of the Russian Revolution and the creation of a new national government, that the Orthodox church was disestablished. Consequently, civil records were kept at town and city offices under the supervision of the Ministry of Internal Affairs of the national government. The birth records note the first name and family name of the child, and the names, ages, address, and occupations of the parents. Registers also exist for marriages, divorces, changes of names, and deaths. From 1874 to 1918 universal military service was established. It resulted in the establishment of draftee lists. All males twenty-one years of age had to present themselves at the local military office in

October of each year. A third of these were enlisted into active duty. The term of service was six years active duty and nine years reserve duty. The records provide the draftee's name, date and place of birth, and father's name. It is a useful resource for all males during a period in which there was no census. The records are located in state and regional archives.

For parts of Galicia and Bukovina, former provinces of Austria, which now constitute the western section of the Ukraine, the Austrian army kept personnel files on all soldiers. See the discussion of Austrian military records in the section on Austria.

Obtaining copies of Russian public records is at best difficult. American citizens seeking such data should write to the Consular Section, American Embassy–Moscow, c/o Dept. of State, Washington, DC 20521 and request the information sheet and order form used to submit requests for copies of public records in Russia. The completed form is returned to the American embassy with a small charge for each requested document. The fee is not refunded even if your request is not fulfilled. Generally, it takes from six months to one year before the American embassy receives a response to a request to Russian officials for a copy of a public document. Frequently the record is reported to be unavailable because of the damage and destruction of public records in World War II.

China

After the American Civil War many Chinese laborers were brought to California and dispatched to remote posts in various western states to assist in the building of railroad lines. However, anti-Chinese sentiment on the Pacific coast led to violence and the first Chinese Exclusion Act, which Congress passed in 1882. The act prohibited the entry into the

United States of Chinese workers for a period of ten years; it was extended for a similar period in 1892, and in 1902 was indefinitely extended. Consequently, the Chinese population of the country declined from 107,000 in 1890 to 75,000 in 1930, which virtually ended anti-Chinese outbursts. The laws were repealed in 1943, and Chinese immigrants were admitted into the United States under the Quota Law of 1921.

Today the cultural contributions of the Chinese community are felt not only in California and Hawaii but also in cities such as New York and Boston. The population of Chinese-Americans now stands at approximately 1,600,000. When researching your Chinese ancestry, you should, of course, first follow the fundamental steps necessary for all persons who research their family history. Talk with older relatives about the family's past, and consult the vital records and census records whenever possible to establish supporting evidence.

Because ancestor worship was an important aspect of Chinese cultural and religious life through the centuries, the preservation of a family's lineage was common. Genealogical records in China have been maintained by families and clans for hundreds of years. Most records include lineage and branches of the family, essentially pedigree charts. Other resources are the ancestral halls for worshipping ancestors, and cemeteries. Other sources for information are the *fang-chih*, or local histories of China, which contain helpful family data. In addition to being geographical, religious, and educational records, the *fang-chih* list prominent leaders from a variety of occupational groups and biographies of eminent officials and families. Before 1949 the census section of the Civil Affairs Department of each precinct had charge of registering all births, marriages, and deaths within its jurisdiction. The records were held by the precinct, and when a family moved to another precinct, it was necessary to inform the census section so that its records could be passed to the next precinct.

Japan

The early story of the Japanese in America is similar to that of the Chinese. Japanese laborers were not allowed to go abroad to work until 1886, and after five years only one thousand Japanese were in the United States. During the period between 1906 and 1924 the Japanese were excluded primarily by the discriminatory laws of the state of California, although it was, in fact, a national policy under the 1907 "Gentlemen's Agreement" of President Theodore Roosevelt. With the passage of the Immigration Act of 1924, such exclusion was enforced by a statute that remained in effect until the McCarran-Walter Act of 1952.

Throughout Japanese history clans have established private academies and libraries to preserve genealogical records, as have Buddhist monasteries and the various governments. Family history has been an essential part of Japan's samurai, or military, tradition since the early seventeenth century.

Registration of vital statistics in Japan is regulated by the comprehensive Family Registration Law. Under the terms of the law, family registration is to be handled by the head of the local government. Information to be included in the registration is: birth, adoption, dissolution of adoptive relations, recognition (generally of a child to be legitimated), marriage, divorce, parental power and guardianship, death and disappearance, resumption of surname by surviving spouse and dissolution of matrimonial relations, disinheritance of a presumptive successor, entry into or separation from a family, acquisition of a name or surname, and transfer of registered locality of family and establishment of a family register. Write to the Civil Affairs Bureau, Minister of Justice, Tokyo, for information on these details.

The family register establishes that all matters relating to a Japanese citizen are recorded from cradle to grave. It is not only the record of the individual's status but also the collective record of all those who are related to that person. Should you have Buddhist ancestry you will want to check the death registers kept in the temples. The dead are given a posthumous Buddhist name. The temple record also serves as an obituary, providing names and other helpful information. The Buddhist mortuary tablets, prepared for ancestor veneration and the remembrance of the dead, are usually found in the family household shrine (*butsudan*) in homes where Japanese Buddhist practices remain strong, and record at least the posthumous names and dates of death of individuals. Family crests, like coats of arms in various European nations, can be important sources of genealogical information. Frequently found on tombstones, mortuary tablets, family documents, and ceremonial dress, the crests do not represent surnames but are connected with family branches in particular regions of Japan.

CHAPTER 15

Odds and Ends to Help Your Search

The Calendar

A stumbling block for many an ancestor hunter, when attempting to check the dates of forebears, is a mysterious discrepancy of either a few days or a year that throws out calculations. If this does not arise, then the double date in some old record may cause the searcher to wonder why those who made the contemporary record did not know whether the child was born in 1701 or 1702. If you have much experience with them, you will note that these double dates occur in the old records only in January, February, and March—never in any other months and never after 1752.

This system of double-dating arose as a result of a change made in the calendar in 1582. Before that date the so-called Julian calendar was used throughout the Christian world. It was established by Julius Caesar, hence its name. This system, which divided the year into 365 days, plus an extra day every fourth year, was officially adopted at the sitting of the Nicene Council in A.D. 325. As it became possible to measure more accurately the length of the solar year, it was found that the Julian system of measuring exceeded the solar year by eleven minutes, or twenty-four hours every 131 years, and three days every 400 years. This excess amounted to about ten days between A.D. 325 and A.D. 1582. Thus the date of the vernal equinox had been thrown back, by that time, from March 21 to March 11, and the calculations for Easter were thrown out. In 1582 Pope Gregory XIII, then head of the Roman Catholic church, ordered that ten days be dropped out of the calendar, thus restoring the equinox to its accustomed date, March 21. To prevent the recurrence of this error, he ordered further that, in every four hundred years, leap year's extra day should be omitted three times. To accomplish this in an orderly fashion it was to be omitted on centennial years of which the first two digits could not be divided by four without a remainder. Thus it was omitted in A.D. 1700, 1800, and 1900, but will not be omitted in A.D. 2000. Moreover, the decree changed the beginning of the new year from March 25 to January 1. This system, known as the Gregorian calendar, now prevails and we are right with the sun.

Following the edict of the Pope, all Catholic countries adopted the new system of reckoning. But England, in difficulties with the Church of Rome and always reluctant to accept a new and untried idea, even though scientifically proved, refused to adopt the new calendar officially, and did not adopt it until 1752, or 170 years later, when the difference between the calendar and the sun was a little more than eleven days. So in English-speaking countries (including the English colonies) and in Russia, the Julian calendar continued to prevail as the official system of counting time. Throughout that time (that is, until 1752) the new year did not begin until March 25, and there was still a difference of eleven days between the English calendar and that used in the rest of Europe.

In spite of this difference in the official calendar, many people began to use the Gregorian system. Hence, in many of the early colonial records you will find double dates, generally written like this: "March 9, 1656/57," indicating that, although it was officially still 1656, some people considered it to be 1657. Governor Winthrop dated a letter to his wife

March 22, 1629; six days later he wrote another and dated it March 28, 1630.

Incidentally, in dates of the seventeenth century you will frequently find the month indicated by its number rather than its name. This was primarily because most of the months had pagan names and hence those names were disliked by the Puritans, and even more by the Quakers, who believe in simplicity carried to its extreme. Since, before 1752, March was considered the first month of the year, even though the twenty-fifth was the day on which the year changed, we must interpret the old records with that in mind. Thus "13th, 2nd month, 1644" becomes "13 April 1644"; or "3:12 mo: 1639" becomes "3 February 1639" (that is, 1640). Generally the day was given first and the month second, but you should always make sure by comparing the date with others in the same record, remembering that there were but twelve months and a possible thirty-one days. If you find that a date is given as "3:28:1644," you know that "3" represents the month—May; but if the record is "3:8:1644," you should try to find in the same record a date that definitely establishes the first figure as that of the month, such as "4:15:1644."

In 1752, when the British government finally decided to recognize the fact that a mistake had been made in calculating the length of the solar year, and to shift into line with the other countries of Europe in the use of the calendar, Parliament passed an act by which the Gregorian system was officially adopted. It is said that there were riots in some of the rural sections of England because the act ordered that eleven days should be dropped out of the calendar following September 2 (making the next day September 14). The people thought that the government was trying to cheat them out of eleven days of their lives!

To cite an example of what this change meant, let us consider the birth date of George Washington. He was actually born, according to the official calendar in force at the time, February 11, 1732. But, with the change in the calendar in 1752, he changed his birthday to conform with the new calendar and thus made it February 22, in order to celebrate, we suppose, the exact anniversary of his birth. Therefore, to state his birth date accurately, we should write: "Born February 11, 1731, O.S. (that is, old style), or February 22, 1732, N.S. (new style)." When attempting to correlate birth records, the genealogist should always remember this difference of eleven days and the change in the beginning of the new year. If your ancestor's gravestone states that he died "August 31, 1810, aged 81 years, 6 months, 19 days" and you figure back from that record and determine that he was born February 12, 1729, and then you find the date of his birth in the vital records of his native town as February 1, 1728, you can account for the discrepancy by this change in the calendar, for February 12, 1729, would be the "new style" of reckoning, and February 1, 1728, the "old style.'

Most people do not change into new style the dates of these old records, when both of the dates (that is, those of birth and death) occurred before the change in the calendar. Even if one date is old style and one new style, it is not necessary to make the change, for it can be designated by the initials "O.S." or "N.S." to indicate that you have noted any discrepancy that you have found. In the case of the double dates occurring between January 1 and March 25, the year is generally designated "$16^{40}/_{41}$."

Frequently this matter of the change in the calendar will explain the birth of two children apparently within too short a period. Thus, if you have collected the data on the births of the children of a family from different sources, you can reconcile them by studying the calendar. Suppose that you find, from one source, that John and Mary Jones had a son, named Henry, born March 27, 1640, and from another record a daughter, named Hannah, born February 28, 1640. This looks very strange until you remember that the February 28, 1640, was "old style" and actually, according to modern reckoning, February 28, 1641; therefore, you can figure that these two children were born eleven months apart, instead of twenty-seven days apart.

Terms of Relationship Used in Early Records

One matter very confusing to those who begin to dig for ancestors in the early records is that of the terms used to designate relationships in ancient wills, deeds, diaries, and letters. Unless you are familiar with the variant meanings these words had in the seventeenth century, you are likely to make some serious errors.

One of the most tricky terms of this sort is "cousin." Today we think of a cousin as the son or daughter of one of our uncles or aunts, or someone more remotely related but descending from a common ancestor, and we speak of "first cousins," "cousins-german," or "own cousins" to indicate an exact degree of cousinship—that is, a son or daughter of a brother or sister of either of our parents. "Second cousin" means a grandchild of our great-uncle or great-aunt, and so forth. The child of a "first cousin" or "own cousin" is our first or own cousin once removed. But in seventeenth-century wills one frequently finds the term "cousin" applied to any relative who is not a brother or sister, son or daughter. Thus a man, making his will in 1650, might call his grandchild "cousin," or he might use the term to refer to a nephew, niece, uncle, aunt, or any other close relative except blood brother, sister, son, or daughter. Thus John Hubbard is called "cousin" in the wills of both Robert Merriam and Mary Merriam of Concord in the seventeenth century. Since no records of the exact relationship have been found, all we

can assume is that John Hubbard was in some way connected with Robert Merriam or his wife Mary and may have
been a nephew.

"Son-in-law" and "daughter-in-law" were terms that
sometimes had a different meaning in seventeenth-century
records. A man was quite likely to call a stepchild (that is, a
child of his wife by a former marriage) "son-in-law" or
"daughter-in-law" in his will.

On the other hand, "son" and "daughter" were sometimes used in that period in the sense in which we use "son-
in-law" and "daughter-in-law." You have to reason out just
what was meant by the term and try to find evidence of the
exact relationship.

"Brother" is another tricky term. Sometimes it meant
blood brother, sometimes stepbrother, sometimes brother-
in-law, and frequently "brother in the church," as it is still
used in some evangelical sects. Wordy old Judge Samuel Sewall, he of the diary, frequently called a man "brother" who
had no degree of relationship with him. He appears to have
attended the funerals of innumerable "brothers" or "sisters"
who were in no way related to him or his several successive
wives. In other records, even in such serious documents as
wills, the term was used to designate even the husband of a
sister-in-law. In a letter written by Thomas Hungerford of
Connecticut in 1657 to Anne, wife of John Leigh, of Ipswich,
Massachusetts, he calls her "sister" and thanks her for her
offer to take care of his motherless daughter, Sarah. On the
basis of this letter it has been assumed that John Leigh's
wife, Anne, was Thomas Hungerford's sister. There is no
other evidence of the relationship, although John Leigh, in
his will dated in 1671, made a bequest to this Sarah Hungerford. It seems more likely that Anne Leigh was a sister of
Thomas Hungerford's first wife, whose maiden surname is
unknown. Thomas Hungerford was about to marry a second
wife in 1657, when this letter was written, so it is quite pos-

sible that he sent his young daughter (Sarah was born about 1654) to her mother's sister and keep with him his son, Thomas Jr. (born about 1648). Neither John Leigh nor his widow Anne mentioned Thomas Hungerford's son or his daughter Hannah (by his second wife) in their wills.

"Mother" and "father" are likewise terms that did not always imply the relationship with which they are associated today. They might mean "mother-in-law" or "father-in-law," or might even refer to a stepparent acquired through the remarriage of a parent.

Frequently old records will refer to "Mrs." or "Mistriss" Sarah Jones, let us say. If you find such a title before a girl's name in a colonial marriage record, it does not mean necessarily that she was a widow or had been married before. In the seventeenth and even in the eighteenth century the title "Mistriss" (often abbreviated to "Mrs." in records) was one of social distinction as a general rule. Its use did not necessarily mean that the woman to whom it was applied was, or had been, married, as it does now. Records of the 1690s exist in which the title was given to an unmarried girl of seventeen who belonged to a family of considerable standing in the community. Sometimes the recorder used the term "widow" if the bride had been married before and had lost her husband, although in some records you will find "Mrs." meaning widowhood. As you work with the records, you will learn to distinguish the meaning and use the title correctly.

In early colonial days, "Mister" (or Mr.) was a title of respect given only to those who held important civil office or were of gentle blood before coming to America. If a man did not act in accordance with the dignity of the title "Mr.," it was taken away from him, as some of the old records show. About the only title that outranked it was "deacon." For instance, in the early records of Plymouth Colony, Dr. Doane's ancestor was called "Mr. John Done," but after he was made a deacon he was always referred to as "Deacon John Done," thus indicating the attitude of the times toward titles.

"Goodman" and "goodwife" were titles applied to those who had the respect of their fellow colonists but who did not quite merit the titles "Mr." and "Mrs." A man who had the right to vote or conduct business in the community was entitled to be called "freeman." When a man was "admitted freeman" in a community, it indicated that he was not an indentured servant any longer (if he had been one) and was free to commit himself in trade and to vote.

The inexperienced genealogist will do well to study carefully all the available records of a family before he or she accepts too literally in the modern sense any of the terms expressing relationship, particularly when he finds them in old documents originally written in the seventeenth century. Inaccurately interpreted or unthinkingly accepted, they may lead you into difficulty and cause you to claim as ancestors people whose blood does not flow in your veins.

The Family Coat of Arms

The use of a coat of arms in the United States is a matter of personal taste. Unless you have a coat of arms that is registered as a trademark in the Patent Office, there is no government authority that can prevent any other individual from using it. Moreover, there is no law by which you can obtain a coat of arms. Since our government does not recognize coat armor, it has become a matter of custom to use a heraldic insignia only from personal choice. In using it, one should abide by the laws governing its use in the country in which it originated. Moreover, laws or customs regarding the right to use arms vary from country to country, so the native land of the family progenitor has a bearing on any "right" to arms.

Heraldry is of truly ancient origin. There is evidence that in ancient Greece and Rome family insignia were used. By the time of the Norman conquest of England, many individuals throughout Europe used such devices. As the use of armor developed and it became impossible to distinguish one man from another when the visor of his helmet was closed, it came to be the custom to wear a surcoat over the metal armor, on which were embroidered the "arms," or insignia, which the individual used to distinguish himself. Usually this was identical with the insignia on the banner that his men carried, and it came to be known as the "coat of arms" of his family, as it was handed on from generation to generation. Gradually laws were made governing the use of coats of arms, and by the fifteenth century a definite code had been established. In the sixteenth century, in England, the College of Arms, under whose jurisdiction the use of coat armor was placed, began a series of "visitations" of the several counties of England to determine what arms were being borne and who was entitled to them. The records of these visitations, containing as they do thousands of pedigrees, are a source of knowledge for the genealogist as well as a record of arms. Since that time, arms have been granted by the Crown on the authority of the College of Arms, and today you must either prove your right to bear a coat that has been confirmed by the College or pay a fee for a grant of arms. In various western European nations there is today a strong interest in heraldry, and many articles and books are published on a variety of aspects of the subject. The key organization promoting professional attention in this field is the International Confederation of Genealogy and Heraldry, François-Louis àWeng, 24 rue Saint Louis-en-L'Ille, F 75004, Paris, France. It is composed of the key institutions in western Europe that pursue these interests. Should you want to pursue your heraldic research further, we would suggest you do so by contacting the center for heraldic study in the particular country from which your ancestors migrated.

(1) England, Wales, and Northern Ireland. The Royal College of Arms, Queen Victoria Street, London, EC4V 4BT grants arms for these areas.

(2) Scotland. The Lord Lyon, Lyon Office, New Register House, Edinburgh, EH1 3YT controls grants of all coats of arms in Scotland. You need to make application to the Lord Lyon for a grant of your Scottish ancestor's coat of arms, or if your ancestor did not have a coat of arms, you make application to receive a grant of arms for that ancestor. After that procedure has been completed, you may request that the arms be reassigned to you.

(3) Republic of Ireland. To check for your ancestral coat of arms, write to the Chief Herald of Ireland, Dublin Castle, Dublin, 2.

(4) Austria. The official use of coats of arms has been forbidden in this country since 1919. Before that, after 1760, arms were restricted to use only by the nobility. For assistance, however, write to: Heroldischgenealogische Gesellschaft "Adler," Haarhof 4a, A 1010, Vienna.

(5) Belgium. Your inquiries should be directed to Le Conseil Héraldique, 85 rue du Prince Royal, Brussels.

(6) France. The Société Française d'Héraldique, 113 rue de Courcelles, Paris, is the center for study in France. The country enjoys a splendid heraldic heritage, particularly during the fifteenth, sixteenth, and seventeenth centuries: the French Revolution and later political developments arrested modern interest in heraldry and abolished the college of arms that had been established in 1406.

(7) Germany. For assistance with questions regarding the coat of arms of your German ancestor write to: Der Herold, Verein für Heroldik, Archivstrasse 12-14, D 1000 Berlin-Dahlem.

(8) Italy. Write to Istituto di Genealogia e Araldica, Via Antonio Cerasi 5ᵃ, Rome, for help in gathering details about your Italian ancestors who may have obtained a coat of arms.

(9) Spain. The Instituto Internaçiónal de Genealógia y Heraldica, Apartado de Correos 12,079, Madrid, is the agency in Spain to which you should send your questions about your Spanish ancestor's right to arms.

For any other country, such as the Netherlands, Sweden, or Switzerland, we suggest you contact the particular nation's embassy in Washington, D.C., for advice on how to go about obtaining heraldic information about your ancestor, and assistance in obtaining it. You will find that the staffs of the embassies are helpful in responding to your important questions.

In using a coat granted or confirmed several centuries ago, you must prove your descent from the family that originally used that coat and establish your right to the same arms. The right to bear arms descends in the male line only. Even if you assume a coat of arms without the authority of a heraldic institution in Europe, England, Scotland, or Ireland, you should use only the arms that have been borne by your paternal line. A woman did not go to war in the Middle Ages and hence did not bear arms and wear coat armor. Therefore, although it is perfectly proper for you to blazon your mother's family arms in your account of her descent, you should not assume those arms as your device. According to the English law, you can quarter your father's arms with your mother's, provided she was an heiress and had no brothers. But we do not propose to go into the matter of quartering arms here, for it is too extensive a subject; in some of the books to which we shall refer you, it is treated fully.

Looking up your surname in some armory (such as Burke's *General Armory*) and assuming that you have a right to the coat of arms described therein is not enough. You must prove your descent from the family to whom those arms were granted or confirmed by the appropriate heraldic institution. If you are willing to go to the expense of having those arms confirmed to you, or if you wish a new coat granted to you, you must apply to an agency such as the College of Arms in London, England, or the Lord Lyon's Court in Edinburgh, Scotland, and go through the same procedure that any English or Scottish person would go through in a similar case.

For example, although your name may be an unusual one, such as Hungerford, you should find proof of the connection of your immigrant ancestor with the family who bore the arms in England. In the case of the Hungerford family, we lack any evidence whatsoever of the English connection of Thomas Hungerford in Connecticut (1639), Thomas in Maryland (1641), or William in Maryland (1642). All were undoubtedly of the same blood as the English family of that name, but until their places in the English pedigrees are established, their descendants have no right (according to English law) to use the Hungerford arms as given in Burke's *General Armory*.

Because of the interest in coat armor in America, the New England Historic Genealogical Society of Boston, Massachusetts has a Committee on Heraldry. Since 1864 this committee has investigated the claims of over seven hundred American families to bear coat armor and has compiled and published a roll of authentic coats of arms. Nine parts of the roll have appeared, carefully illustrated with drawings of the arms. This is as near as we come on this side of the ocean to anything like the distinguished English College of Arms.

We should note a book or two that may be useful to you in your preliminary efforts to identify your ancestor's coat of arms. An excellent book on the use of coats of arms is Thomas Woodcock's and John Robinson's *Oxford Guide to Heraldry* (1988). Another helpful volume is *The Right to Bear Arms*, which was published anonymously in England several years ago. The standard book on heraldry is Charles Boutell's *Manual of Heraldry*—there is a revised edition by J. P. Brooke-Little (1973). Another good one is Francis J. Grant's *Manual of Heraldry* (1924). Of the older armories, the best known is Sir John

Bernard Burke's *The General Armory of England, Scotland, Ireland, and Wales* (1878), generally referred to as Burke's *Armory*. The 1884 edition was reprinted in 1969. It is useful because it attempts to list all known coats of arms ever used in the British Isles. A brief, interesting, and informative little book is that by Sir Anthony R. Wagner, K.C.V.O., D. Litt., Clarencieux King-of-Arms, the College of Arms, London, *Heraldry inEngland* (King Penguin Books, 1946). Here is one sentence from it: "An honest pedigree, however unambitious, and a new shield [that is, grant of arms] though without pretence to nobility, may warm its owner's heart, make him hold his head higher and feel himself the heir of a great tradition" (page 24).

For further assistance you will want to consult the Library of Congress's Coats of Arms Index, which is located in the Local History and Genealogy Reading Room. The index includes more than one hundred thousand illustrations of coats of arms found in various publications in the library. The *Heraldry Index of the St. Louis Public Library* is another excellent resource to appropriate depictions drawn from its collections gathered since the early days of the twentieth century. For other countries we would suggest the following: for Scotland, Sir Thomas Innes's book, *Scots Heraldry*; for France, the *Grand Armorial de France*; for Germany, *Genealogische Handbuch des Adels*; for Italy, Giustino Colaneri's useful book, *Bibliografia araldica e genealogica d'Italia*; and for Spain the reference work *Heraldic and Genealogical Encyclopedia: Spanish American* is helpful for arms of families not only in Spain but also in the various Latin American countries.

Bound Boys and Orphans

Several have asked what it means when one discovers a tradition, or the fact, that great-grandfather, let us say, was a "bound boy" or an "indentured servant," or was taken from an orphanage. The old, reliable *Century Dictionary* (10 vols., 1896), a useful tool for quick reference because it includes phrases and illustrative quotations as well as words, defines "bind" (in this sense) as "to indenture as an apprentice: often [used] with out." A son was "bound out" by his father, his widowed mother, or his guardian to give him training in some craft or trade, or perchance to relieve the parent from the expense of feeding and clothing him during his minority. Orphanages regularly bound out boys and girls in the same way, that they might be trained to support themselves. This system of indentured apprenticeship undoubtedly had its origin in the trade guilds of the Middle Ages. During the course of the centuries, various laws governing and controlling it have been enacted, but we need not go into its history here—if you are interested, read the short but excellent article in the 11th edition of the *Encyclopaedia Britannica* as an introduction, and then Abbot Emerson Smith's *Colonists in Bondage: White Servitude and Convict Labor in America, 1607-1776* (1947), noting especially the bibliographical appendix, pages 397-417. Consult too Peter Wilson Coldham's valuable *Complete Book of Emigrants in Bondage, 1614-1775* (1988).

For our purpose, it is sufficient to say that, from early colonial days, a boy might be "bound out" to a master, who, under the terms of the indenture (or legal agreement), had to provide him training in his craft or trade and give him board, lodging, and clothes, and perhaps pay him a stipulated sum at the end of his term. This was usually seven years or, in some instances, until the boy came of age. A farmer lacking sufficient help would take a boy in this way to help him with the farm work, or a girl to help his wife spin and weave and cook; a goldsmith, or printer, or papermaker would do the same to get assistants and to train them. The boy so indentured would, in seven years, learn the craft and be able to take care of himself at the end of the contract. A widow, bereaved of her husband and left with little support, might bind out one or more of the elder children in order to provide them with a trade and at the same time relieve herself of their support.

An indentured servant was generally one who, wanting to migrate to America, the land of golden opportunities, where he thought he would have a better chance of improving his condition than he would in his native country, would sell his services (the only asset he might have) to someone by indenturing himself as a servant in return for the passage money he needed to get to the New World. By this indenture he contracted to work for the man who advanced the money for a specified number of years. Some of the passengers on the famous *Mayflower* were such servants, Dr. Doane's ancestor, George Soule, among them.

Some masters were exacting, severe, even cruel and inhuman in their treatment of their apprentices and indentured servants, in fact using them like slaves; others were fair and kindly, even though they may have been strict and insistent upon full service and good workmanship; and some went further and treated their bound boy or girl as a member of the family.

Although it may be difficult, it is not always impossible to find the parentage of a bound boy, or an orphan. Indentures of apprenticeship were generally matters of public record, so the records of them may be found in county courthouses or other repositories such as the state archives—the custodianship of such records varies in different periods and in the several states. In some, for instance, there is an orphans' court in the county organization; in others the records may be kept in some division of the municipal government. See, for example, pages 55-58 in Rosalie Fellows Bailey's *Guide to Genealogical and Biographical Sources for New York City (Manhattan) 1783-1898* (1954) for her account of the records of orphans and apprentices in that city. Perhaps the best way to locate records of indenture or orphanage is to write to the county clerk and ask for information—failing that, try the secretary of state at the state capitol. Again, let us warn you, in writing to an official for the records of a specific individual, give in concise form all the data you have and especially the approximate date, if you do not have a specific date.

To descend from a bound boy, an orphan, or an indentured servant is nothing to be ashamed of or sensitive about. Poverty is not a disgrace, nor is orphanage, whatever the circumstances that brought it about. Not all children in orphanages were illegitimate or of unknown parentage, but all were wards of the state through no fault or act of their own and should be respected as human beings and treated with sympathy and understanding, if for no other reason than that they were deprived of parental affection and normal family life.

Illegitimate and Adopted Children

Speaking of illegitimate and adopted children: we have been asked how such cases should be dealt with in a genealogy or family history. This may well become a moot point when the genealogies of many twentieth-century families are compiled, considering some attitudes now prevalent. Many illegitimate children are acknowledged by their fathers, or their fathers are identified in records. In some instances they even bear the father's name. In fact, in the New England colonies, an illegitimate birth was frequently recorded under the mother's name and the child given its father's surname; in some instances the birth may be recorded under both names, paternal and maternal. We have found such cases in Rhode Island records. An illegitimate child is in no way to blame for the accident of his or her birth, though in times past many were stigmatized by a cruel society. In our time, we trust, we are less censorious and more willing to accept men and women on their merits. Certainly in the compilation of a genealogy, illegitimate or adopted children bearing the surname of the family should be given full treatment if they live to adulthood and have progeny and hence are carried forward as heads of family groups. Although adopted children usually do not have the "blood," they too bear the name and hand it down to their descendants. When the actual parentage of an adopted child is known, it should be recorded in the genealogy. That is what we have advised when we have been consulted. The fact of illegitimacy or adoption can be given in a footnote, with as much detail as the compiler decides to use. When such a person is carried forward as the head of a family group, such information need not be repeated or amplified if the compiler has any qualms about it.

During the past few years there have appeared in newspapers and magazines happy and sad accounts of adopted children seeking reunion with their biological parents and birth mothers searching for a long-relinquished child. It is usually a story of anxiousness and frustration; of restrictions established by law in the various states; of bureaucratic procedures rigidly fixed by social agencies; of the adoptee's innate question, "Who am I?" and the natural parent's right to privacy. A strong advocate of the adopted person's right to know is Jayne Askin, an adoptee herself.

She has written an important how-to book on the subject with Bob Oskam: *Search: A Handbook for Adoptees and BirthParents* (1982); here she recounts her own painful but persistent search to find and know her biological parents. Another book about traveling the same path, *Lost and Found: The Adoption Experience* (1979) by Betty Jean Lifton, focuses on the experiences of other adoptees in their search for blood relatives. It is an eloquent and thoughtful volume that speaks at once about the genealogical questions confronting an adoptee and the urgent need for compassionate revision of the present rules governing adoption. Carol Schaefer's book *The Other Mother: A Woman's Love for the Child She Gave Up for Adoption* (1991) shatters the myth that all unwed mothers go on to lead normal and untouched lives. She tells of her search for the son she didn't raise and of his love for the mother he didn't know. It is a poignant and powerful testament to the bonding power of motherhood.

If you decide to search for your birth parents are you prepared emotionally to accept whatever you find? Perhaps you will encounter a birth parent who must for their own reasons deny the relationship, or a birth father who possibly never knew of your birth. You may find a birth mother who is unable to identify which man of many is your birth father, or a family with an "undesirable" background. Are you strong enough to risk rejection, with no possible escape into fantasy or rationalization to soften the impact? Or if you relinquished a child and are now searching for it, are you able to accept that a grown child may have interests and a lifestyle much different from your own, and may carry resentment or bitterness about your abandonment?

In response to demands by adoptees searching for their birth parents a number of states have enacted, during the past ten years, statutes that grant to the birth parent or to the adult adoptee, upon application to the respective state department of vital statistics, the right to see the original birth certificate, which had previously been sealed. The applicant is also provided upon request a true copy of the original document without official certification. The excellent guide by Jayne Askin mentioned above addresses how to begin the search, the agencies you can turn to for support and assistance, your rights under the various state laws, how much it may cost, and the search and support groups that are active throughout the United States.

I should also note that between 1853 and 1929 the Children's Aid Society of New York sent more than one hundred thousand orphaned or abandoned children from New York City to homes in the cities, towns, and farms in the West. The children were participants in a social experiment called the Orphan Train Movement, a forerunner of today's foster-care system. During those seventy-six years many children roamed the streets of New York uncared for, left to feed and clothe themselves. They became bootblacks, newspaper boys, streetwalkers, and domestics. They were often illiterate and were considered a menace to society.

New York City during the period experienced a rapid influx of European immigrants. The Irish, German, Italians, Jews, and Slavs, among others, found new homes in overcrowded neighborhoods, particularly on the Lower East Side, and even newer dangers. Sanitation was nonexistent and diseases like typhoid, cholera, and influenza took thousands of lives. Often families were wiped out, and any surviving children were on their own.

For the Children's Aid Society, the notion of putting children who had done no wrong into an institution was detested. The solution of the organization was to send them to America's farm belt and match them with good homes and foster parents, who often became adoptive parents.

Today many of those sent West on the Orphan Trains are seeking their ancestors. The Orphan Train Heritage Society of America (4912 Trout Farm Road, Springdale, AR 72764) is the central clearinghouse for information about the movement. The society publishes a newsletter, maintains a growing file of records on orphaned, abandoned, and homeless children, and holds an annual reunion every autumn.

Where to Go to School

Opportunities for instruction in family history research have increased considerably in recent years. Today, across the United States and Canada public libraries, state and local historical and genealogical societies, adult education centers, and colleges and universities offer courses for those searching for their ancestors. Probably your nearby library or historical society can help you locate a course being offered in your area. Before taking such a course, it is well, however, to have gathered at least a few records of your progenitors, gained a little experience, and know what your problems are. In many of these, in addition to lectures, there is some type of laboratory work, and you are graded, in part at least, on the way you handle a problem. The instructor may assign to you a case that will involve using the kinds of records he or she has been discussing, or may have you take one of your own problems and apply to it the principles you have been taught and expect you to use the appropriate sources in your efforts to find the solution. This is good practice, for you have expert guidance in your searching.

In Washington, D.C., the National Archives in cooperation with the National Genealogical Society offers a series of monthly lectures on various subjects from September through April, which are taped and available on loan to members of the Society. Also the National Archives and the Society cosponsor the National Institute on Genealogical Research held each summer at the Archives. Drawing on the important resources available for research use in the Washington neighborhood, the course usually covers the techniques of genealogical research, research in various geographical areas and in special fields, with visits to special libraries such as the Daughters of the American Revolution Library in Memorial Continental Hall in Washington, the Library of Congress on Capitol Hill, the Maryland Hall of Records in Annapolis, and the Virginia State Archives in Richmond. For information about the program and registration forms write to the National Archives and Records Administration, Education Branch, Washington, DC 20408.

At least one large university—Brigham Young University, in Provo, Utah—offers a special course of studies in genealogy and research techniques as part of a four-year course leading to a degree. The university also offers through the Department of Independent Study a program of study leading to a certificate in genealogical studies on completion of course requirements. Write to Independent Study, 206 Harmon Building, Brigham Young University, Provo, UT 84602, for detailed information. In August of each year the university holds a genealogy and family history seminar which offers a variety of courses for students. Introductory and advanced study, and instruction on special topics of genealogical interest are presented. For additional information write to Genealogy and Family History Seminar, Brigham Young University Conference and Workshops, 136 Harmon Building, Brigham Young University Provo, UT 84602.

The National Genealogical Society has offered for a number of years for its members an excellent home study course in genealogy. For details write to the society at Glebe House, 4527 17th Street, Arlington, VA 22207. Another excellent resource for instructional opportunities is Thomas Jay Kemp's *Home Study Courses of Interest to Genealogists and Local Historians* (1986). One of the valuable results of such courses is fellowship with other hunters and the opportunity to talk over some of your problems with them. Clarifying a problem in your own mind in order to state it clearly to someone else helps you see it more objectively. And sometimes having a day or week or two in which to do nothing but pursue an elusive ancestor is fun and refreshing.

The Spacing of Generations

Questions are sometimes asked about the number of generations that are likely to occur in a given span of years, say a century. We generally figure three or four generations to a hundred years—in rare instances only two, in others five. The average span between one generation and the next is about twenty-five to thirty years, so, in the space of 350 years, you can estimate that there will be about twelve generations. At the tercentenary of the landing of the Pilgrims at

Plymouth, most of the applicants for membership in the Society of Mayflower Descendants were of the tenth generation in descent, few were of the ninth, few of the twelfth.

There are, of course, exceptions to any rule of thumb. Only a short time ago we read in the newspaper about a boy of twelve who was willing to help support his newborn child, whose mother was thirteen. Occasionally one hears of other instances of extraordinarily youthful parentage. Maurice Berkeley, who later became Lord Berkeley, was born in 1281 and married in 1289 at the age of eight to an heiress of considerable property, who was also eight. Their first child, Thomas, was born about 1291: he was thirty-five when he succeeded his father in the peerage. His son, another Maurice, also married at the age of eight another heiress, but this young couple was not permitted to live together for several years.

In the days of increasing longevity and youthful marriages, one quite frequently sees in the newspapers pictures of "five generations" — say a great-great-grandmother seated in the center of a group, holding an infant in her arms. She is usually in her eighties, if not her nineties, and the infant is a few months old. Five generations in less than a century! True, but the span between each generation is still twenty to thirty years. Say the great-great-grandmother was born in 1900; her son, the great-grandfather, in 1925; his daughter, the grandmother, in 1947; her daughter, the mother, in 1968; and the infant in 1990.

At the other extreme, it is not unusual for a man to be forty, fifty, or even sixty before he marries or his first child is born; and in rare, but nonetheless authentic, cases an octogenarian may father children. The late Richard T. Ely, a noted economist, was born in 1854. He married his second wife in 1931 when he was seventy-seven. Before he died in 1943 he had fathered a son and a daughter by that wife, the youngest born when he was about eighty-four years old — two generations in eighty-four years.

Names

Because we are occasionally asked about surnames, their meaning or origin, we shall take a little space (beyond the mention in chapter 1) to briefly introduce the subject, knowing full well that what we write is but a shadow of what you should know if you become really interested in the subject.

Surnames did not come into general use until about the thirteenth and fourteenth centuries, although there are traces of them long before that. The earlier names were usually locative, referring to a place. Such names as De Courtenay (later just Courtenay) indicated that the men so called were of the noble family ruling a region and having a chateau of that name in France. Descendants who came to England in the days of the early Norman kings kept the designation of their "hometown" as their name. This type of name belongs to one of the four main classes of surnames as the specialists in the study of names arrange them. It is called a toponym; this category has two subclasses: the locative, derived from the name of a place, as Courtenay is, and the topographical, derived from the designation of a physical or geographical feature, such as Hill or Wood. Another class consists of patronymics (rarely, matronymics, names derived from the mother's name), names inherited from the father like Johnson or Adams (that is, Adam's son, the suffix having been dropped sometime over the centuries). Another class is the occupational surname, derived from the occupation of the bearer, such as Chandler (candlemaker), Sherman (shear man, one who sheared cloth: note that shearer was one who sheared sheep). The fourth class is made up of nicknames, pet names, diminutives. Many names that seem strange to us today fall in this class, such as Calef (a calf), White or Blount (a blond), Tubbe (a fish found off the coast of Cornwall, where there was a family of this name). Some names may be classified in two categories, such as Robinson

(Robin, a nickname or diminutive for Robert, to which the patronymic suffix has been added).

Changes in spelling through the years have so altered the original form of some names that it is difficult to discover the earliest form and hence the meaning, unless one is a scholar versed in onomatology (the history of names). Therefore, it is best to consult a good book on the subject. The best, a combination of an excellent and readable essay on surnames and a lengthy list, is the late P. H. Reaney's *Dictionary of British Surnames* (1961). Dr. Reaney's dictionary is not as extensive as we might wish, although it runs to several hundred pages. It does not include many Irish or Scottish names. For the Scottish, see George Black's *Surnames of Scotland*, published as a bulletin of the New York Public Library in 1966; and for the Irish, Edward MacLysaght's *Surnames of Ireland*, published in Shannon, Ireland, by the Irish University Press in 1969. The latter is not as comprehensive as Dr. Black's. Two additional valuable volumes are J. N. Hook's *Family Names: How Our Surnames Came to America* (1982), and Elsdon C. Smith's *American Surnames* (1986).

There is always a tendency among us amateurs to make assumptions. However, assumptions in genealogy, especially in claiming relationship because of identity of family names, are treacherous. As Dr. Black observes in his discussion of the name Stewart (Stuart and any other spelling), many noblemen, as well as successive sovereigns, had stewards. Steward (Stewart) is an occupational surname. Stewards were not uncommon in noble households in both England and Scotland. Hence the word may have become a surname almost simultaneously in different areas. Therefore, not all Stewarts (Stuarts) are Scots, nor do they all descend from a common progenitor, or even a family of stewards, although the office of steward was sometimes hereditary. So it is with many other surnames. In Dr. Doane's case (the name means a dune, or hill), he found Doanes whose name was originally Dohn, the progenitor having come from Germany, and others who came from various parts of England and Scotland, some spelling the name Don, some Doun, some Doone, any of which may be transformed into Doan or Doane, as some have. So do not rely upon a name alone.

APPENDIXES

Bibliography

The following lists of books are not to be regarded as exhaustive. They are intended to serve as a guide to the most used books in each indicated field. The individual starting out to search for ancestors must remember that no one book can tell him or her how to work out his or her lines, for each line presents its own problems. Therefore, these lists suggest the starting points for further research in books, once the hunter has reached the point where he or she can begin to work with printed material. You will note that no histories of individual families are suggested. For references to printed genealogies of specific families, consult especially the bibliographies listed in sections C and D. Section E lists the better-known general magazines of genealogical interest. Section F contains listings of atlases and gazetteers, which are indispensable tools for understanding the history of the western world. Maps were guides to the explorers and to our ancestors as they traveled from the Old World to the New, and from the Atlantic coast across the Great Plains and Rocky Mountains to the Pacific coast. Section G notes key reference works for the study of heraldry.

A. Handbooks and Guides

American Society of Genealogists. *Genealogical Research: Methods and Sources.* Rev. ed. 2 vols. Washington, D.C., 1980, 1983.

Ancestry's Red Book: American State, County, and Town Sources. Edited by Alice Eicholz. Salt Lake City, Utah, 1989.

Andereck, Paul A., and Pence, Richard A. *Computer Genealogy: A Guide to Research through High Technology.* Salt Lake City, Utah, 1985.

Arthur, Stephen, and Arthur, Julia. *Your Life and Times: How to Put a Life Story on Tape. An Oral History Handbook.* Baltimore, Md., 1987.

Askin, Jayne, with Bob Oskam. *Search: A Handbook for Adoptees and Birth Parents.* New York, 1982.

Baxter, Angus. *In Search of Your British and Irish Roots: A Complete Guide to Tracing Your English, Welsh, Scottish, and Irish Ancestors.* Baltimore, Md., 1986.

_____. *In Search of Your German Roots: A Complete Guide to Tracing Your Ancestors in the Germanic Areas of Europe.* Baltimore, Md., 1987.

_____. *In Search of Your European Roots.* Baltimore, Md., 1988.

_____. *In Search of Your Canadian Roots.* Baltimore, Md., 1989.

Beard, Timothy Field, with Denise Demong. *How to Find Your Family Roots.* New York, 1977.

Bentley, Elizabeth Petty. *County Courthouse Book.* Baltimore, Md., 1990.

Berry, Ellen Thomas, and Berry, David Allen. *Our Quaker Ancestors: Finding Them in Quaker Records.* Baltimore, Md., 1987.

Black History: A Guide to Civilian Records in the National Archives. Compiled by Debra L. Newman. Washington, D.C., 1984.

Blockson, Charles L., and Fry, Ron. *Black Genealogy.* Englewood Cliffs, N.J., 1977.

Currer-Briggs, Noel. *A Handbook of British Family History: A Guide to Methods and Sources.* Second ed. Saffron-Walden, England, 1979.

_____. *Worldwide Family History.* London, 1982.

Camp, Anthony J. *Wills and Their Whereabouts.* London, 1974.

_____. *Everyone Has Roots: An Introduction to English Genealogy.* Baltimore, Md., 1978.

Cerny, Johni, and Eakle, Arlene. *Ancestry's Guide to Research Case Studies in American Genealogy.* Salt Lake City, Utah, 1985.

Cerny, Johni, and Elliott, Wendy. *The Library: A Guide to the LDS Family History Library.* Salt Lake City, Utah, 1988.

De Platt, Lyman. *Genealogical and Historical Guide to Latin America.* Detroit, Mich., 1978.

Ethnic Genealogy: A Research Guide. Edited by Jessie C. Smith. Westport, Conn., 1983.

Everton, George B., Sr. *A Handy Book for Genealogists.* Eighth ed. Salt Lake City, Utah, 1991.

Falley, Margaret Dickson. *Irish and Scotch-Irish Ancestral Research: A Guide to the Genealogical Records, Methods and Sources in Ireland.*

Evanston, Ill., 1962. Vol. 1, Repositories and Records; vol. 2, Bibliography and Family Index.

Fletcher, William. *Recording Your Family History: A Guide to Preserving Oral History and Using Audio and Video Tape.* Berkeley, Calif., 1990.

Genealogical Resources in the New York Metropolitan Area. Edited by Estelle M. Guzik. New York, 1989.

Greenwood, Val D. *The Researcher's Guide to American Genealogy.* Second ed. Baltimore, Md., 1990.

Groene, Bertram Hawthorne. *Tracing Your Civil War Ancestor.* Winston-Salem, N.C., 1973.

Guide to Records in the National Archives of the United States Relating to American Indians. Compiled by Edward E. Hill. Washington, D.C., 1981.

Hamilton-Edwards, G. K. S. *In Search of British Ancestry.* Fourth ed. Baltimore, Md., 1983.

_____. *In Search of Scottish Ancestry.* Second ed. Baltimore, Md., 1984.

_____. *In Search of Welsh Ancestry.* Baltimore, Md., 1986.

Helmbold, F. Wilbur. *Guide to Researching Your Family History.* Birmingham, Ala., 1976.

Heraldic Artists Ltd. *Handbook on Irish Genealogy: How to Trace Your Ancestors and Relatives in Ireland.* Edited by Donal Begley. Sixth ed. Dublin, 1984.

Jarboe, Betty M. *Obituaries: A Guide to Sources.* Second ed. Boston, Mass., 1989.

Jonasson, Eric. *Tracing Your Icelandic Family Tree.* Winnipeg, Manitoba, 1975.

_____. *The Canadian Genealogical Handbook.* Second ed. Winnipeg, Manitoba, 1978.

Kirkham, E. Kay. *Simplified Genealogy for Americans.* Salt Lake City, Utah, 1977.

Kurzweil, Arthur. *From Generation to Generation: How to Trace Your Jewish Genealogy and Personal History.* New York, 1980.

Lichtman, Allan J. *Your Family History: How to Use Oral History, Personal Family Archives, and Public Documents to Discover Your Heritage.* New York, 1978.

Linder, Bill R. *How to Trace Your Family Tree.* New York, 1978.

Meyer, Mary K., editor. *Meyer's Directory of Genealogical Societies in the U.S.A. and Canada.* Eighth ed. Mt. Airy, Md., 1990.

Mitchell, Brian. *A Guide to Irish Parish Registers*. Baltimore, Md., 1988.

Mitler, Olga. *Genealogical Research for Czech and Slovak Americans*. Detroit, Mich., 1978.

Moody, David. *Scottish Family History*. Baltimore, Md., 1990.

Moulton, Joy Wade. *Genealogical Resources in English Repositories*. Columbus, Ohio, 1988.

Neagles, James C. *Confederate Research Sources: A Guide to Archive Collections*. Salt Lake City, Utah, 1986.

_____. *The Library of Congress: A Guide to Genealogical and Historical Research*. Salt Lake City, Utah, 1990.

Neagles, James C., and Neagles, Lila L. *Locating Your Immigrant Ancestor: A Guide to Naturalization Records*. Logan, Utah, 1986.

New England Genealogical Research: A Guide to Sources. Compiled by Kip Sperry. Bowie, Md., 1988.

Newman, John J. *American Naturalization Process and Procedures, 1790-1985*. Indianapolis, Ind., 1985.

Nielson, Paul Anton. *Swiss Genealogical Research: An Introductory Guide*. Virginia Beach, Va., 1979.

Rillera, Mary Jo. *The Adoption Searchbook*. Second ed. Logan, Utah, 1985.

Rose, James, and Eicholz, Alice. *Black Genesis*. Detroit, Mich., 1978.

Rottenberg, Dan. *Finding Our Fathers: A Guidebook to Jewish Genealogy*. New York, 1977.

Ryan, James G. *Irish Records: Sources for Family and Local History*. Salt Lake City, Utah, 1988.

Ryskamp, George R. *Tracing Your Hispanic Heritage*. Riverside, Calif., 1984.

Sack, SallyAnn Amdur. *A Guide to Jewish Genealogical Research in Israel*. Baltimore, Md., 1987.

Schlyter, Daniel M. *A Handbook of Czechoslovak Genealogical Research*. Buffalo Grove, Ill., 1985.

Schweitzer, George K. *Revolutionary War Genealogy*. Knoxville, Tenn., 1982.

_____. *War of 1812 Genealogy*. Knoxville, Tenn., 1983.

_____. *Civil War Genealogy: A Basic Research Guide for Tracing Your Civil War Ancestors*. Knoxville, Tenn., 1984.

The Source: A Guidebook of American Genealogy. Edited by Arlene Eakle and Johni Cerny. Salt Lake City, Utah, 1985.

Steel, D. J., assisted by Mrs. A. E. F. Steel. *Sources for Scottish*

Genealogy and Family History. In *National Index of Parish Registers,* vol. 12. London, 1970.

Stevenson, Noel C. *Search and Research.* Salt Lake City, Utah, 1977.

Streets, David H. *Slave Genealogy: A Research Guide with Case Studies.* Bowie, Md., 1986.

Stryker-Rodda, Harriet. *How to Climb Your Family Tree: Genealogy for Beginners.* New York, 1977.

Sturm, Duane, and Sturm, Pat. *Video Family History.* Salt Lake City, Utah, 1989.

Szucs, Loretto, and Luebking, Sandra N. *The Archives: A Guide to the National Archives Field Branches.* Salt Lake City, Utah, 1988.

Tracing Your Ancestry: A Step by Step Guide to Genealogical Research in the National Archives. Rev. ed. Washington, D.C., 1985.

Walch, Timothy. *Our Family, Our Town: Essays on Family and Local History Sources in the National Archives.* Washington, D.C., 1987.

Williams, Ethel W. *Know Your Ancestors: A Guide to Genealogical Research.* Rutland, Vt., 1960.

Wright, Norman E. *Building an American Pedigree: A Study in Genealogy.* Provo, Utah, 1974.

Young, Tommie M. *African-American Genealogy: Exploring and Documenting the Black Family.* Clarksville, Tenn., 1980.

_____. *Afro-American Genealogy Sourcebook.* New York, 1987.

Yurdan, Marilyn. *Tracing Your Ancestors (British).* Newton Abbot, England, 1988.

_____. *Irish Family History.* Baltimore, Md., 1990.

Zabriskie, George O. *Climbing Your Family Tree Systematically.* Salt Lake City, Utah, 1969.

B. Reference Books

Barton, H. Arnold. *The Search for Ancestors: A Swedish-American Family Saga.* Carbondale and Edwardsville, Ill., 1979.

Black, George F. *The Surnames of Scotland: Their Origin, Meaning, and History.* Fourth ed. New York, 1983.

Colket, Meredith B. *Founders of Early American Families: Emigrants from Europe, 1607-1657.* Rev. ed. Cleveland, Ohio, 1985.

Coldham, Peter Wilson. *The Complete Book of Emigrants, 1607-1660.* Baltimore, Md., 1987.

_____. *The Complete Book of Emigrants, 1661-1699.* Baltimore, Md., 1990.

_____. *The Complete Book of Emigrants in Bondage, 1614-1775.* Baltimore, Md., 1988.

DeBreffny, Brian. *Irish Family Names.* Dublin, 1982.

Dobson, David. *The Original Scots Colonists of Early America, 1617-1783.* Baltimore, Md., 1989.

Dubester, Henry J. *State Censuses: An Annotated Bibliography of Censuses of Population Taken after the Year 1790, by States and Territories of the United States.* Washington, D.C., 1948.

Filby, P. William. *Passenger and Immigration Lists Bibliography, 1538-1900: Being a Guide to Published Lists of Arrivals in the United States and Canada.* Second ed. Detroit, Mich., 1988.

_____, editor. *Passenger and Immigration Lists Index.* Multivolume. Detroit, Mich., 1981—.

_____, compiler. *Directory of American Libraries with Genealogy or Local History Collections.* Wilmington, Del., 1988.

Fitzhugh, Terrick V. H. *The Dictionary of Genealogy.* Totowa, N.J., 1985.

Franklin, W. Neil, compiler. *Federal Population and Mortality Census Schedule, 1790-1890, in the National Archives and the States: Outline of a Lecture on Their Availability, Content, and Use.* Washington, D.C., 1971.

Fucilla, Joseph G. *Our Italian Surnames.* Evanston, Ill., 1949.

Gannon, Peter S. *Huguenot Refugees in the Settling of Colonial America.* New York, 1985.

Germans to America: Lists of Passengers Arriving at U.S. Ports, 1850-1859. Edited by Ira A. Glazier and P. William Filby. Twelve vols. Wilmington, Del., 1988—.

Haley, Alex. *Roots.* New York, 1976.

Hassall, W. O. *History through Surnames.* Oxford, 1967.

Hook, J. N. *Family Names: How Our Surnames Came to America.* New York, 1982.

Jacobus, Donald Lines. *Genealogy as Pastime and Profession.* Second ed. Baltimore, Md., 1968.

Kaganoff, Benzion C. *A Dictionary of Jewish Names and Their History.* New York, 1977.

Kemp, Thomas Jay. *International Vital Records Handbook.* Baltimore, Md., 1990.

Kirkham, E. Kay. *Some of the Military Records of America Before 1900: Their Use and Value in Genealogical and Historical Research.* Salt Lake City, Utah, 1964.

_____. *The Land Records of America and Their Genealogical Value.* Provo, Utah, 1972.

_____. *A Survey of American Church Records*. Fourth ed. Logan, Utah, 1978.

_____. *Our Native Americans and Their Records of Genealogical Value*. 2 vols. Logan, Utah, 1980, 1984.

Lifton, Betty Jean. *Twice Born: Memoirs of an Adopted Daughter*. New York, 1975.

_____. *Lost and Found: The Adoption Experience*. New York, 1979.

MacLysaght, Edward. *The Surnames of Ireland*. Sixth ed. Shannon, Ireland, 1969.

Matthews, Constance M. *English Surnames*. New York, 1967.

Maudell, Charles R. *The Romance of Spanish Surnames*. New Orleans, La., 1967.

Morgan, T. J., and Prys, Morgan. *Welsh Surnames*. Cardiff, 1985.

Parker, J. Carlyle. *City, County, Town and Township Index to the 1850 Federal Census Schedules*. Detroit, Mich., 1979.

Reaney, Perry H. *A Dictionary of British Surnames*. London, 1961.

Rosenstein, Neil. *The Unbroken Chain: Biographical Sketches and the Genealogy of Illustrious Jewish Families from the 15th-20th Century*. New York, 1976.

Round, J. Horace. *Family Origins and Other Studies*. 1930, reprint. Baltimore, Md., 1970.

Scottish Family Histories Held in Scottish Libraries, compiled by Joan P. S. Ferguson. Edinburgh, 1986.

Sims, Clifford S. *The Origination and Signification of Scottish Surnames*. Reprint. Rutland, Vt., 1969.

Smith, Clifford Neal. *A Calendar of Archival Materials on the Land Patents Issued by the United States Government, with Subject, Tract, and Name Indexes, 1788-1810*. Federal land series, vol. 1. Chicago, Ill., 1973.

_____. *Federal Bounty-Land Warrants of the American Revolution, 1799-1835*. Federal land series, vol. 2. Chicago, Ill., 1973.

Smith, Clifford Neal, and Piszczan-Czaja Smith, Anna. *Encylopedia of German-American Genealogical Research*. New York, 1976.

_____. *American Genealogical Resources in German Archives: A Handbook*. New York, 1977.

Smith, Elsdon C. *American Surnames*. Reprint. Baltimore, Md., 1986.

Stahl, Abraham. *Jewish Family Names*. Second ed. Tel Aviv, 1985.

Stern, Malcolm H. *Americans of Jewish Descent: A Compendium of Genealogy*. New York, 1971.

_____. *First American Jewish Families: 600 Genealogies, 1654-1977.* New York, 1978.

Stevenson, Noel C. *The Genealogical Reader.* Salt Lake City, Utah, 1958.

_____. *Genealogical Evidence: A Guide to the Standard of Proof Relating to Pedigrees, Ancestry, Heirship, and Family History.* Rev. ed. Laguna Hills, Calif., 1989.

Stewart, George R. *American Given Names: Their Origin and History in the Context of the English Language.* New York, 1979.

Tepper, Michael. *American Passenger Arrival Records: A Guide to the Records of Immigrants Arriving at American Ports by Sail and Steam.* Baltimore, Md., 1988.

Wagner, Sir Anthony. *English Genealogy.* Second ed. Oxford, 1972.

The Wuerttemberg Emigration Index. Compiled by Trudy Schenk, Ruth Froelke, and Inge Bork. Salt Lake City, Utah, 1986.

Woulfe, Patrick. *Irish Names and Surnames.* Baltimore, Md., 1969.

C. Indexes to "Buried" Genealogies

A Survey of American Genealogical Periodicals and Periodical Indexes. By Kip Sperry. Detroit, Mich., 1978.

Almanach de Gotha: annuaire généalogique diplomatique et statistique. 1763-1944. Published at various locations.

The American Genealogical Index. Edited by Fremont J. Rider. 48 vols. Middletown, Conn., 1942-52. (Indexes the individual names in a selected list of several hundred family histories and the federal census of 1790.)

The American Genealogical-Biographical Index. Edited by Fremont J. Rider. Middletown, Conn., 1952—. (Continuation of preceding; now being published. In addition to providing the histories of more families, it includes all the names in the *Boston Evening Transcript,* 1906-11, and 63 volumes of lists of Revolutionary War soldiers and a few other military rosters. This useful tool will probably extend to at least 300 volumes.)

Bibliographia genealogica americana: An Alphabetical Index to American Genealogies and Pedigrees Contained in State, County, and Town Histories, Printed Genealogies, and Kindred Works. By Daniel S. Durrie. 1868; second ed., rev. 1878; third ed., rev. Albany, 1886 (supplement, 1888).

Biography and Genealogy Master Index. Edited by Barbara McNeil. Detroit, Mich., 1981.

Genealogical Periodical Annual Index. Compiled by Laud C. Towle. Bowie, Md., 1962—.

The Grafton Index of Books and Magazine Articles on History, Genealogy, and Biography Printed in the United States on American Subjects during the Year 1909. New York [ca. 1910].

Index to American Genealogies and to Genealogical Material Contained in All Works Such as Town Histories, County Histories, Local Histories, Historical Society Publications, Biographies, Historical Periodicals, and Kindred Works. Fourth ed., rev., Albany, N.Y., 1900 (supplement, 1900-1908).

Index to Genealogical Periodical Literature, 1960-1977. By Kip Sperry. Detroit, Mich., 1979.

Index to Genealogical Periodicals. By Donald Lines Jacobus. 3 vols. New Haven, Conn., 1932-53. (The third volume contains the late Mr. Jacobus's "Own Index," a key to many excellent studies of ancestral lines buried in the lineages of individuals, such as Ferris's *Dawes-Gates Ancestral Lines.*) Baltimore, Md., 1973.

Index to Indian Wars Pension Files, 1892-1926. By Virgil D. White. 2 vols. Waynesboro, Tenn., 1987.

An Index to Mexican War Pension Applications. Transcribed by Barbara S. Wolfe. Indianapolis, Ind., 1985.

Index to Old War Pension Files, 1815-1926. By Virgil D. White. 5 vols. Waynesboro, Tenn., 1987.

Index to War of 1812 Pension Files. Transcribed by Virgil D. Wolfe. Waynesboro, Tenn., 1989.

The Library of Congress Index to Biographies in Local Histories. Microfilm. 40 rolls. Baltimore, Md. References extracted from state and regional histories and biographical collections from every part of the United States.

Munsell's Genealogical Index. South Norwalk, Conn., 1933.

Periodical Source Index. Edited by Michael B. Clegg and Curt B. Witcher. Fort Wayne, Ind., 1985.

D. Bibliographies

American Jewish Genealogy: An Annotated Bibliography of Books on Jewish Local History, and Other Subjects of Use to Genealogists. Compiled by Janice M. Regenstein. Wichita, Kans., 1981.

Bibliography of Genealogy and Local History Periodicals with Union List of Major U.S. Collections. Edited by Michael B. Clegg. Fort Wayne, Ind., 1990.

Bibliography of Irish Family History and Genealogy. Edited by Brian DeBreffny. Cork, 1974.

Bibliography of Lists of New England Soldiers. Compiled by Mary Ellen Baker. Addenda by Robert MacKay. Boston, Mass., 1977.

Brigham, Clarence S. *History and Bibliography of American Newspapers, 1620-1820.* 2 vols. Worcester, Mass., 1947.

_____. *Additions and Corrections.* Worcester, Mass., 1961.

Connecticut: A Bibliography of Its History. Edited by Roger Parks. Hanover, N.H., 1986.

Filby, P. William. *A Bibliography of American County Histories.* Baltimore, Md., 1985.

_____. *American and British Genealogy and Heraldry: A Selected List of Books.* Third ed. Boston, Mass., 1983. *Supplement I, 1982-85,* Boston, Mass., 1987.

Freidel, Frank, ed. *Harvard Guide to American History.* Rev. ed. 2 vols. Cambridge, Mass., 1974.

Generations Past: A Selected List of Sources for Afro-American Genealogical Research. Compiled by Sandra M. Lawson. Washington, D.C., 1988.

Heiss, Willard, and Hamm, Thomas D. *Quaker Genealogies: A Selected List of Books.* Boston, Mass., 1985.

Humphrey-Smith, Cecil R. *A Genealogist's Bibliography.* Baltimore, Md., 1985.

Jewish Genealogy: A Sourcebook of Family Histories and Genealogies. Compiled by David S. Zubatsky. New York, 1984.

Jewish Genealogy Worldwide: An Annotated Bibliography of Books on Jewish Local History and Other Subjects of Use to Genealogists. Compiled by Janice M. Regenstein. Wichita, Kans., 1981.

Kaminkow, Marion J. *Genealogies in the Library of Congress: A Bibliography of Family Histories of America and Great Britain.* Baltimore, Md., 1974.

_____. *United States Local Histories in the Library of Congress: A Bibliography.* Four vols. Baltimore, Md., 1975.

_____. *Genealogies in the Library of Congress: A Bibliography (supplement, 1972-1976).* Baltimore, Md., 1977.

_____. *Genealogies in the Library of Congress: A Bibliography (second supplement, 1976-1986).* Baltimore, Md., 1987.

_____. *A Complement to Genealogies in the Library of Congress: A Bibliography.* Baltimore, Md., 1981.

Kemp, Thomas Jay. *Connecticut Researchers Handbook.* Detroit, Mich., 1982.

Library of Congress Local History Bibliography. 5 vols. Baltimore, Md., 1975.

Maine: A Bibliography of Its History. Edited by John D. Haskell, Jr. Hanover, N.H., 1977.

Massachusetts: A Bibliography of Its History. Edited by John D. Haskell, Jr. Hanover, N.H., 1976.

New England: A Bibliography of Its History. Edited by Roger Parks. Hanover, N.H., 1989.

New England: Additions to the Six State Bibliographies. Edited by Roger Parks. Hanover, N.H., 1989.

New Hampshire: A Bibliography of Its History. Edited by John D. Haskell and T. D. Bassett. Hanover, N.H., 1979.

New York Public Library. *Dictionary Catalog of the Local History and Genealogy Division, the Research Libraries of the New York Public Libraries.* 18 vols. Boston, Mass., 1974.

_____. *United States Local History Catalog.* 2 vols. Boston, Mass., 1974.

Newberry Library, Chicago. *The Genealogical Index.* 4 vols. Boston, Mass., 1960.

Rhode Island: A Bibliography of Its History. Edited by Roger Parks. Hanover, N.H., 1983.

Vermont: A Bibliography of Its History. Edited by T. D. Seymour Bassett. Hanover, N.H., 1983.

Schreiner-Yantis, Netti, editor. *Genealogical and Local History Books in Print.* Fourth ed. 3 vols. (first supplement, 1989). Springfield, Va., 1985.

E. Current Magazines and Serials of General Interest

American Genealogical Periodicals: A Bibliography with a Chronological Finding List. By Lester J. Cappon. New York, 1964—.

American Genealogist. 1923—.

Avotaynu: The International Review of Jewish Genealogy. Teaneck, N.J., 1985—.

Genealogical Journal. Utah Genealogical Association. Salt Lake City, Utah, 1972—.

Journal of Genealogy. Robert D. Anderson, publisher and editor in chief. Omaha, Neb., 1976—.

National Genealogical Society Quarterly. 1912—.

New England Historical and Genealogical Register. 1847—.

New York Genealogical and Biographical Record. 1870—.

Toledot: The Journal of Jewish Genealogy. 1977—.

F. Atlases and Gazetteers

Adams, James T. *Atlas of American History.* New York, 1943.

The American Heritage Pictorial Atlas of United States History. New York, 1966.

Cappon, Lester J. *Atlas of Early American History: The Revolutionary Era, 1760-90.* Princeton, N.J., 1976.

The Columbia Lippincott Gazetteer of the World. New York, 1962.

Gaustad, Edwin Scott. *Historical Atlas of Religion in America.* Rev. ed. New York, 1976.

Paullin, Charles O. *Atlas of the Historical Geography of the United States.* Edited by John K. Wright. Washington, D.C., and New York, 1932.

Shepherd, William R. *Historical Atlas.* Ninth ed. New York, 1964.

U.S. Geological Survey. *National Atlas of the United States of America.* Washington, D.C., 1970.

Webster's Geographical Dictionary. Springfield, Mass., 1962.

G. Heraldry

Boutell, Charles. *Boutell's Heraldry.* Revised by J. P. Brooke-Little. New York, 1973.

Brooke-Little, John P. *An Heraldic Alphabet.* Rev. ed. London, 1975.

Burke, Sir John Bernard. *Burke's Genealogical and Heraldic History of the Landed Gentry, Including American Families with British Ancestry.* London, 1939.

_____. *The General Armory of England, Scotland, Ireland, and Wales: Comprising a Registry of Armorial Bearings from the Earliest to the Present Time.* London, 1884. Reprinted, 1969.

The Complete Peerage. Edited by Vicary Gibbs. 13 vols. in 14. London, 1910-59.

Fox-Davies, Arthur C. *A Complete Guide to Heraldry,* 1909. Reprinted, revised, and annotated by J. P. Brooke-Little. New York, 1969.

Grant, Francis J. *The Manual of Heraldry.* Edinburgh, 1962.

Heraldry Index of the St. Louis Public Library. 4 vols. Boston, Mass., 1980.

Innes, Sir Thomas. *Scots Heraldry: A Practical Handbook on the Historical Principles and Modern Application of the Art and Science.* Second ed. Baltimore, Md., 1971.

London, H. S. *The Right Road for the Study of Heraldry.* Second ed. London, 1960.

Rietstap, Johannes B. *Armorial général; précède d'un dictionnaire des termes du blason.* 1861. Reprint. 2 vols. Baltimore, Md., 1972.

Rolland, Victor, and Rolland, H. V. *General Illustrated Armorial.* 1903-26. Reprint. 6 vols. in 3. Baltimore, Md., 1967.

_____. *Supplement to the Armorial General.* 1904-54. Reprint. 9 vols. in 3. Baltimore, Md., 1969-71.

A Roll of Arms: Registered by the Committee on Heraldry of the New England Historic Genealogical Society. Parts 1-9. Boston, Mass., 1928-79.

von Volborth, Carl A. *Heraldry of the World.* London, 1973.

Woodcock, Thomas, and Robinson, John Martin. *The Oxford Guide to Heraldry,* Oxford, 1988.

State Offices of Vital Statistics

Local records of births, marriages, and deaths are key sources of information for you in your search for your ancestors. During the twentieth century, particularly since the establishment of the Social Security system, record-keeping by each state has been considerably expanded and improved. The following list of state offices of vital statistics is presented for your convenience and should be consulted first in your quest for personal data. Do remember, however, that the records of the offices of vital statistics of the various states should be supplemented or complemented by the use of town or county records. For example, many county clerks' offices, to this day, are the repositories of marriage records.

When you write to a state, county, or town record office, be as precise as possible about the kind of information you are seeking: names, dates, and addresses. Ask for a "full copy" of the birth, marriage, or death certificate, since you want a complete copy of the information that is on file regarding your ancestor.

Because the procedures and fees charged for obtaining copies of records from the various offices of vital statistics vary, it is best to write in advance requesting information about such details.

Alabama
   Center for Health Statistics
   State Department of Public Health
   434 Monroe Street
   Montgomery, AL 36130
   (Births, deaths: 1908–
   Marriages: Aug. 1936–; earlier, Probate Judge, County Court House)

Alaska
Department of Health and Social Services
Bureau of Vital Statistics
P.O. Box H-02G
Juneau, AK 99811
(Births, marriages, deaths: 1913–)

American Samoa
Registrar of Vital Statistics
Vital Statistics Section
Government of American Samoa
Pago Pago, AS 96799
(Births, marriages, deaths: 1900–)

Arizona
Vital Records Section
Arizona Department of Health Services
P.O. Box 3887
Phoenix, AZ 85030
(Births, deaths: July 1909–; before 1909, abstracts from county clerk
Marriages: clerk of superior court of county where license was
issued)

Arkansas
Division of Vital Records
Arkansas Department of Health
4815 West Markham Street
Little Rock, AR 72201
(Births, deaths: Feb. 1914–
Marriages: 1917–)

California
Vital Statistics Section
Department of Health Services
410 N Street
Sacramento, CA 95814
(Births, marriages, deaths: July 1905–; earlier at county record-
er's office)

Canal Zone
Panama Canal Commission
Vital Statistics Clerk
APO Miami, FL 34011
(Births, marriage, deaths, divorces: May 1904–Sept. 1979)

Colorado
Vital Records Section
Colorado Department of Health
4210 East 11th Avenue
Denver, CO 80220
(Births, deaths: 1910–
Marriages: a statewide index of records for all years except 1940-67. Write to county clerk for copies)

Connecticut
Vital Records
Department of Health Services
150 Washington Street
Hartford, CT 06106
(Birth, marriages, deaths: July 1, 1897–; prior records with town and city clerks and in the Barbour Collection at the State Library in Hartford)

Delaware
Office of Vital Statistics
Division of Public Health
P.O. Box 637
Dover, DE 19903
(Births, marriages, deaths: 1930–)

District of Columbia
Vital Records Branch
Room 3009
425 I Street NW
Washington, DC 20001
(Births: 1874–
Deaths: 1855–, except none during Civil War
Marriages: Marriage Bureau, 515 5th Street NW, Washington, DC 20001)

Florida
Department of Health and Rehabilitative Services
Office of Vital Statistics
1217 Pearl Street
Jacksonville, FL 32202
(Births: 1865–
Deaths: 1877–
Marriages: June 6, 1927–; earlier, write to county judge's office)

Georgia
  Georgia Department of Human Resources
  Vital Records Unit
  Room 217-H
  47 Trinity Avenue SW
  Atlanta, GA 30334
  (Births, deaths: 1919–
  Marriages: June 9, 1952–; earlier, county clerks or clerk of the or-
  dinary court at county courthouse)
Guam
  Office of Vital Statistics
  Department of Public Health
  and Social Services
  Government of Guam
  P.O. Box 2816
  Agana, GU, M.I. 96910
  (Births, marriages, deaths: Oct. 16, 1901–)
Hawaii
  Office of Health Status Monitoring
  State Department of Health
  P.O. Box 3378
  Honolulu, HI 96801
  (Births, marriages, deaths: 1853–)
Idaho
  Vital Statistics Unit
  Idaho Department of Health and Welfare
  450 West State Street
  Statehouse Mail
  Boise, ID 83720
  (Births, deaths: 1911–
  Births, deaths: 1907-11, county recorder
  Marriages: 1947–; prior, at county recorder's office)
Illinois
  Division of Vital Records
  Illinois Department of Public Health
  605 West Jefferson Street
  Springfield, IL 62702
  (Births, deaths: 1916–
  Marriages: 1962–
  Earlier births, marriages, deaths at county clerk's office)

Indiana
  Vital Records Section
  State Board of Health
  1330 West Michigan Street
  P.O. Box 1964
  Indianapolis, IN 46206
  (Births: Oct. 1907–
  Deaths: 1900–
  Births and deaths prior, health officer of county or city
  Marriages: 1958–; prior, clerk of circuit court or clerk of superior
  court)
Iowa
  Iowa Department of Public Health
  Vital Records Section
  Lucas Office Building
  321 East 12th Street
  Des Moines, IA 50319
  (Births, marriages, deaths: 1880–)
Kansas
  Office of Vital Statistics
  Kansas State Department of Health and Environment
  900 Jackson Street
  Topeka, KS 66612
  (Births, deaths: July 1911–; prior, at county clerk's office
  Marriages: May 1913–; prior, probate judge of county)
Kentucky
  Office of Vital Statistics
  Department for Health Services
  275 East Main Street
  Frankfort, KY 40621
  (Births, deaths: 1911–
  Marriages: July 1958–; prior, clerk of county court)
Louisiana
  Vital Records Registry
  Office of Public Health
  325 Loyola Avenue
  New Orleans, LA 70112
  (Births, deaths: July 1914–
  Marriages: 1946–; prior, clerk's office of parishes [counties])

For New Orleans:
  Bureau of Vital Statistics
  City Health Department
  City Hall
  Civic Center
  New Orleans, LA 70112
  (Births: 1790–; deaths: 1803–; marriages)

Maine
  Office of Vital Records
  Human Services Building
  Station 11
  State House
  Augusta, ME 04333
  (Births, marriages, deaths, 1892–; earlier, town clerk's office)

Maryland
  Division of Vital Records
  Department of Health and Mental Hygiene
  Metro Executive Building
  4201 Patterson Avenue
  P.O. Box 68760
  Baltimore, MD 21215
  (Births and deaths: 1898–
  Marriages: June 1951–; earlier, clerk of circuit court in county
  where license was issued)

Baltimore City Health Dept.
  Bureau of Vital Records
  Municipal Office Building
  Baltimore, MD 21202
  (Births, deaths: 1875–)

Massachusetts
  Registry of Vital Records and Statistics
  150 Tremont Street
  Room B-3
  Boston, MA 02111
  (Births, marriages, deaths: 1896–; earlier, write to the Massachu-
  setts Archives at Columbia Point, 220 Morrissey Boulevard, Bos-
  ton, MA 02125)

For Boston:
    City Registrar
    Registry Division
    Health Department
    Room 705, City Hall Annex
    Boston, MA 02133
    (Births, deaths: 1639–)

Michigan
    Office of the State Registrar and Center for Health Statistics
    Michigan Department of Public Health
    3423 North Logan Street
    Lansing, MI 48909
    (Births, marriages, deaths: 1867–; earlier, county clerk's office)

Minnesota
    Minnesota Department of Health
    Section of Vital Statistics
    717 Delaware Street SE
    P.O. Box 9441
    Minneapolis, MN 55440
    (Births, deaths: 1908–; earlier, clerk of district court of county, or
    City Health Dept. for Minneapolis or St. Paul
    Marriages: 1958–; earlier, clerk of district court)

Mississippi
    Vital Records
    State Department of Health
    2423 North State Street
    Jackson, MS 39216
    (Births, deaths: Nov. 1, 1912–; earlier, circuit clerk of county
    Marriages: 1926–; earlier, circuit clerk of county where license
    was issued)

Missouri
    Department of Health
    Bureau of Vital Records
    1730 East Elm Street
    P.O. Box 570
    Jefferson City, MO 65102
    (Births, deaths: 1910–; earlier, county clerk's office
    Marriages: July 1948–; earlier, recorder of deeds of county where
    license was issued)

Montana
  Bureau of Records and Statistics
  State Department of Health and Environmental Sciences
  Helena, MT 59620
  (Births, deaths: 1907–; earlier, county clerk's office
  Marriages: July 1943–; earlier, clerk of district court where license was issued)
Nebraska
  Bureau of Vital Statistics
  State Department of Health
  301 Centennial Mall South
  P.O. Box 95007
  Lincoln, NE 68509
  (Births, deaths: 1904–
  Marriages: 1909–; earlier, clerk of county court)
Nevada
  Division of Health-Vital Statistics
  Capitol Complex
  505 East King Street #102
  Carson City, NV 89710
  (Births, deaths: 1911–; earlier, office of county recorder of each county
  Marriages: office of county recorder of each county)
New Hampshire
  Bureau of Vital Records
  Health and Human Services Building
  6 Hazen Drive
  Concord, NH 03301
  (Births, marriages, deaths: 1640–)
New Jersey
  State Department of Health
  Bureau of Vital Statistics
  South Warren and Market Streets
  CN 370
  Trenton, NJ 08625
  (Births, deaths: June 1878–
  Marriages: state office or county clerk's office
  Births, marriages, deaths: May 1848-May 1878, Archives and History Bureau, State Library Division, State Dept. of Education, Trenton, NJ 08625)

New Mexico
   Vital Statistics
   New Mexico Health Services Division
   1190 St. Francis Drive
   Santa Fe, NM 87503

   (Births, deaths: 1880–; earlier, county clerk's office
   Marriages: county clerk's office in county where license was issued)

New York
   (except for New York City)
   Vital Records Section
   State Department of Health
   Empire State Plaza
   Tower Building
   Albany, NY 12237

   (Births, deaths: 1880–; earlier, City Registrar of Vital Statistics
   Births, deaths before 1914 for Albany, Buffalo, Yonkers: City
   Registrar of Vital Statistics
   Marriages: 1880-1907; May 1915–; for 1908-April 1915: county
   clerk's office where license was issued
   Marriages, from 1880 through 1907 for Albany, Buffalo, Yonkers:
   city clerk's office)

New York City, Borough of Bronx
   Bronx Bureau of Vital Records
   1826 Arthur Avenue
   Bronx, NY 10457

   (Births, deaths: 1898–; 1865-97 in
   Municipal Archives
   Office of City Clerk
   1780 Grand Concourse
   Bronx, NY 10457
   Marriages: 1914–)

New York City, Borough of Brooklyn
   Brooklyn Bureau of Vital Records
   Municipal Building
   Brooklyn, NY 11201

   (Births, deaths: 1898–; 1866-97 in
   Municipal Archives

Office of City Clerk
208 Joraleman Street
Brooklyn, NY 11201
Marriages: 1866–)

New York City, Borough of Manhattan
Bureau of Vital Records
Department of Health of New York City
125 Worth Street
New York, NY 10016

(Births, deaths: 1898–; births: 1866-97; deaths: 1798-1897 in
Municipal Archives
Marriage License Bureau
Room 265, Municipal Building
New York, NY 10007
Marriages: 1866–; 1847-65 in Municipal Archives)

New York City, Borough of Queens
Queens Bureau of Vital Records
90-37 Parsons Boulevard
Jamaica, NY 11432

(Births, deaths: 1898–
Office of City Clerk
120-55 Queens Boulevard
Kew Gardens, NY 11424
Marriages: 1898–)

New York City, Borough of Staten Island
Staten Island Bureau of Vital Records
51 Stuyvesant Place
St. George
Staten Island, NY 10301

(Births, deaths: 1898–
City Clerk's Office
Borough Hall
St. George
Staten Island, NY 10301
Marriages: 1898–)

North Carolina
Department of Environment, Health and Natural Resources
Division of Epidemiology

Vital Records Section
225 North McDowell Street
P.O. Box 27687
Raleigh, NC 27611

(Births, deaths: Oct. 1913–
Marriages: 1962–; earlier, register of deeds in county where marriage was performed)

North Dakota
Division of Vital Records
State Capital
600 East Boulevard Avenue
Bismarck, ND 58505

(Births, deaths: July 1893–; earlier, clerk of district court
Marriages: July 1925–; earlier, county judge of county)

Ohio
Division of Vital Statistics
Ohio Department of Health
G-20 Ohio Department Building
65 South Front Street
Columbus, OH 43266

(Births, deaths: Dec. 20, 1908–; earlier, county probate court where event occurred
Marriages: Sept. 1949–; earlier, county probate court)

Oklahoma
Vital Records Section
State Department of Health
1000 Northeast 10th Street
P.O. Box 53551
Oklahoma City, OK 73152

(Births, deaths: Oct. 1908–
Marriages: county clerk of court where license was issued)

Oregon
Oregon Health Division
Vital Statistics Section
P.O. Box 116
Portland, OR 97207

(Births, deaths: July 1903–
Marriages: 1907–; earlier, county clerk's office where license was issued)

Pennsylvania
  Division of Vital Records
  State Department of Health
  Central Building
  101 South Mercer Street
  P.O. Box 1528
  New Castle, PA 16103

  (Births, deaths: 1906–; earlier, register of wills, orphan's court, in county where birth or death occurred
  Marriages: 1941–; earlier, marriage license clerk, county courthouse)

  Births, deaths, Pittsburgh, 1870-1905:
  Office of Biostatistics
  Pittsburgh Health Department
  City-County Building
  Pittsburgh, PA 15219

  Births, deaths, Philadelphia, 1860-1915:
  Vital Statistics
  Philadelphia Department of Public Health
  City Hall Annex
  Philadelphia, PA 19107

Puerto Rico
  Department of Health
  Demographic Registry
  P.O. Box 11854
  Fernandez Juncos Station
  San Juan, PR 00910

  (Births, marriages, deaths: July 22, 1931–)

Rhode Island
  Division of Vital Records
  Rhode Island Department of Health
  Room 101, Cannon Building
  3 Capital Hill
  Providence, RI 02908

  (Births, marriages, deaths: 1853–; earlier, town clerk's office where birth, marriage, or death occurred)

South Carolina
  Office of Vital Records and Public Health Statistics
  South Carolina Department of Health and Environmental Control

2600 Bull Street

Columbia, SC 29201

(Births, deaths: 1915–; earlier, county health dept., City of Charleston

Births: 1877–

Deaths: 1821–

Marriages: July 1, 1950–; earlier, county probate judge where license was issued; July 1911–)

South Dakota

State Department of Health

Center for Health Policy and Statistics

Vital Records

523 East Capital

Pierre, SD 57501

(Births, deaths: July 1905–

Marriages: July 1905–; earlier, county clerk of court where license was issued)

Tennessee

Tennessee Vital Records

Department of Health and Environment

Cordell Hull Building

Nashville, TN 37219

(Births, deaths: 1914–; earlier, county clerk's office

For Nashville, June 1881–;

For Knoxville, July 1881–;

For Chattanooga, 1882–

Deaths: 1914–

For Nashville, July 1874

For Knoxville, July 1887–

For Chattanooga, Mar. 6, 1872

Marriages: July 1945–; earlier, county court clerk's office, where license was issued)

For Memphis:

Shelby County Health Department

Division of Vital Records

Memphis, TN 38105

(Births: April 1874-87

Nov. 1898-Jan. 1914

Deaths: May 1848-Jan. 1914)

Texas
  Bureau of Vital Statistics
  Texas Department of Health
  1100 West 49th Street
  Austin, TX 78756

  (Births, deaths: 1903–; earlier, county clerk's office
  Marriages: county clerk's office where license was issued)

Utah
  Bureau of Vital Records
  Utah Department of Health
  288 North 1460 West
  P.O. Box 16700
  Salt Lake City, UT 84116

  (Births, deaths: 1905–; earlier, county clerk's office
  Births, deaths: Salt Lake City, Ogden, 1890-1904, write to the City
  Board of Health
  Marriages: county clerk's office where license was issued)

Vermont
  Vermont Department of Health
  Vital Records Section
  60 Main Street
  Box 70
  Burlington, VT 05402

  (Births, deaths: 1760–
  Marriages: 1857–; earlier, contact town clerk's office in town
  where license was issued)

Virginia
  Division of Vital Records
  State Health Department
  P.O. Box 1000
  Richmond, VA 23208

  (Births, deaths: 1853-Dec. 1896; June 4, 1912–; contact city or town
  health department for period between Dec. 1896 and June 4, 1912
  Marriages: 1853–; earlier, clerk of county circuit court where license was issued)

Washington
  Vital Records
  1112 South Quince
  P.O. Box 9709, ET-11

Olympia, WA 98504

(Births, deaths: July 1907–; earlier, office of county auditor where event occurred
Marriages: 1968–; earlier, office of county auditor where license was issued)

West Virginia
Vital Registration Office
Division of Health
State Capital Complex Building 3
Charleston, WV 25305

(Births, deaths: 1917–; earlier, clerk of county court where event occurred
Marriages: 1921–; earlier, clerk of county court where license was issued)

Wisconsin
Vital Records
1 West Wilson Street
P.O. Box 309
Madison, WI 53701

(Births, deaths: 1852–
Marriages: April 1835–)

Wyoming
Vital Records Services
Hathaway Building
Cheyenne, WY 82002

(Births, deaths: July 1909–
Marriages: May 1941–; earlier, county clerk's office in county where license was issued)

Locations and Areas Served by the National Archives and Records Administration Branches

Several kinds of federal records are a vital source of genealogical information: census records, military records, pension records, bounty land records, passenger arrival lists, passport applications, and others. Many of these materials have been microfilmed and may be consulted at the National Archives Building in Washington, D.C., or at one of the regional archives located throughout the United States. The following list notes the location and geographical areas served by the regional archives. We suggest that you write to the Chief, Regional Archives, at the regional archives nearest you and request a list of the materials in their collections available for your use. The materials may be used in the search room of the regional archives or borrowed by your local public library on the interlibrary loan order service for your use in your hometown. There is no charge for these services. An indispensable aid to the riches of the National Archives and Records Administration is the *Guide to Genealogical Research in the National Archives* (1985). Your local library may have a copy of this book, or it can be purchased for a small charge from the National Archives Trust Fund, National Archives Building, Washington, DC 20408.

Washington, D.C.
  National Archives and Records Administration
  Washington, DC 20408

National Archives—New England Region
  380 Trapelo Road
  Waltham, MA 02154
  (Serves Connecticut, Maine, Massachusetts, New Hampshire, Rhode Island, and Vermont)

National Archives—Northeast Region
Building 22, Military Ocean Terminal
Bayonne, NJ 07002
(Serves New Jersey, New York, Puerto Rico, and the Virgin Islands)

National Archives—Mid-Atlantic Region
9th and Market Streets, Room 1350
Philadelphia, PA 19107
(Serves Delaware and Pennsylvania; for microfilm loans also serves District of Columbia, Maryland, Virginia, and West Virginia)

National Archives—Southeast Region
1557 St. Joseph Avenue
East Point, GA 30344
(Serves Alabama, Florida, Georgia, Kentucky, Mississippi, North Carolina, South Carolina, and Tennessee)

National Archives—Great Lakes Region
7358 South Pulaski Road
Chicago, IL 60629
(Serves Illinois, Indiana, Michigan, Minnesota, Ohio, and Wisconsin)

National Archives—Central Plains Region
2312 East Bannister Road
Kansas City, MO 64131
(Serves Iowa, Kansas, Missouri, and Nebraska)

National Archives—Southwest Region
501 West Felix Street (building address)
P.O. Box 6216 (mailing address)
Fort Worth, TX 76115
(Serves Arkansas, Louisiana, New Mexico, Oklahoma, and Texas)

National Archives—Rocky Mountain Region
Building 48, Denver Federal Center (building address)
P.O. Box 25307 (mailing address)
Denver, CO 80225
(Serves Colorado, Montana, North Dakota, South Dakota, Utah, and Wyoming)

National Archives—Pacific Sierra Region
1000 Commodore Drive

San Bruno, CA 94066
(Serves California except southern California, Hawaii, Nevada except Clark County, and the Pacific Ocean area)

National Archives—Pacific Southwest Region
24000 Avila Road, 1st Floor (building address)
P.O. Box 6719 (mailing address)
Laguna Niguel, CA 92677
(Serves Arizona; the southern California counties of Imperial, Inyo, Kern, Los Angeles, Orange, Riverside, San Bernadino, San Diego, San Luis Obispo, Santa Barbara, and Ventura; and Clark County, Nevada)

National Archives—Pacific Northwest Region
6125 Sand Point Way NE
Seattle, WA 98115
(Serves Idaho, Oregon, and Washington)

National Archives—Alaska Region
654 West Third Avenue, Room 012
Anchorage, AK 99501

Census Records

Since 1790 the federal government has undertaken a census of the population every ten years. The schedules for censuses between 1790 and 1870, a microfilm copy of the 1880 schedules, the existing fragments of the 1890 schedules (the 1890 census was nearly completely destroyed by fire), and microfilm copies of the 1900, 1910, and 1920 schedules are at the National Archives.

For the period between 1790 and 1840 the census schedules give only the name of the head of household. Other family members are recorded by age and sex but are not named. The 1850 and 1860 schedules list slave owners and the age, sex, and color of each slave but not the name. The 1850 census is important because it was the first census to record the names of all free persons in the household, and to ask for state, country, or territory of birth for them. Additional information is included with each succeeding census after 1850.

Mortality schedules were compiled for the censuses of 1850, 1860, 1870, 1880, and 1885, which show the name, the month and cause of death, and the state, territory, or country of birth of each person who died during the year that preceded the taking of each of the censuses. The National Archives has microfilm copies of the mortality schedules for many of the states; for those states not represented, inquire for the materials at the appropriate state archives or state historical society.

The Works Progress Administration during the 1930s produced an index system for the 1880, 1900, and 1910 censuses called Soundex. It is a helpful aid to readers searching for their ancestors because it gathers surnames that sound the same but that may be spelled differently. The surnames are arranged by the Soundex code and then alphabetically by the first names. You should consult the leaflet at the National Archives or at one of the regional archives regarding the procedures to follow when using the Soundex system.

In recent years many indexes to census records have been edited by Ronald V. Jackson and Garry R. Teeples and published by Accelerated Indexing Systems, Salt Lake City, Utah (and other private firms). You should check those references before searching the records themselves. You may use microfilm copies of the various federal census records at the National Archives or its several regional archives centers, or the film may be borrowed and used at your local public library or at the family history centers of the Church of Jesus Christ of Latter-day Saints. It is also possible to purchase from the National Archives microfilm rolls of the federal census schedules at a modest charge.

In many states a census has been taken halfway between the federal censuses. For example, in New York there was a census in 1855, another in 1865, and so forth. The ancestor researcher should hunt around and try to find out what censuses have been taken in the locality in which he or she is interested. A helpful book in this regard and one that you should look at before undertaking work with this kind of material is the *United States Census Compendium* compiled by John "D" Stemmons and published in 1973 by Everton Publishers, P.O. Box 368, Logan, UT 84321. It is a directory of census records, tax lists, petitions, oaths of allegiance, church members, directories, poll lists, and so on, which can be used as a census. The book notes the various material available for each state and for each county within the state, and identifies the name and location of the agency where the material may be consulted by a researcher.

Population Schedules Missing, 1790 to 1820
This list of missing schedules is presented to save the ancestor hunter time and postage in writing to Washington, and in the hope that by lucky chance some reader of this book may find one or more of these schedules and notify the Bureau of the Census of the find so that copies may be made.

Census Records of 1800, 1810, and 1820 at the National Archives,
Washington, D.C.
(figures indicate number of volumes)

State Schedules	1800	1810	1820
Connecticut	2	3	3
Delaware	1	1	1
District of Columbia (in Maryland)	1	–	1
Georgia	–	–	5
Illinois	–	–	2
Indiana	–	–	3
Kentucky	–	4	8
Louisiana	–	1	2
Maine	3	2	4
Maryland	3	4	7
Massachusetts	4	5	8
Michigan	–	–	1
Mississippi	–	–	1
New Hampshire	1	2	2
New Jersey	–	–	–
New York	8	9	18
North Carolina	5	6	6
Ohio	–	–	11
Pennsylvania	7	11	18
Rhode Island	1	1	1
South Carolina	2	2	3
Tennessee	–	(1 county)	3
Vermont	2	2	3
Virginia	–	6	11

1790 Schedules Missing
Delaware (all)
Georgia (all)
Kentucky (all)
Maryland (Alleghany, Calvert, and Somerset counties)
New Jersey (all)
North Carolina (Caswell, Granville, and Orange counties)
Tennessee (all)
Virginia (all—the printed volume of schedules is made up
of state tax lists, not census).

1800 Schedules Missing
Georgia (all)
Indiana Territory (all)
Kentucky (all)
Maine (part of York County)
Maryland (Baltimore County outside of the city of Baltimore)
Massachusetts (part of Suffolk County)
Mississippi Territory (all)
New Hampshire (parts of Rockingham and Strafford counties)
New Jersey (all)
Northwest Territory Ohio River (all)
Pennsylvania (parts of Westmoreland County)
South Carolina (Richland County)
Tennessee (all)
Virginia (all)

1810 Schedules Missing
District of Columbia (all)
Georgia (all)
Illinois Territory (all except Randolph County)
Indiana Territory (all)
Louisiana (all)
Maine (part of Oxford County)
Michigan (all)
Mississippi (all)
New Jersey (all)
New York (Cortland and part of Broome counties)
North Carolina (Craven, Green, New Hanover, and Wake counties)
Ohio (all)
Pennsylvania (parts of Bedford, Cumberland, and Philadelphia counties)
Tennessee (all except Rutherford County)
Virginia (Cabell, Grayson, Greenbrier, Halifax, Hardy, Henry, James, King William, Lee, Louisa, Mecklenburg, Nansemond, Northampton, Orange, Patrick, Pittsylvania, Russell, and Tazewell counties)

1820 Schedules Missing
Alabama (all)
Arkansas Territory (all)
Georgia (Franklin, Rabun, and Twiggs counties)

Indiana (Daviess County)
Maine (parts of Penobscot and Washington counties)
Missouri (all)
New Hampshire (Grafton and parts of Rockingham and Strafford counties)
New Jersey (all)
North Carolina (Currituck, Franklin, Montgomery, Randolph, and Wake counties)
Ohio (Franklin and Wood counties)
Pennsylvania (parts of Lancaster and Luzerne counties)
Tennessee (Anderson, Bledsoe, Blount, Campbell, Carter, Claiborne, Cocke, Grainger, Green, Hamilton, Hawkins, Jefferson, Knox, McMinn, Marion, Monroe, Morgan, Rhea, Roane, Sevier, Sullivan, and Washington counties)

Note

The following substitutes for the missing census schedules of 1790 have been compiled from tax lists.

Delaware: Reconstructed 1790 Census of Delaware. Compiled by Leon DeValinger. Washington, D.C., 1954. (National Genealogical Society, Special Publication No. 10.)

Kentucky: *"First Census"* of Kentucky, 1790. Compiled by Charles B. Heinemann and Gaius Marcus Brumbaugh. Washington, D.C. [ca. 1940].

Kentucky: *"Second Census"* of Kentucky, 1800. Compiled by G. Glenn Clift. Frankfort, Ky., 1954.

Vermont: *Heads of Families at the Second Census of the United States Taken in the Year 1800: Vermont.* Montpelier, Vt., 1938.

INDEX

Index

The names of fictitious people and imaginary places mentioned in the text are not included in this index. Titles of books mentioned in the text are listed, followed in parentheses by the name of the author or editor. Names of places are not usually included.

Gilbert H. Doane (1897–1984) wrote *Searching for Your Ancestors* in 1937. He was director of university libraries, director of the library school, and professor emeritus at the University of Wisconsin.

James B. Bell, author, lecturer, and historian, is former director of the New England Historic Genealogical Society and the New York Historical Society.